The Complete Guide to
Hunting Knives

Durwood Hollis

Published by

700 E. State Street • Iola, WI 54990-0001
Telephone: 715/445-2214

www.krause.com

Please, call or write us for our free catalog of antiques and collectibles publications.
To place an order or receive our free catalog, call 800-258-0929. For editorial comment and further
information, use our regular business telephone at (715) 445-2214.

Library of Congress Catalog Number: 2001086560
ISBN: 0-87349-228-5

Printed in the United States of America

Columbia River Knife & Tool has been in the business of making quality, user-friendly knives since 1994. Featured on the cover are their new Pro-Hunter series knives. Former Alaskan guide, turned custom knifemaker, Russ Kommer has created three high-performance styles, a folder, semi-skinner with a guthook, and a trout and bird blade. The blades and frames of all three knives are composed from AUS-6M stainless steel. The handle scales are formed of injection-molded Zytel, which provides a lightweight, sturdy, and comfortable fit in the hand. The fixed blade is a great trout and bird knife, which along with the semi-skinner, features a ring hole for the user's little finger to go in. This feature allows the knife to stay on the hand, so there's no need to search for where you put down your knife during caping, skinning, and gutting procedures. Kommer has also designed the CRKT Bear Claw and Kommer Grind Big Eddy fillet knives. The Pro-Hunter line will be available to consumers in 2002. To see more of Columbia River Knife & Tool's product line filled with strong, durable work and sport knives, you can go to their Web site www.CRKT.com or call toll free in the U.S. and Canada: 1-800-891-3100 to locate a dealer near you.

Dedication

For my wife, Anita, whose kind words and gentle smile have always been my inspiration. And for my children, Dustin, Brendan, Karlynda, Kristin, Dianté, and my millennium daughter, Kailea Makena Hollis, who are all so full of life that they make an old man young again.

Acknowledgment

I would like to thank all of those in the handmade and production cutlery community who provided assistance in the development of this work. Men of the forge, like Edmund Davidson, Ed Fowler, Russ Krommer, and Loyd Thomsen, all were a wealth of information.

Likewise, I am indebted to C. J. Buck (Buck Knives), Dave Brands (Coast Cutlery), Matt Foster (Gerber Legendary Blades), John Ferril (Grohman Cutlery), Harriet Kelokski (Kellam Cutlery), Doug Flagg (Kershaw kai Cutlery), Charles Allen (Knives of Alaska), David Bloch (Outdoor Edge Cutlery), Joyce Laituri (Spyderco), and Jessica Hall (United Cutlery) for their cooperation and support.

Many thanks to Dave Staples of Outside Images for his help in facilitating the flow of information to my office. And to the management team at Schrade Cutlery for their willingness to put up with all of my cutlery inquisitiveness.

I certainly want to thank outdoor writers Craig Boddington, Steve Comus, John Higley, Jim Matthews, Tom McIntyre, Bob Robb, Dan Schmidt, and the late Peter Hathaway Capstick for freely sharing their own thoughts on hunting knives.

My thanks goes out to outdoor professionals, Duwane Adams and John Winter, for sharing their hunting camps with me. From those experiences much of the material contained herein was drawn.

I am also appreciative of the assistance provided by Steve Shackelford (editor, *Blade* magazine), and Joe Kertzman (managing editor, *Blade* magazine) in encouraging me to move forward with this project.

Special thanks is extended to Jon Cox of the Brunton Company and Buck Knives for allowing me to use their line art drawings.

Finally, to the editors of Krause Publications, Books Division, for providing me with the opportunity to forge this work on outdoor cutlery and game care.

Table of Contents

Foreword

Since man first stepped into existence, the fabrication and use of tools have separated us from other hominids. Our ability to modify and use objects to further specific endeavors has become the very definition of human existence. Whether it is a fire-hardened stick, a piece of bone, or a chipped stone, such tools were essential to the manipulation of the environment.

However, tool use alone does not imply the human elements of forethought and planning. A chimpanzee that wets a twig with saliva uses it to extract ants from an underground burrow is in fact using a tool. Likewise, a sea otter using a rock to crack open a bivalve in search of food also performs an act of tool use. In either of these instances, however, both animals lack the ability to meet unforeseen contingencies. The ants may not stick to the twig, and repeated attempts to break the bivalve shell may meet with failure.

With their limited concept of time and dependance on instinct, animals cannot with any depth of understanding, draw upon the past and take into account the future. Man alone combines innate intelligence with conscious deliberation and forethought to develop and use the implements necessary for survival.

Stone tools, used by our prehistoric ancestors, are the most significant evidence of mankind's existence. Other implements, made from organic materials (wood or bone), were subject to the forces of nature and lost to modern discovery. Stone tools persist in the archeological record, and without exception these implements are associated with hunting activities.

The very first "tools" used by early man were no doubt naturally fractured pieces of sharp stone. These chips were simply picked up and the sharp edges used in the butchering of game. Such tools—especially those chipped from a quartz core or matrix—were amazingly sharp. Over the course of time, certain individuals learned to break chips free from larger rocks, creating more user-friendly, single-face cutting implements.

Next in the development of human-manufactured cutting implements came handaxes. Held in the grip-pocket of the hand, these symmetrically-formed tools resembled an inverted drop of water. The rounded end offered a sufficient gripping surface, with the opposite end serving as the cutting edge. In time, the idea of hafting (attaching) a handaxe to a handle made from antler, bone, or wood, came into existence. The added length of the handle increased impact force and enhanced cutting power, both considerable assets when chopping through bone.

A remarkable step forward in the evolution of cutting implements came as man the toolmaker learned to chip, or "knap" stone. The knapping of small pieces off of a larger stone core was a laborious process. However, early stone smiths soon realized that by chipping off nonessential parts, it left them with a precisely-crafted tool.

D. Hollis

Author Durwood Hollis has spent a lifetime in the field with rifle, bow and arrow, rod and reel, and a camp skillet in his hands. In every activity, a knife has played a significant role. Fixed-blade or folder, it doesn't seem to matter to this avid sportsman. The only thing that's important, he feels, is a "sharp edge and a steady hand."

To be sure, different kinds of stone reacted differently to the knapping process. Chert, flint and obsidian, with their micro-crystalline structures, were the most easily manipulated. Using controlled pressure, the stone surface could be made to fracture in a precise manner. This allowed the stone knapper to impart direction and dimension to the process. The result was the creation of a wide variety of shapes and sizes of tools, some of which had extremely fine cutting edges.

Other types of stone—basalt and slate being prime examples—did not respond well to attempts at chipping. Sandstone or a similar abrasive was used to grind basic shapes and finalize edge configurations. Less likely to break under a load or when subject to impact, basalt and slate tools were often used for heavy-duty cutting assignments.

While stone implements represented a major leap forward in human cultural florescence, there were drawbacks. When knapped into usable configurations, stone blades were thin, brittle and easily broken. Still, stone cutting tools persisted for millennia. With the discovery of copper about 4000 B.C., and the subsequent use of the raw ore as blade material (worked cold, or heated and poured into a form), another leap forward in blade development was achieved. In comparison to stone, copper offered enhanced blade impact resistance and extended edge life.

Accidentally, or purposefully by experimentation, other ores found their way into molten copper. When cooled and formed into tools, some of these new metal composites, or alloys, were found to be superior to pure copper. The discovery of new alloys was the stimulus for continued research, resulting in the ultimate development of bronze—a mixture of copper and tin.

Bronze became the metal of choice for ornamentation, tools, and weaponry beginning about 3000 B.C. in the Mediterranean area. Two thousand years later, in 1000 B.C., the discovery of iron was responsible for a whole new era of cutting tools. Shortly thereafter, the carbonization of this metal gave rise to the development of steel and the accompanying skills of alloying, heat treating and tempering.

The stonesmiths and workers of raw ores and alloys from our prehistoric and historic past are not unlike the bladesmiths of today. The modern practices of forging and stock removal differ only in the materials used and the level of manufacturing sophistication. Both the manufacturing techniques and the end product are quite similar. When examined retrospectively, prehistoric chipping grounds and historic metal forges were nothing less than primitive cutlery manufacturing facilities.

By no means is this book a commentary on the cultural development of man. However, the killing and butchering of prey are important parts of human existence. At the center of these activities, knives, axes, and other cutting tools continue to be as important to the hunter today as they were when the timeline of man first began.

In the chapters ahead, you'll read about knife blade and handle materials, the basic elements of knife manufacturing, knife configuration, blade shapes, edge grinds, edged tool selection, field use, edge restoration, the use of heavy duty cutting implements (axes and saws), as well as field shears, and cutlery selection for hunting camp. To assist your understanding of field use, this book contains extensive descriptive and illustrative material on the issues of field dressing, skinning, field butchering, and trophy knifework. Furthermore, most of us who hunt have, at one time or another, dropped a line in a creek, river, or lake. For this reason, I've also included a chapter on edged tools for the angler.

When hunting success results in game care, the selection and use of edged tools will become a paramount consideration. No matter how we rationalize our presence on the killing grounds, the nobility of the act lies in our commitment to utilize what we harvest. In the hunting field, the sharpened edge is the controlling factor. Without it, the hunt is nothing more than an exercise in futility.

Whether a shard of volcanic glass, or blade of finely-crafted steel, a cutting tool is the single defining cultural element that sets man apart from all other creatures. With such an implement in hand, our first ancestors made their mark in the pages of time. Modern man continues to have no less the need.

Durwood Hollis,
Rancho Cucamonga, California, January 1, 2001.

Preface

We might try to deny it in today's urbane and cultured society, but all of us are hunters at heart, right down to the root of our genetic core. The nature of the beast is that we are also fascinated with everything about the hunt, especially the gear involved with the practical aspects of the pursuit. In hunting camps around the globe, and I suspect through all time, hunters have sat by fires and considered the merits of the gear that makes us better at our hunter role. We discuss calibers and ballistics, bows and broadheads, clothing and boots, and everything else that surrounds this primal activity. However, there is only one piece of equipment common to all hunters everywhere and throughout the ages. From flaked flint to crafted steel, the knife alone is the common thread that knits all hunters into one fabric. And it is the responsibility of that sharpened edge to turn downed-game into end-game—a product for the larder.

My friend and hunting companion, Durwood Hollis, recognized that distinction early in his outdoor writing career. This interest in edged tools has taken him around the world and into a variety of hunting camps. Of course, there was game to hunt, but it was the blade that always fascinated him. During his travels, Durwood took the time to visit cutlery factories and small custom knife shops alike. What he learned was forged into columns and articles that have appeared in all of the major hunting and fishing magazines for more than twenty years.

At a very personal level, Durwood Hollis has been my own knife and knife-use encyclopedia. Whenever I had questions, I simply dialed his number on the telephone: How do you get an edge on the skinning knife? How do you box skin a coyote? Where can I get a knife designed for turkey hunting and what features should I look for? There were no stupid questions for Durwood. And he always seemed to have the answers, because he'd made the same inquiries himself of experts around the world.

I've been with Durwood when he has grilled a hunting guide about why a particular type of blade was used. The guide hadn't thought much about it. He just knew what worked best. Durwood would fire questions in rapid succession. And during the course of time it took to field dress, skin and butcher a particular game animal—years of knife experience had been brought to light.

When Durwood told several of his regular hunting partners and fellow outdoor writers that he was going to write this book, our reaction was a unanimous "it's about time!" *The Complete Guide to Hunting Knives* is a distillation of Durwood Hollis's vast experience with blades and their use. I don't think a better person could have been selected to write this volume. If there's a problem with the book, it's probably the fact that it should have been written a decade ago. I know that such an undertaking could have saved Durwood many hours on the telephone and visits from guys like me who had knife-related questions and knew that he had the answers—as does this book.

Jim Matthews, *Outdoor News Service*

The heart of a knife is the steel from which it is wrought. Its soul is the manifestation of the knifemaker's skill at the forge. (Pictured: a clip-pattern Damascus blade knife with box elder wooden handle and fossilized antler spacers, made by Loyd Thomsen).

Chapter 1
Basic Blade Composition

"Steel: a hard, tough metal composed of iron alloyed with various small percentages of carbon and often variously with other metals, as nickel, chromium, manganese, etc., to produce hardness, resistance to rusting, etc."
(Webster's New World Dictionary, 3rd College Ed., 1993.)

The very core of any knife is the blade material. It is here, in the cold silence of steel, that the soul of the knife and its maker rest. More than just iron, carbon and diffused alloys, blade steel comes to life in the forge and becomes greater than what it once was. To be sure, each step of production (forging, quenching and tempering) is a significant component of the entire process. However, one cannot diminish the significance of the basic elements of steel. A look at the process of steel production and what it takes to transform raw iron into premium blade steel will offer insight into the heart of the matter.

By definition, steel is iron alloyed with a small percentage of carbon. The initial step in the creation of steel utilizes heat in a controlled environment. Carbonization occurs when the carbon is absorbed into the molten iron. Then other elements are added to the mix until a particular formulation is achieved that maximizes the unique qualities required for optimum steel performance. The primary elements that can be found in suitable blade steels are: Carbon, chromium, cobalt, copper, manganese, molybdenum, nickel, phosphorous, silicon, sulphur, tungsten, and vanadium. Each of these elements imparts special properties to the steel itself.

Carbon increases hardness, improves wear-resistance, which in turn enhances edge retention and the tensile strength of the steel. Chromium provides resistance to corrosion if the formulation has 13% or more present. This element also increases hardness, tensile strength and overall toughness. Cobalt is often used to intensify the individual effects of other components, permitting quenching at higher temperatures and increasing strength. Copper is another element that provides a measure of corrosion resistance. Manganese is used to remove oxygen from the molten metal, and increase's hardenability, wear resistance and tensile strength. Molybdenum is used to add corrosion resistance, increase strength, hardness, hardenability, toughness, and machinability. Nickel provides added strength and toughness. Phosphorous also

improves the strength, machinability, and hardness of the steel. Silicon is another de-oxyifier and de-gasifier that removes contained oxygen from molten steel. It also increases the strength of the steel. Sulphur, when used even in minute quantities, improves the machinability of the steel. Tungsten adds strength and enhances hardenability, and vanadium increases strength, toughness, and wear resistance.

Jennifer Thomsen-Connell

The hammer falls and the sparks fly—it's all part of the knife making process for the hand forger.

Heat Treating: While certain elements have the potential for specific properties, these properties are only manifested when the steel is appropriately heat treated and tempered. Initially, the steel must be heated to a nonmagnetic stage (referred to as "critical temperature") in a controlled environment. That environment, the forge, provides the venue where heat can be maintained at a certain temperature for a specific period of time. The effect of this controlled heat results in the total saturation of all elements and the establishment of the grain structure within the steel. It is here that mistakes made in the initial forging process will become manifest.

Tempering: After heat treating, the steel is too hard and brittle to work adequately. Tempering is necessary to achieve its optimal level of hardness and toughness. However, there must be a necessary balance between hardness and toughness. Hardness is accompanied by resistance to deformation. Toughness increases the ability of the material to resist impact. If the steel is too hard, it will shatter. If the steel is too tough, it will deform rather than fracture. Tempering is nothing more than a reheating process that slightly softens the steel to relieve undue stress.

This process is accomplished through additional reheating and quenching of the steel. After thorough heat saturation, the quenching process is used to rapidly cool the heated steel from critical temperature. A variety of materials—water, oil, and salt immersion—can be used as quenching mediums. Just like individual steel formulations have different critical temperatures, they also respond differently to the quenching environment. Some steels may even need to be placed in a sub-zero environment for a specific period of time to completely stabilize their grain structure.

Rockwell Testing: Once the tempering process is completed, the relative hardness of the steel can be measured precisely by a Rockwell testing machine. This procedure involves impressing a diamond-tipped needle under controlled tension directly into the blade after final tempering. The amount of pressure it takes to achieve penetration is measured and assigned a Rockwell number. The higher the number, the more resistant the blade will be to edge deterioration. This results in extended edge life, but it will definitely be harder to resharpen the blade. Conversely, the lower the number, the less resistance to edge erosion. Which means the blade will dull quickly, but demand less effort to resharpen.

Jennifer Thomsen-Connell

Small and monitored by hand in the home shop, or large and computer-controlled, the forge is where it all happens.

There are several different Rockwell measurement scales. Knife steel is computed on the Rockwell "C" scale. Blades testing below Rc 52 (Rockwell "C" scale) are relatively soft, while those at Rc 60 are extremely hard. Even a couple of points on the scale can mean a huge difference when it comes to edge longevity or ease of sharpening. Cutlery manufacturers continually search for a steel that offers both extended edge retention and sharpening ease, however, no such steel formulation exists. If a knife holds its edge for a long period of time, it will be difficult to sharpen when the need arises. Conversely, if a knife is easy-to-sharpen, expect limited edge life. Edge retention and sharpening ease are at opposite ends of the blade hardness continuum.

Stainless Steel: While there are a number of different steels used in the cutlery industry, the vast majority of hunting knives are crafted from one of the following stainless formulations: 420, 440A, 440C, AUS-6, AUS-8, 154 CM, ATS-34, or ATS-55. A look at each of these steels and their individual elements will illuminate both their differences and similarities.

420 stainless steel has a fairly low carbon (0.15%) and chromium (12.00-14.00%) content, when compared to 440A or 440C. The steel composition contains no molybdenum, which both of the other 400 series steels have in their formulations. Correspondingly, it is tempered to a lower Rockwell reading (Rc 52-56) than either 440A or 440C stainless steel. Unlike harder stainless formulations, this steel is soft enough to be relatively easy to sharpen. Furthermore, knives made from 420 stainless are

The Rockwell test machine impresses a diamond-pointed stylus under load into a steel blade. The amount of resistance is measured on the "C" scale.

Jennifer Thomsen-Connell

From raw cable to a finished billet of Damascus steel takes patience, sweat and hours of intensive labor.

amazingly affordable. Correspondingly, this steel has several features that former carbon steel knife owners can well appreciate.

440A stainless steel provides a significant increase in both carbon (0.60-0.75%) and chromium (0.16-0.18%) content, when compared to the aforementioned 420 formulation. It also has molybdenum (0.75%), which is absent in 420 stainless. The increase in carbon offers greater strength, hardness and improves edge retention. The addition of the molybdenum enhances the carbon properties and improves corrosion resistance. Likewise, the increase in chromium augments hardness, strength, and provides greater resistance to corrosion. Most 440A blades offer their best performance at Rc 55-57.

440C stainless steel has even more carbon content (0.95-1.20%) than either 440A or 420. This increase is the only basic difference between 440C and the other two 400 series stainless products. This distinction can be realized in increased hardness, greater tensile strength, and improved edge retention. Properly tempered, a 440C blade will be hardened in Rockwell range of Rc 58-60. When it comes to edge life, clearly the high-carbon content of 440C gives it the edge over both 420 and 440A stainless.

AUS-6 stainless steel is similar to 420 stainless, but with a higher carbon content (0.55-0.65%). While slight amounts of nickel (0.49%) and vanadium (0.10-0.25%) are also present, I am not sure there is enough to make a noticeable difference. The chromium content (13.0-14.5%) is nearly identical to 420, so resistance to corrosion will be similar. An affordable higher-carbon version of 420, this steel is always a good bet.

AUS-8 stainless steel offers an even higher carbon content (0.70-0.75%), with a hint of molybdenum (0.10-0.30%) added. The chromium content (13.00-14.50%) is the same as AUS-6, so there shouldn't be any difference in corrosion resistance. The higher carbon allows this steel to Rockwell at Rc 58-59, giving it a slight edge over AUS-6. All things being nearly equal, in my experience there's little difference between the two steels.

ATS-34/154CM stainless steels are so similar in formulation and performance that any minor difference isn't worth mentioning. Both are high-carbon (ATS-34/1.05%, 154CM/1.00-1.10%) steels, with similar chromium content (ATS-34/14.00%, 154CM/13.00-15.00%). Other minuscule differences in the alloys exist, but both Rockwell in the Rc 59-61 range. Both ATS-34 and 154CM are definitely tough steels, and knives made from either one will be costly to produce. These added production costs will be reflected in the final retail price.

ATS-55 stainless steel is just ATS-34 with the addition of a little cobalt (0.40%) and copper (0.20%). The cobalt adds a point or two to the Rockwell (Rc 60-62) range, and the copper

Kershaw selected AUS-6A stainless steel for use in their fixed-blade hunters.

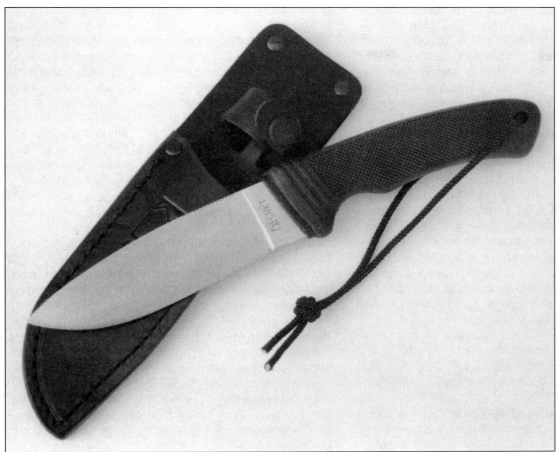

High-chromium, high-carbon stainless steel offers excellent performance with low maintenance—the right choice in a field knife. This representative from Columbia River Knife & Tool (Bridger Model 2001) line is a fine example of this approach.

D. Hollis

increases corrosion resistance. Other than that, there's not much difference between ATS-34 and ATS-55. In comparison to 400 series formulations, ATS' steels have the capacity for better edge retention. However, the lower chromium content makes them more vulnerable to corrosion.

In a knife blade, the relationship of one stainless steel to another is evident. The addition of carbon provides greater edge retention potential, but you lose a measure of ductility. Likewise, increases in chromium enhance corrosion resistance, but you give up toughness. While 420 makes a serviceable blade, its edge retention capability is eclipsed by 440A, 440C and the high-carbon AUS formulations. And the extremely high carbon content of both ATS-34, ATS-55, and 154 CM provides greater edge retention capability than any of the 400 or AUS series steels. When it comes to corrosion resistance, the high-chromium formulation of both 440A and 440C provides more corrosion-resistance than 420 stainless, AUS steels, ATS steel, and 154 CM.

Some years ago, I had the pleasure of spending a week hunting elk in the Bridger-Teton Wilderness with outfitter and guide, John R. Winter. On one stormy evening, we ran into what seemed like a gathering of bull elk. Several mature bulls were heard bugling all around us. My hunting partner was the first to score on a nice 5x4 satellite bull—then my turn came. Just as the light was fading, a great 6x6 bull came up a nearby ridge with his cows. The shot wasn't difficult, but the bull fell on a steep slope. Compelled by circumstances to work in a near vertical environment, which made the assignment even more challenging, we undertook basic field care.

John decided to use both his knife and my knife. "We'll have to work fast. The day is almost done. I'll do the cutting, you handle the sharpening," he announced. After the knives switched hands a couple of times, the difference between the blade steels was evident. While both knives were stainless and possessed similar shapes and edge profiles, the edge on my knife held up much longer than the edge on John's favorite blade. Furthermore, when it came to ease of sharpening, it took some serious calories to put my keen cutter back into the game. John's knife, however, came to life after only a few strokes with the diamond rod. Right then and there, I gained a thorough understanding of the relationship between edge retention and ease of sharpening.

Carbon and Carbon/Alloy Steel: At this point, some mention should be made regarding carbon and carbon/alloy steel knives. Several different carbon and carbon/alloy steels—D-2, 0-1, 0-6, W-1, W-2, 1045 through 1095, 5160, 52100 and others—are used by custom makers and found in some factory offerings. Carbon steels basically contain iron with the addition of carbon and manganese. Carbon/alloy steels have the same formulation with the addition of the elements, chromium and vanadium, in varying amounts. The one single factor that separates carbon and carbon/alloy steel from stainless steel is that to qualify as stainless, the chemical composition of the steel must have at least 13% chromium in its formulation. A quick look at some of the most popular carbon steel used by knifemakers can offer some insight into their basic differences.

0-1: Carbon steel makes a very decent blade and has a reputation for being more forgiving when worked than other simple alloys. This steel heat-treats easily and offers good service as a knife blade under most conditions.

0-6: Carbon steel is considered a step up from 0-1, in that it has a finer crystalline structure with extremely hard graphitic particles. This provides enhanced toughness and better wear resistance over 0-1.

W-1, W-2, and Steel 1045-1095: Carbon steels that all provide a solid level of toughness. Any one of these steels can be found put to use as truck springs, files, and road grader blades. All are very simplistic, yet they make good, strong knife blades that can withstand considerable abuse.

5160: Carbon steel is typically found used in springs. It has about 1% chromium in its formulation, allowing deep hardening. This is a tough steel that when brought to its full potential at Rc-60, offers fantastic edge retention.

A-2: Carbon steel is tougher than 0-1, which is the result of a small percentage of chromium in the formulation. Offering excellent wear-resistance, this steel is a little more difficult to work than 0-1, but it makes a great blade.

D-2: Carbon steel has a strong chromium component (12%). While not enough chromium to qualify as stainless, it resists staining better than other carbon steels. This tool steel has outstanding wear resistance and is often used in handmade knives.

Spring steel (leaf and coil), ball bearings (other bearing steels), cast off files, plow shears (other steel farm implement components), as well as saw steels are the most common sources of carbon and carbon/alloy steels used in knife blades. These are not complex steel formulations. Best of all, they are relatively easy to forge, heat-treat favorably, and make fine blades.

Epoxy coating, Parkerizing, as well as the application of molecularly-bonded titanium coatings are often used to protect a carbon steel blade. No matter how effective these treatments are in providing primary protection, nevertheless, a carbon steel blade will still demand more user maintenance to keep it free from rust and staining than a stainless blade. Knife blade maintenance may not be a big deal to some. After all, most firearms are made from blued carbon steel and keeping them free from rust isn't such a bother. Others may find the added time it takes to keep a carbon steel blade clean and rust-free a nuisance that can easily be avoided by simply using a stainless steel product.

Damascus Steel: Somewhere between the 4th and the 7th Century, layer forging of steel developed. Early steel smiths discovered that by combining hard and soft steel formulations together, they could achieve great cutting ability and enhanced ductility. Later, decorative effects were created by folding and twisting the laminated steel.

When steel is intensively forged, it will begin to exhibit surface markings. If etched with acid, these markings can be enhanced so that they are plainly visible to the human eye. Since the markings resemble fine ripples seen in water, this became known as "watering" or "damask" and was connected with finely worked steel. Because the Western World was first exposed to this steel in the Middle East, probably near Damascus in modern-day Syria on one of the east-west trade routes, the descriptive terminology "Damascus Steel" was commonly used.

The city of Damascus is located in the modern-day country of Syria. This metropolitan area has a long history as a commercial trading center. Several cultures, most notably Babylonian, Egyptian, and Roman, had an influence in this area. The actual point of origin for hammered steel is probably obscured by both time and these multiple cultures. However, the city of Damascus wasn't really known for cutlery manufacture. In fact, this was the trading crossroads for the textile industry. When European Crusaders plundered the region, among all of the wonderfully patterned and brocade fabrics that they returned home with, the most highly prized was a wavy-patterned silk known as "damask." Since many of the edged weapons of war that were also seized had a similar patterned appearance, it is understandable how the label, "damask" steel, easily evolved. Over time, no doubt, the term "damask" was transformed into "Damascus."

Typically, Damascus is made by forging different steels (carbon, carbon/alloy, or stainless steel) together into a single billet. The knifemaker must start with good, clean stock. Sometimes varying thicknesses of steel are used. The edges are trued and clamped together. The ends can then be wired wrapped, or welded together, to prevent any shifting of the stack. Then the layered steel is heated in the forge, fluxed sparingly, heated again, and when it turns the color of hot honey and begins to bubble, it is quickly hammered on the anvil. This process is repeated until all of the steel layers are completely welded together. When this has been accomplished, the resultant billet can be cut into two pieces, stacked one on top of another, and forged again. The process can be repeated over and over again until the desired number of steel layers is welded together. Depending on the particular pattern desired, the steel can be twisted, grooved, or drilled at different stages of the forging process. The fewer the layers of steel, the bolder the pattern. This is often a desirable feature in a large knife. In a small knife, however, additional layers can serve to enhance the pattern. The great thing about this steel is that every knife is unique unto itself, and the patterns achieved in the forging process are limited only by the creative imagination of the maker.

Hammer, twist and turn are all part of Damascus steel's secret.

Jennifer Thomsen-Connell

In addition to using layers of flat steel stock, wire rope or steel cable can be used to produce rather interesting Damascus patterns. The only difference is that the material is initially forged in the round. This means that the forger must constantly turn the piece to prevent it from splaying out in all directions. Once the cable is completely welded, it can then be forged flat and used like layered Damascus. When properly forged and etched, cable Damascus is magnificent with very good edge holding properties.

There are many variables that come into play when forging Damascus steel. Most problematic situations, like trapped flux, cold spots when welding, and cracks ("cold shuts"), are manifest when the forger doesn't take the time necessary to properly work the steel. It is common for a knifemaker to spend days devoted to the creation of a Damascus knife. Forging, heat treating, tempering and etching Damascus isn't a race to be run—it is a course that must be followed.

I can recall the words of knifemaker Jim English who said in an interview that, "Damascus is like no other steel I've ever worked with. It is as though it were alive and takes its own form. The knifemaker only serves to free what is already inherent in the steel."

Obviously, the time and effort that it takes to produce a single billet of Damascus steel are several times that of other steels. Why then are so many willing to pay more for what admittedly is a dated technology? The answer may lie in the fact that the time-honored tradition of hammer-welding steel somehow mitigates the cost. At least for some, Damascus steel is without a peer and a "must-have" blade material at any cost.

The Last Word

Differences between blade steels are often not readily evident to the average hunter. If you only use your knife occasionally, then edge retention probably isn't going to be your most important priority. Out of the factory box, almost any knife—carbon, carbon/alloy steel or stainless steel—will hold its edge through basic field dressing chores. However, just try to use the same knife to field dress, skin, cape, and bone-out meat. Then and there, you'll gain real respect for the steel formulation, as well as the heat treatment and tempering process that went into the production of that edged tool.

The ability of your knife to gain and hold its edge is primarily a reflection of the steel formulation. Despite complex combinations of alloyed elements, each providing in part specific properties, every steel is a compromise. Knifemaker Wayne L. Goddard put it best when he stated: "In the search for the ultimate alloy composition in steel it seems that, more often than not, it is necessary to give up something to get something else." (*Blade* magazine, "Carbon and Carbon Alloy Knife Steels," 12/91, pg. 48.)

When Blade Steel Isn't Steel

The use of materials other than steel as knife blade material is on the rise. The folks at Boker USA were among the first to introduce ceramic blades to the sporting cutlery market. A few years ago I had the opportunity to use a Boker ceramic blade knife on a deer hunt. Wildlife officials determined that the area I selected to hunt could support a two-deer limit. With the appropriate license and two deer tags in my pocket, I was determined to give the new ceramic knife a real workout. On the first morning in the field, I managed to score on a pair of forked-horn bucks. In short order, I field-dressed, skinned, and boned-out both deer without any perceptible deterioration of the ceramic blade edge. Later in the day, I used that same knife to slice up a tomato for sandwiches at lunch. If that isn't a testimony to incredible edge retention, then I don't know what is.

Ceramic blades do have their drawbacks. If dropped on a hard surface, or subjected to lateral stress, a ceramic blade can, and will fracture. Although, if you treat a ceramic blade like a premium knife blade should be treated, most likely you won't ever have any problems. Finally, short of spending some real calories with a diamond sharpener, or sending the knife back to the factory for re-sharpening, ceramic blades are nearly impossible to sharpen. In spite of all of this, ceramic is a wonderful blade material if used properly as a cutting tool.

Another new blade material is, interestingly enough, called Talonite®. Camillus pioneered this material in the production cutlery market. A unique combination of cobalt and chromium carbides in a cobalt matrix, Talonite® will not rust—ever! Because the cobalt matrix only requires a Rockwell hardness of Rc 45-47, a Talonite® blade is very easy to sharpen. The relatively "softer" cobalt is easy to remove during the sharpening process, quickly exposing the "harder" chromium carbides. Reportedly, this material will hold an edge 12 times longer than an adequately heat-treated ATS-34 stainless blade. Expect to pay a premium price for a knife with a Talonite® blade, but it might just be well worth the added expense.

Another material that has found its way into the cutlery industry is titanium. This element was first discovered in 1791 by William Gregor, a British mineralogist. It is silver, or dark-gray in color. From a knifemaker's standpoint, titanium's properties of extreme light weight (40% lighter than steel), absolutely rust-free in any environmental venue, enhanced ductility, and fantastic edge retention (reportedly a titanium blade will retain its edge three times longer than an ATS-34 blade), are highly desirable. The rarity of titanium has driven its cost sky high, so it has yet to make a significant impact as blade material (Boker USA offers a limited number of both kitchen and sporting knife models with titanium blades). However, smaller knife components (handle scales, screws, liners, etc.) are already being produced out of this material.

I am sure we haven't seen the end of continued developments in this arena. The search for the ultimate blade material is sure to be elusive and never ending.

Boker USA

This magnificently-designed ceramic blade folder from Boker features lightweight titanium handle scales.

Boker USA

The unique crystalline surface of the titanium blade on this Boker Orion folder blends artistry, innovation and craftsmanship. Complete with clothing clip and liner lock, this knife weighs just 2.4 ounces.

To bring out the very best in knife steel, like the 420 high-carbon stainless in this Schrade Zumbo Elk folder, both heat and cold are used.

Chapter 2

Fire and Ice

While steel may be the heart of a knife blade, heat treatment is the breath of life.

At the beginning of the previous chapter, I stated that "blade steel comes to life in the forge and becomes greater than what it once was." The nature of iron is to remain in its natural state and resist the inclusion of all other elements, including carbon. Over time, iron has a tendency to leech out all other constituents. To produce steel, the inclusion of carbon within the iron matrix must take place. Ancient metallurgists learned that working wrought iron (iron without a carbon content) over a charcoal forge activated the process of carbonization, or carbon absorption. Carbon has certain advantageous properties, which allow the crystalline structure to easily combine with other elements. The most simple steel formulation—iron combined with a small percentage of carbon—reacts even more dynamically if subjected to intense heat (heat treatment), combined with material appropriate quenching (continued internal matrix development) and the relief of heat-produced internal stress (tempering).

Fire: Steel that has not been subjected to the heat treatment process consists of iron combined with carbon. In this state, a portion of the contained carbon is boned to the iron as iron carbides, commonly known as cementite. The iron that remains is called ferrite and is composed of iron crystals with carbon atoms compressed into the existing intervals. When steel is subjected to extreme heat in a controlled environment, the individual structure of the cementite and the ferrite is reformed into austenite (named after the English metallurgist, Sir William C. Roberts-Austen).

As the temperature within the steel increases, the nature of the granular structure will also increase in size. To obtain the properties necessary for blade steel, the large austenite granules must be converted to martensite (a term that is derived from the name of an early metallurgist, Adolf Martens). This occurs when the steel is heated to a nonmagnetic state.

To permit the heat to completely infiltrate the steel matrix, it must be "soaked" in the furnace. The "soak time" will depend entirely on how consistently the heat has permeated the steel structure. If heat penetration is uneven, the result will be a hard outer shell and a soft inner core. For consistent hardness to occur all of the contained austenite must be converted to martensite. The amount of time it takes for complete heat absorption is directly related to the individual steel formulation.

In major cutlery production facilities, the application of heat is conducted in a large furnace with a number of similar blades undergoing the process simultaneously. The entire procedure is computer-controlled, with quality assurance as an integral component of the operation. Individual

Jennifer Thomsen-Connell

Large or small, a forge does one thing—it provides the heat necessary for blade work.

21

knifemakers may conduct this process in their shops, but on a much smaller (often one knife at a time) scale. As an alternative, blades can be sent to an outside facility specializing in heat treatment. Either way, makers must implement their own Rockwell testing program to ensure the consistency of the outside vendor's service product.

Ice: After heating to this critical temperature—which in carbon steel is about 1425 to 1500 degrees, and several hundred degrees higher in stainless formulations—the steel is quickly cooled by liquid immersion or exposure to room temperature. This cooling activity is referred to as the quenching process. When the internal temperature of the steel rises, carbon and any other components of the admixture disperse throughout the iron environment. Quickly cooling, or quenching the heated steel is responsible for trapping the carbon within the iron matrix, resulting in the transformation of the larger granules of austenite into a fine martensite structure.

This conversion process will continue as the internal steel temperature continues to drop lower and lower. With stainless steel, the process is enhanced by subjecting the heated steel (within two hours after removal from the furnace) to a cryogenic, or sub-zero temperature quench. If the hot steel is not moved out of the furnace to the freezer quickly, the austenite will stabilize and the continued conversion to martensite will not occur. Without this cryogenic quench the retained austenite produces a grain structure within stainless steel that microscopically looks like large boulders. After quenching in a sub-zero environment, the conversion of austenite to martensite results in a grain structure production resembling fine sand. The outcome of this superior grain structure produces a consistent blade edge that resists chipping and fracturing.

The only way to ensure that this process is being conducted properly is by sacrificing a blade and conducting a microscopic examination of the internal steel grain structure. This is something that an individual knifemaker is loath to perform. Unlike the external Rockwell examination that leaves an infinitesimal test imprint on the blade, internal matrix analysis results in the total loss of the blade. Furthermore, the expenditure related to laboratory analysis must be factored along with other production costs. In most instances, these are steps

Jennifer Thomsen-Connell

The force of the hammer and the heat of the forge is life-giving to knife steel.

Basic Steps in Manufacturing a Knife

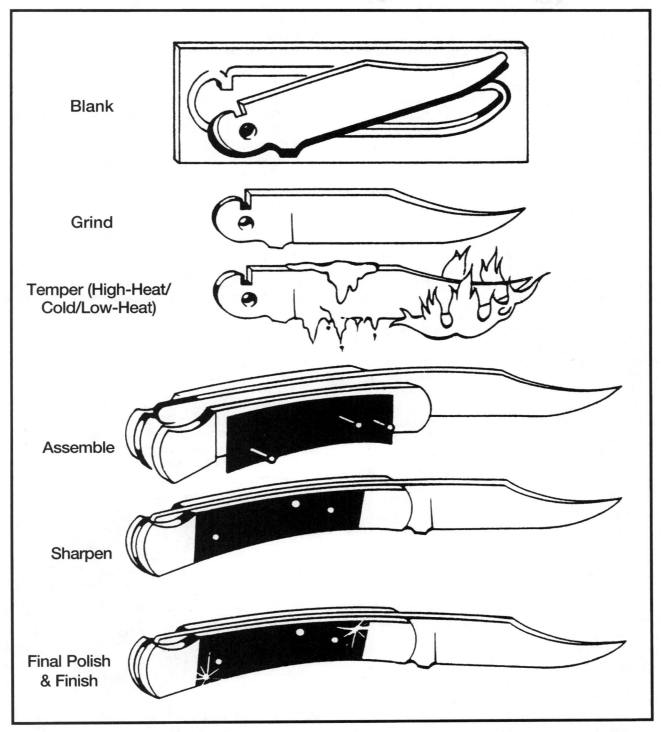

Blank

Grind

Temper (High-Heat/
Cold/Low-Heat)

Assemble

Sharpen

Final Polish
& Finish

Buck Knives

beyond the ability and means of individual knifemakers. A certain level of confidence in one's own ability to apply heat, quench and temper steel properly is absolutely necessary. Likewise, if these procedures are carried out by someone other than the maker, that same degree of trust must be extended to the facility providing those services. Absent a scientific means of assurance, the final evaluation of an individual knifemaker's skill, or choice of a service provider in this realm, can only be seen in blade edge performance.

More Heat: Subjecting steel to extreme temperature and sudden quenching creates stress within the metal. Under the microscope, this stress can be seen as cracking, molecular twisting, and asymmetrical expansion or contraction, or all of the aforementioned. While the application of heat may produce an extremely hard steel, it lacks toughness and may crack, or fracture when force is applied. The alleviation of internal stress and the inelastic nature of the steel is accomplished through annealing or tempering. The process trades a degree of hardness for an enhancement of toughness or ductility. This "drawing" out of internal stress is performed at a low heat and any retained austenite will be converted to martensite. To ensure that this conversion process and stress relief is total, the process is often repeated. Repetitive tempering, depending on the number of times the process is duplicated, is referred to as "double," or "triple draw."

Tempering is one more step in the creation of a superior performance in blade steel. It is something that cannot be rushed, sidestepped or avoided because of cost considerations, or lack of requisite skill sets. The degree of heat application, the length of time heat is applied, and the necessary number of tempering applications is precise science—not guesswork. Each steel formulation necessitates different tempering procedures. There isn't a one-works-for-all tempering process. If variables are not adjusted or controlled, blade toughness will adversely be impacted. An inadequately tempered blade may have superior edge retention properties, but the probability of chipping or fracturing during normal use will be exacerbated. This is just one more reason why a knifemaker needs to have not just some, but *all* of the right stuff.

Rockwell Testing: While early metalsmiths knew that steel was much harder than iron, no precise objective measurement system was available to them. Different steel alloys do manifest significant differences to the eye, but the eye alone gives no insight to an actual measurable degree of hardness. Traditionally, the only way to judge the hardness of a particular piece of steel blade was to use a file or sharpening stone. At best, this resulted in a subjective impression, rather than an objective measurement. Furthermore, if a finished blade is touched by a file, it will mar the finish.

Certainly, this lack of precise knowledge was also a problem for those working with other metals and even nonmetallic materials like hard plastics. The answer came in 1919, when Stanley P. Rockwell developed a hardness-testing device. Rockwell was a metallurgist, employed in a New England ball bearing fabrication facility. In an effort to determine the hardness and uniformity of bearing races, Rockwell built a test machine that could quickly and precisely measure the hardness of every kind of metal and nonmetallic materials. The Rockwell test (as it came to be called) was discussed briefly in the previous chapter. To better understand this process of examination, it will be covered in greater detail in the following paragraphs.

Rockwell testing consists of four steps. First, before actual test readings are achieved, a spherical penetrator tip (hardened steel or diamond-tipped) is directly applied to the material being tested with a minor force load. This minor force load flattens any surface imperfections or distortions at the test point. This allows complete accuracy during the actual hardness measurement phase of the test. In an actual test, the penetration or indentation into the surface of a knife blade is extremely small. Second, a major force load (this can vary depending on the particular material being tested and test scale used) is applied to the penetrator. Third, the major load is withdrawn, keeping the minor load in place. Fourth, the depth of penetration under the major load is measured, and converted reciprocally into an actual hardness reading—Rockwell number. The shallower the penetration, the harder the material and the higher the Rockwell test reading. Conversely, the deeper the penetration, the softer the material and the lower the Rockwell test reading.

D. Hollis

The heat treating process is designed to bring out what lies hidden in the steel. This Remington folder is an example of that potential.

Since the test machine can be used on a wide range of materials, there are a number of different Rockwell test scales, types of penetrators, and anvils. The American Society for Testing & Materials (ASTM) has standardized the test for each Rockwell hardness scale and provided a letter designation for each. The Rockwell "C" scale is the one used for testing knife blades. The hardness range for most useable blades is between Rc 50 to Rc 63. Blades testing at the lower end of this scale will respond to edge restoration efforts easily, but offer limited edge retention. Blades testing at the upper end of the scale will be difficult to manually sharpen, but will provide extended edge life.

Rockwell testing is an appropriate and needful quality assurance step. There's no doubt that you can produce a quality blade without going through this procedure. The question remains, however: Can that excellence be replicated consistently? Without adequate manufacturing controls (Rockwell testing is just one of many such controls), the answer is not solidly in the affirmative.

After the Fire Has Gone Out

You will note that hardness and toughness are at opposite ends of the steel spectrum. No steel known to man provides both. The best that can be achieved is that through the processes of heat exposure, quenching and tempering a harmonious blend of both qualities is produced.

A blade is heat treated to harden it and make it resistant to wear. In actual use, however, toughness and ductility are essential. Toughness provides impact resistance, and ductility produces movement instead of breach. Most of us want our knives to be resistant to wear, hence an overwhelming desire for edge retention. In the real world, however, a knife blade is subject to both impact and force. Absent the inherent ability to respond in a meaningful manner to such stress, the blade will shatter or fracture.

The heat treatment process, which includes both quenching and tempering, is designed to produce the very best in blade performance. Depending on just how those procedures are conducted, the end result may, or may not, reflect the total potential inherent in a particular steel. Poorly executed, heat treatment is the bane of the cutlery industry. Performed with knowledge, skill and precisely controlled and monitored, the same procedure is a boon to those who demand nothing less than the very best.

When you're challenged by a backcountry game-care chore, the only tool for the job is a quality knife. Responsible management of harvested consumables is completely dependent on edged tools. When you're cold, the best cloth and insulation won't help if they're not fashioned into the proper garment. Likewise, without adequate heat treatment, the finest knife steel in the world is about as useful as mud flaps on an alligator.

Jennifer Thomsen-Connell

Either blanked in a multi-ton press or hammered on an anvil (Damascus steel forging shown), heat is the uniting force behind any steel.

To be safe and comfortable, a knife handle must fit the grip pocket of your hand and possess enough texture so it won't slip during use.

Chapter 3
Hold On!

Even if your knife can cut, the handle is the controlling factor when it comes to user comfort, efficiency and safe use.

As a knife owner, you may not realize the importance of handle materials, construction, and design. Traditionally, far more significance has been focused on the blade than the knife handle. Even the best steel. The knife configuration and the cutting edge can be negated by a faulty grip design. If components like the pommel (the end cap) or guard inhibit placement of the hand, or the shape of the handle is too fat or skinny, the full cutting potential of the tool may never be realized.

The form of any product, or component thereof, should follow function. Through the science of ergonomics,

attached directly to the frame and provide the point of contact for the hand.

Handle Materials: Natural materials—animal in origin (leather, horn, antler, and bone), derived from marine environments (coral, mother-of-pearl, abalone, and ray skin), naturally occurring (amber, wood, and stone), as well as manufactured materials both metal (aluminum,

Ed Fowler

Custom maker, Ed Fowler likes sheep horn handles on his rugged fixed-blade knives. The convoluted horn surface offers an adequate grip without being uncomfortable.

we now understand that an elliptical shape fits the grip pocket geometry of the human hand. Furthermore, when wrapped around an object the interior of the hand tapers somewhat at either extremity. And this taper is more pronounced toward the back edge of the hand. Knowing this and incorporating it into an adequate handle design seemingly has escaped some knifemakers. The knife handle controls the level of energy imparted by the hand into the blade. Depending on the design's direction, some handle configurations, more than others, are adaptable and proficient at performing this function. The farther the departure from known hand biotechnology, the greater the impact on knife performance.

Handle Core: The handle core in a fixed-blade design is the blade tang. The tang is nothing more than a rearward extension of the blade. There are many different tang configurations including: thin "rat tail" tangs, split "double" tangs, and full-length/full-width tangs. In a folder, the blade tang is quite abbreviated and serves only as a hinge-point for the blade. A folding knife handle can be the skeletonized knife frame, or more commonly—a pair of handle scales. These scales are

titanium, etc.) and synthetic (molded thermoplastic and phenolic resin laminates)—are used as the substance of knife handles.

Some of the material—bone, leather, antler, and horn—are available in good supply and are relatively inexpensive. Others—ivory and oosic—are extremely limited in availability and are tightly regulated. Correspondingly, they are more costly to obtain as handle materials.

Oval washers, cut from a tanned cowhide and treated to inhibit the growth of fungus, are commonly used as knife handle material. The washers are contained between the blade guard and the pommel, stacked one upon another, along the entire length of a fixed-blade knife tang until the desired handle length is achieved. Shaped and polished, leather washers add a distinctive look to a knife. If constantly subjected to moisture, over time leather can dry-out and cracks will appear between the washers. The regular application of leather preservative is needed for protection and to prevent this from happening. Despite upkeep considerations, leather resists impact, provides an adequate gripping surface and takes minimal upkeep.

Horn, in the form of wild sheep, buffalo, African and Asian antelope horn, as well as domestic sheep and cow horn, is widely seen on both custom and production knives. The color of horn varies from almost translucent to deep black, with a myriad of shades from grey to brown. Horn is easily shaped and can be polished without a need for a surface sealer. This natural material is also resistant to impact and relatively impervious to moisture.

Bone is another widely used handle material. There is an entire industry in South America that collects cow shinbone from slaughterhouses. The bone is cleaned, thoroughly dried and then shipped to custom and production cutlery manufacturers all over the globe. Bone is commonly used for folding knife scales and it can be tinted a rainbow of shades. Likewise, bone can be "chipped" and colored to resemble stag. The worst part about working with bone is the smell. When put to the grinder it reeks appallingly.

Antlers from various *Cervidae* species (deer and elk) have been used for centuries as knife handle material. Antlers from male Sambar deer (also known as chital stag, are the most common type found on knife handles. A native of India, this deer produces extremely hard and dense cranial growths. While it must be cleaned and cured to prevent cracking, it is a superior handle material that is without peer for warmth and texture. I have personally used North American deer antlers on knife handles. While it is more porous than Sambar stag, if harvested from a recently killed animal, it works well. Likewise, North American elk and European red deer (also a member of the elk family) antler is also suitable material for knife handles. Ray Simonson (Kopromed cutlery) is now bringing red deer antlers from Poland into this country. With the current restrictions imposed by India on the collection and export of stag, knifemakers might be well advised to use this and other antler materials as a future substitute for Sambar stag.

Ivory is basically extremely dense animal dental material. That's right, it's a tooth. Elephant, fossil mastodon, hippopotamus, walrus, whale, African wild hogs (warthog, bush pig, giant forest hog), and wild boar ivory are all solid choices for knife handle materials. Restrictive international laws that govern access to elephant ivory, the most common source of handle ivory, are already in place. Fossilized mastodon ivory, while not as common, isn't covered by such restrictions. Walrus and whale ivory, once part of a thriving scrim-

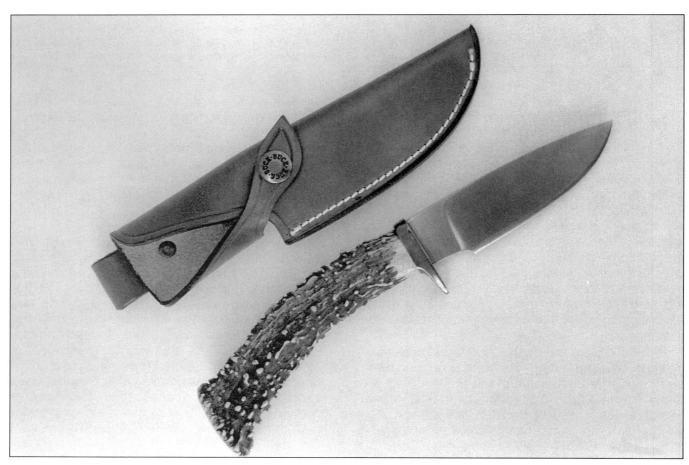

D. Hollis

This drop-point hunter from the Buck Custom Shop features a heavily-textured California mule deer antler handle which affords superior hand-to-knife contact.

shaw trade, are also difficult to obtain. On the other hand, hippo, African wild hog and boar ivory can be more easily acquired. Ivory generally "yellows" with age and it can absorb oils and salts from your hand. Nevertheless, it still provides a dramatic look to a knife and is in great demand with custom makers.

Mother-of-pearl is often used as handle scales on folders. This material is derived from a marine bivalve. It is naturally curved and not available in large sizes. Similarly, abalone shell, another ocean-dwelling mollusk is also curved and must be used in small lengths. Both of these materials are very beautiful when cleaned and polished, each imparting its own look when used on a knife handle. The only weakness is that this material will crack and break if subjected to impact.

Several orders of cartilaginous marine fishes with flattened bodies, eyes on the upper surface, widely expanded fins at either side of the body, and a slender or whip-like tail are known as rays.

The skin from these fish is rough like coarse sandpaper and has been used as a wrap over a wooden handle core on knives and swords of Japanese origin. While it provides excellent hand-to-knife contact, over time, ray skin can crack and peel. It is an improvement, however, over a wooden handle surface.

Several different naturally-occurring materials, such as amber (fossilized tree sap), stone, and wood from a variety of sources have all found their way onto knife handles. Of these materials, wood is the most commonly used on both fixed-blade and folding knives. Several exotic tropical hardwood—cocobolo, ebony, lignum vitae, bubinga, jacaranda, and others—are found as handle material in both factory and custom knives alike. Other woods—desert ironwood, thuya burl, rosewood, maple, walnut, hickory, ash, birch, buckeye, sandalwood, orange, cherry, and pear—are among other woods that can be used. Most woods are easily polished, but may need a finish for protection. Some woods, however, have a large enough oil content that when finished there is no need for an external sealer. Warm, rich, and often magnificent in presentation pieces, wood has a sustaining presence as knife handle material.

Many exotic hardwoods are used as knife handle material. Of these, cocobolo, ebony and rosewood are occasionally used on factory knives. Curly maple is widely used by many Nordic cutlery producers. However, bubinga, desert ironwood, and lignum vitae are generally only found on handmade knives. Hardwood veneer can be laminated and bonded with a clear acrylic resin. Not unlike linen or paper Micarta®, this is a very durable handle material that needs no sealer. Known in the industry as Pakkawood®, this laminate is available in a wide range of colors and is easily polished to a high gloss. It is quite popular as a handle material with some cutlery producers.

The following inset provides a brief look at the prominent features of some of the most popular wood handle materials. Of course, other woods—African blackwood, Osage orange (Bois D'Arc), cordia, kingwood, partridgewood, Brazilian walnut (Pau Ferro), tulipwood, wenge, zebrawood, and ziricote—are also part of a wider selection of handle materials. Each has its own forté, often dramatic but usually cosmetic. However, the material cost usually restricts the use of most of these woods to custom knifemakers.

Opinel

The traditional pocketknife of France, the Opinel folder, uses locally obtained hardwood for handle material. Affordable and easily machine-shaped to precise dimensions, wood is often the choice of many knifemakers, both factory and custom.

Exotic Wood Knife Handle Materials

Bubinga: An African hardwood that is very tough, with extremely fine grain. Generally, this wood has a pinkish or reddish cast, but it can vary in color manifesting rich shades of lavender and deep purple. The color is often in stripes, not unlike Zebrawood. A self-polishing wood, but it should be sealed.

Cocobolo: A hardwood that is a favorite with many knifemakers. This wood is a rich brown with some pink and red tones. The wood itself is extremely hard and buffs to a wonderful gloss without any oil or sealer. It tends to darken with age and use, but continues to maintain a marvelous luster from the contained natural wood oil.

Curly Maple: Often used on knives produced by Swedish, Finnish and other Nordic manufacturers. Very fine grain and extremely dense. This wood has a wonderful curled figure. Left in the natural state, or stained, curly maple manifests a beautiful luster.

Ebony: This wood comes in both black and brown and is fantastically dense and heavy. Occasionally, you can find ebony that has light streaks throughout which break up the monotone color. A popular handle material with custom makers, it shapes and buffs well.

Desert Ironwood: Another extremely hard wood that requires metalworking tools to work. This material features a rich, chocolate brown color with black streaks. The wood can be polished to a high gloss and needs no sealant. This material is in high demand with many knifemakers.

Lignum Vitae: This is some of the toughest wood around (has been used for bearing material). Lignum vitae is so dense, in fact, that it will not float in water. Colored with brown, tan and olive tones, the wood has an opulent, silky look. While it can be polished, an occasional oil treatment will keep it from checking.

Mesquite: This desert wood features a great deal of burl with a bold swirling pattern. Considering that the burl portion is most often used, there are few problems associated with shaping and polishing this wood.

Rosewood: This hardwood is available from various areas, including India, Brazil and Central America. Naturally rich with oil, the wood is self-polishing and doesn't require a sealer. It comes in a variety of colors, with the presence of streaking, marbling and growth lines clearly manifest.

Various metals are currently used as knife handle materials. A steel blade tang can even be skeletonized and serve as a handle. Hollow aluminum handles with removable end caps are popular in survival knives (you can pack a lot of neat stuff into a hollow knife handle). Typically, a hollow-handle knife has a very short blade tang, making the junction of the blade and handle quite weak. This is the most common failure of many commercial hollow-handle survival knives. Knifemaker Chris Reeve overcomes this problem by crafting his hollow-handle knives from a single bar of stock. In this manner, the blade, guard, and handle are one continuous piece. Probably best when used as handle scales on a folder, aluminum and titanium can be anodized in a wide range of colors and patterns. These metals are extremely lightweight, absolutely rustproof, and can be manufactured in an infinite range of configurations.

Synthetic materials, both resin-impregnated laminates and molded thermoplastics, have seen wide use as knife handle materials, particularly in factory-made knives. Cost, availability, and customer preference are all part of the expanded use of synthetics. Micarta®, a phenolic resin laminate developed by Westinghouse for use in the manufacture of electronic circuit boards, is nothing more than multiple layers of fabric, wood, or paper impregnated with a resin. Incredibly strong and able to withstand anything that Mother Nature can throw at it, this stuff makes great knife handles. Furthermore, when polished, the various layers of base material exhibit a nice contrast (not unlike Damascus steel). Similarly, carbon fiber fabric can also be resin-impregnated. This material is equally as tough as Micarta® and is available in a number of interesting patterns. And like other impregnated materials, once shaped and polished, it needs no surface protection.

When wood impregnated with a resin, rather than referring to it as Micarta®, it is marketed as Pakkawood®, Staminawood®, or Fibron®. Since the resin is distributed (impregnated) throughout the layered wood, the maker needs only to shape and polish the material to produce a suitable and long-lasting finish. Any subsequent scratches or blemishes in the finish that occur through use can be sanded and polished out by the user. The only problem with this stuff is that it's as smooth as glass. Used on many folders, common plastic handle scales offer a colorful, but less than an

United Cutlery

Made from black Spanish Micarta®, the handle on this Hibber Pro Guide Hunter has finger-grooves for enhanced hand-to-knife contact.

D. Hollis

While Micarta® can be slippery if smooth finished, when bead blasted it enhances the gripping surface markedly.

adequate gripping surface.

Thermoplastic, often referred to as thermomelt (heat-flow) materials, sees wide use as handle material on many factory knives. A product like Delrin® is a thermoplastic that can be molded in a variety of sizes and shapes. Another synthetic, Zytel®, combines chopped glass fibers in a nylon resin. This material is very strong, yet pliable to a degree. A closed-cell foam, Hypalon®, is used as handle material on some fixed-blade knives. Very comfortable to grip, yet nonabsorbent, it makes a great handle material. Probably the most popular and widely used synthetic in the cutlery industry is Kraton®. This material has a resilient (rubber-like), slightly tacky feel to it that offers a superior gripping surface. Even better, it can be molded directly on a fixed-blade knife tang and folding knife frames.

Handle Components: Most fixed-blade knives have both a forward blade guard, or quillion, and an end cap or pommel. Positioned at the leading end of the handle, the guard is designed to prevent the leading finger from coming into contact with the blade edge. Folders have no such handle components. Folding knife handle scales may be so shaped as to act as a blade guard. As an alter-

native, a metal (brass, stainless, nickel-silver) bolster is often situated at the juncture of the blade and the handle. Similarly, another bolster can be placed at the rear of the knife handle. Bolsters serve as anchor points for the pins, rivets and/or screws that attach the knife handle, handle scales, and blade together.

End caps or pommels are located at the terminus of the handle. Made from cast aluminum, brass, nickel-silver, horn, antler crown, or other material, the pommel maybe screwed or pinned to the blade tang, or affixed with glue directly to the handle. A handle molded from synthetic material may have a swell at the butt, thus eliminating the need for capping the end. The role the pommel serves in a sporting knife is grip containment and esthetic balance to the knife design.

While they may not be noticeable, most knife handles have various attachment pins located in strategic positions. At the hinge point of blade movement, folders have a main pin or Tommy pin that connects the blade tang to the handle frame. Additional smaller pins can be used to attach the bolster(s), scales, and liners to the handle frame. Some types of knives use screws rather than pins and others employ glue, solder, or epoxy to affix various handle components. Fixed-blade knives are treated similarly, with guard, handle, and end cap pinned directly to the tang. Thermoplastics can be molded onto the tang in such a manner that the material flows completely around and through the tang. In this manner, there is never a worry about the handle coming loose. Getting all of the component handle parts to fit and blend into a single unit can be challenging for the maker. One of the marks of a quality knife is just how well these individual components come together. Basically, a knife handle shouldn't appear attached. It must look like it grew there!

A knife handle is the controlling factor that dominates the cutting force of the blade. If the handle is too small, it prevents an adequate grip. Likewise, if the handle is poorly shaped, it will be uncomfortable to use for an extended period of time. The handle must also have enough texture to provide hand contact adhesion. Smooth handle materials, when wet, can be as slick as glass. Field dressing an animal, cleaning and fileting fish, or using a knife in the rain, can all compromise knife-to-handle contact. The worst of all situations is a sharp knife without adequate handle control. It's like trying to control a speeding vehicle without brakes or a steering wheel.

What's the best handle material? Finding an answer to that is like attempting to resolve a question like, "how many angels can dance on the head of a pin?" I do know that a poorly designed

Wenger Swiss Army Knives use aluminum for the handle scales on their basic military issue folder.

handle, with less than a satisfactory surface to which the hand can be clasped, will make it nearly impossible to use the knife efficiently and in a safe manner. In the field, situations are never ideal. Combine muscle fatigue, failing light and moisture, and you have an accident waiting to happen.

A few years ago, a gentleman of considerable means rode into deer camp. He was an experienced horseman and hunter. His gear was top quality and he knew how to use it. Somewhere along the way, he had purchased a custom knife with a Wyoming jade handle. It was a magnificent piece, made even more dramatic by the polished stone handle. Obviously, it had set him back more than just few bucks.

After a couple of hours at the campfire one night, he suggested that we hunt together on the following day. He had seen a huge buck twice just above a particular rim, but every time the deer had slipped away before he could get a shot off. Describing the spot where the buck had bedded on the two previous days, it seemed that the deer could bail out in several directions. Two hunters just made more sense than one. Shortly after dawn on the following day, I found myself in the company of my newly-acquired associate.

About an hour into the hunt, my friend ran smack into the animal unexpectedly and missed an easy shot. The buck then whirled around and disappeared over a nearby rim. As luck would have it, I was just below that rim and was able to get on the deer before it was swallowed up by the timber. To abbreviate a somewhat lengthy story, I was the one who ended up shooting the buck.

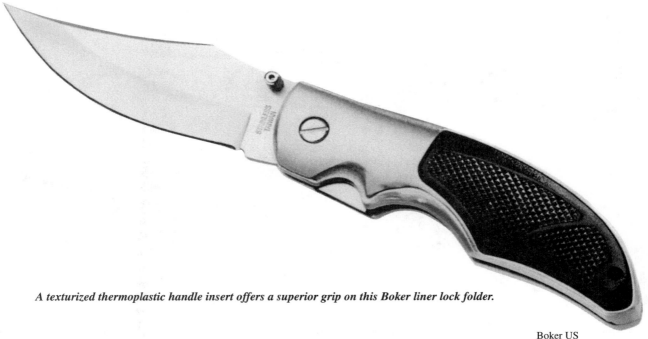

A texturized thermoplastic handle insert offers a superior grip on this Boker liner lock folder.

After unloading my rifle and setting it aside, I validated my deer license and prepared to field dress my kill. About that time, my friend came up and volunteered to handle the gutting chores with his new knife. Since the thought of taking off a warm down coat and getting bloody wasn't my idea of a good time, I took him up on his offer.

The jade-handled knife was just the right size and shape and it had a decent piece of steel in it. About the time my compatriot was elbow-deep into the chest cavity, attempting to sever the windpipe, he suddenly jumped back like he had been bitten by a rattlesnake.

"What happened," I asked?

"I just dropped my knife. The knife handle got really slippery—what with the blood and all. I just couldn't hold on to it," he replied.

While he hadn't noticed (things happen that way with a sharp knife), his hand was dripping more than just deer blood.

"You better let me have a look at your hand. I think you've cut yourself," I said.

Indeed, the hunter had inflicted a shallow laceration across two of his fingers. Nothing life threatening, but it needed a little attention. I wrapped his hand up with a clean handkerchief, fished his knife out of the deer, and finished gutting the animal with my own blade.

After we got back to camp, I had an opportunity to give his hand some proper first aid. While a few butterfly closures took care of the wound, I could see that his pride was hurt far more than his hand.

"What am I going to do with that knife now? That jade handle is too smooth to use safely" he asked.

"Take it to a place that mounts pictures and ask them to put it under glass in a shadow box," I volunteered.

That is what he did. The knife with the Wyoming jade handle had finally found its rightful place in the scheme of things. My then new friend is now an old friend. We've hunted together many times since and his hand still bears the scar from that day so long ago—and the jade-handled knife is still on the wall.

Some handle materials are truly beautiful, but often impractical. In the outdoors a knife handle can be abused. Furthermore, if you're a hunter, your favorite edged tool is definitely going to get bloody. Moreover, the elements of nature and time can wreak havoc on many natural knife handle materials. This alone can demand a heightened level of user maintenance. All of these factors should be considered in your choice of a knife handle.

An outdoor knife needs to be solidly constructed with a handle that offers both comfort and a secure grip. A molded synthetic, particularly Kraton®, is a great choice in a "using" knife. About the only thing that can damage this material is heat (campfire, Coleman stove, a lantern, etc.). Wet or dry, most synthetics won't slip in your hand. And the resilient surface is just downright comfortable. I will admit, Kraton® and its molded siblings and cousins are not the best looking handle materials, but they work! And in an outdoor knife, that's what you want.

Schrade uses molded Staglon handles on two of their Uncle Henry fixed-blade favorites.

Images Group/Schrade

H. Rexroat Photography

Stag handle scales offer both beauty and functional texture to the handle on this Gary Biggers tapered-tang, drop-point hunter.

Okay, let's get personal with this thing. My own preference in knife handle material is stag. It offers the best gripping surface available. Furthermore, it can't be matched for uniqueness and beauty. I will admit that stag can fracture if dropped on a hard surface. It doesn't hold up when placed in the garbage disposal (the untimely demise of an extremely nice Puma folder I once owned occurred in this manner). Other than these detractors, it is a superior handle material. When compared to the cost of knives with molded handles, the price of a stag-handled knife can be staggering. Additionally, you may have to look a little farther than your local Wal-Mart to find such a knife. Believe me, the price and the search will be long forgotten when you put that knife to use.

Your choice in a knife should include some consideration of the handle design, construction and material. That selection may well be your best insurance against an accidental injury. Believe me, if such an event can happen—it will! And when it does, expect it to cost far more than you could have ever imagined!

Buck Knives

Cut from rugged Cordura® Plus nylon, the fabric sheath for this Buck Mentor fixed-blade knife needs little care and offers superior protection.

Chapter 4
On the Belt

A knife sheath has much more value than just a carrying container.
How it's made and what it's made from should be an integral part of knife design itself.

Early on in my term as a knife owner, I learned a couple of valuable lessons about knife sheath design. The first lesson came one fall during waterfowl hunting season in a stubble field near Springville, Utah. A local farmer had given me a tip on a particular field where a drove of mallard and pintail ducks congregated every morning to feed. It seems that shortly after dawn, the ducks swarmed into the field from nearby Provo Lake. Well, I planned to meet the hoard come the following morning.

I arose in predawn darkness and assembled my hunting gear. In short order, shotgun, shells, and decoys were tossed into my tiny Volkswagen (I was in college in those days). I grabbed my duck call and a brand new sheath knife. The knife had been touted by the manufacturer as "an ideal bird blade." With its delicate stainless steel blade and warm rosewood handle, it was all that and then some. After threading my belt through the sheath, I jumped in my little *bug* and hit the road.

Arriving at the predetermined hunting location, I parked near a small group of trees to screen the car from view. The eastern sky was "pinking up" as I made my way out to the middle of the field. In short order, I set out the decoys, and pulled some cut corn stalks over me as camouflage. Right on schedule the ducks appeared like black flies on the tundra.

was awesome shooting and in little more than 30 minutes, I had my limit.

Somewhere between laying flat on my back, jumping up to shoot, and bending over repeatedly retrieving birds, however, my little *gem* of a knife had fallen out of its sheath. Needless to say, I was sorely crestfallen. Not only had the knife cost me more than a college student could afford, it was also a *nice* knife. In an attempt to rectify the loss, I retraced my steps. I did my best. No matter, that beautiful piece of stainless and rosewood would remain a lost treasure forever.

Later that morning, I tried to find some meaning in the whole episode. The reason for the loss was self-evident. Carried in a normal upright position on the belt, the knife sheath provided adequate restraint. The sheath designers hadn't planned, however, on the wearer laying down in a stubble field. In that position, the knife had simply slipped out of the sheath. The sheath itself was made out of top grade leather, tightly stitched and reinforced at all points of strain, and oil-treated. If there was ever a quality sheath, this was it. The faults lie not in the materials or construction, but in the design. Absent some type of closure or retaining mechanism, the sheath depended entirely on friction to contain its contents. Turned upside-down, the knife simply fell out of the sheath. It was an expensive lesson, but one I haven't forgotten through all the years.

The only bad part about it, there was no cover available for a blind. The

The top-grain leather sheath by Kershaw utilizes two retention straps for added knife sheath security.

Kershaw kai Cutlery

only way to hunt the field had been to lie flat on the ground and wait for each flight of birds. When the hunting is good, no one gives much thought to such issues. It's just part of being a duck hunter. It

Lesson number two came a few years later. I had stopped by a local gun shop to purchase a hunting license and a box of rifle shells for an upcoming deer hunt. The last thing on my mind was anything to do with a knife. At the same time, another customer was contemplating a new knife purchase. After making a thorough comparison of different models, he made his choice. It just so happened and this particular individual and I arrived at the cash register at the same time.

After paying for our purchases, this guy decided to show me his most current acquisition. After providing me with a thorough tour of the knife features, he started to return the knife fully into its place of containment. Holding the sheath with one hand, with the other hand he pushed (shoved is more like it) the knife all the way into the sheath. Well, you can guess what happened next. In an instant, the sharp knife blade cut right through the sheath and into the palm of the new knife owner's hand. There was a *howl* of pain and then a gush of blood. Prompt first aid kept a bad situation from becoming worse but the guy had still cut himself really deeply.

Unfortunately, the sheath design hadn't incorporated some type of internal barrier to prevent the blade from *bailing out* right through the leather. Furthermore, the new owner had neglected to obey the first rule of knife ownership—*don't shove knives in the direction of your own anatomy*. It could have been worse. In the field, he might have fallen on the knife with even more serious results! Right then and there, I learned that there was more to knife sheath design than meets the eye.

If there is a failure in the cutlery industry, it's that knife sheaths and carrying cases are often nothing more than afterthoughts. It's a shame to see a champagne quality knife in a beer budget sheath. Made the *right way* and with the *right stuff*, as much time and expense should go into the design, materials and construction of a sheath, as that of the knife for which it is intended. Made any other way, the sheath or carrying case fails to be an integral part of a larger paradigm.

Whatever material sheathed the blades of early man, you can bet it offered protection to both man and blade alike. It probably didn't take too many generations of lost and damaged blades and lacerated body parts to make sure of that. In all likelihood, the first blade edge coverings were made from vegetation—thick leaves, heavy vine, or wood. In time, as the knowledge of animal hide preservation developed, leather became the sheath material of choice. Recently, other materials have come to the forefront of knife sheath and carrying case manufacture. Plastics, nylon webbing, and various woven materials are all rivals, along with leather, for their own niche in the market. Even so, leather has maintained its preeminent position in the industry.

Leather has many features that make it a superior knife sheath material—not the least of which

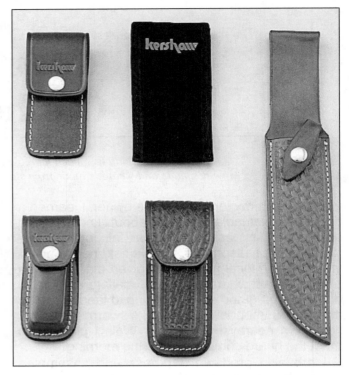

Kershaw kai Cutlery

Leather or synthetic, a knife sheath can be made out of many materials. All of these Kershaw sheaths feature reinforced stitching, snap or hook and loop closures and the best in workmanship.

is its traditional use. Leather is available in many types and grades. And here's the rub—some manufacturers go for the bottom line when selecting sheath leather. The bottom line is profit and the cost of sheath leather is one place they often pinch pennies. I've seen well-designed knives, made out of quality material, housed in a leather sheath that had the consistency of damp cardboard. It might have only meant a few dollars more for top-grain, oil-tanned leather, but the manufacturer stepped-down, rather than stepping-up. That choice turned what could have been, into something cheap and shoddy.

The best leather sheath material feels, smells and looks like what it is. Charles Allen, president of Knives of Alaska, is proud of the unique designs his firm markets. Enough pride, in fact, to carry the same quality over to the sheaths that contain his fine blades. Allen uses only the best leather and it shows. Alaska is a demanding environment and not just any leather will hold up to the dampness and omnipresent rain. Ordinary leather would quickly dry out, crack and become unserviceable. Charles insures that his knives receive the protection they deserve by using top-of-the-line leather. Even more than that, his sheaths are closely stitched with heavy waxed synthetic thread and reinforced at every corner and point of wear. Charles Allen isn't unique in the cutlery industry, but there are enough poor quality leather sheaths on the market to make you wonder why others don't follow his example.

Knifemaker Loyd Thomsen has a real commitment to his knife sheaths. "There's no way I am going to forge a Damascus blade by hand, finish it, and then put it in a cheap sheath. No way! Cattle are my family business and I have the pick of my own hides from which to choose. Only the best ones are kept for my handmade knives. Likewise, I make all of my own sheaths—start to finish. There's nearly as much put into the design, construction and tooling of the sheath as there is the knife to which it is mated. A quality knife deserves a quality sheath. To put a knife in anything else, cheapens the knife and the knifemaker."

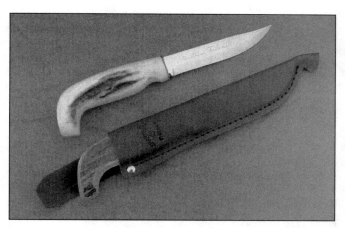

Kellam Knives

The Wild Lynx fixed-blade from Kellam Knives is housed in a traditional Lapland leather sheath that covers the blade and most of the knife handle.

When making a quality knife sheath, Loyd Thomsen emphasized the importance of cleanliness when handling raw (tanned) leather. The oils from your skin can stain leather irreparably. Also, the leather cutting block, cutting and tool implement must be kept clean and free from stains, oil and glue.

Loyd Thomsen's sheaths are all made from leather in the seven to eight ounce range (7/64" to 1/8" thick). He orders his leather directly from the tannery, usually one or two complete cowhides at a time. Thomsen's sheaths are made from a single piece of leather, except for the welt

Boker USA

A clip can be used in place of a sheath to safely attach a folding knife to the belt, pocket edge, or even a boot top.

Leather Tanning Processes

Hides are shipped to the tannery salted down to absorb all of the moisture and blood left after skinning. This prevents the hide from spoiling during shipping. Some hides are tanned with the hair left on the skin (taxidermists use this type tanning process), other hides are tanned in such a manner that all of the hair is removed from the skin. After tanning, you can find wire cuts scars, faded brands, or other blemishes on the tanned hides. Most leather processors use one (or more) of the six tanning processes listed below:

Chrome Tanned: This process uses soluble chromium salts, primarily chromium sulfate to tan the leather.

Vegetable Tanned: Vegetable materials, derived from tree bark and various plants are used in this tanning process. The vegetable formulation may be specific to an individual tannery.

Alum Tanned: Colorless aluminum salts are used in the tanning process. This process is used primarily for lace leather.

Chrome Oil Tanned: Leather is chrome tanned (as described above), then treated with an oil preservative.

Vegetable Chrome Retanned: Leather is first vegetable tanned (as described above), then retanned in chromium salts.

Chrome Vegetable Tanned: Leather is first chrome tanned (as described above), then vegetable tanned.

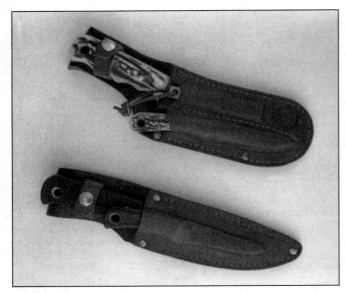

D. Hollis

Featuring the finest oil-tanned leather, closely stitched with waxed synthetic thread, and reinforced at every point of strain, sheaths that house Knives of Alaska-edged products reflect the quality of the knives they contain.

(a heavier piece of leather sewn between the leather edges where the blade edge might cut the stitching). Even the leather snap keeper that retains the knife handle is a contiguous piece of leather that is part of the larger sheath itself. This way, there's never any fear of the snap keeper becoming separated from the sheath. The entire sheath, including the snap keeper and the belt loop are all made from one continuous piece of leather, hand tooled and hand stitched. That's the Loyd Thomsen way, and he's proud of it!

Of course, there are lots of ways to make a knife sheath. Most production factories stamp sheaths out by the thousands, machine glue and stitch, dye, and then imprint each sheath with their own logo. It's a simple process, but sometimes things get sloppy. I've spent good money for quality knives that rattled around in their sheaths. And some sheaths fell apart after just one season of use. Obviously, there are good sheaths—and bad! Likewise, there are many ways to build a knife sheath. Whatever construction method is used, the sheath should not just hold and protect, it should also enhance the knife.

In all candor, leather does have its share of problems. Over time it can stretch, stain, and rot if subjected to moisture. Even with the best of care, leather can age and sometimes not too gracefully. Recently, synthetic materials have been used for sheath materials. Heavy nylon webbing works well if it has a hard liner. Webbing comes in a variety of colors, widths and can be hot-cut to seal the thread ends. Moisture and ultra violet rays don't seem to affect it, and short of exposure to exces-

sive heat, synthetic webbing is a solid choice in both sheath and carrying case material. Most webbing has a military appearance to it, so this seems to fit the look of the new generation of so-called "tactical" knives.

Other materials that are used for the construction of knife sheaths and carrying cases are nylon Cordura®, Ballistic Cloth®, and many others. These woven materials are tough, easy-to-clean, and won't rot or stretch—ever! And from a manufacturer's standpoint, they are inexpensive and easy to mass-produce. Probably best suited for the construction of belt cases for folders, any of these materials are good choices. However, it might not suit a high-end knife, or something with a more traditional look.

Another choice in sheath materials is a molded synthetic like ABS plastic, Zytel® and Kydex®. These materials are beyond tough in their ability to provide extended service under the most extreme conditions. Likewise, they are inert and resistant to almost everything but extreme heat. Easy to manipulate so that they are adaptable to a wide range of knife shapes and sizes, these materials are particularly suited for military and tactical applications. Once again, however, a molded synthetic sheath doesn't look quite right on some knives. It may be just a matter of taste, but I wouldn't swap the quality leather sheath on a handmade, stag-handled, drop-point skinner for a piece of plastic—no way! Even so, molded sheaths are here to stay, both in the low-end cutlery market and the high-end tactical knife scene.

One type of knife that goes well with a molded synthetic sheath is a filet knife. Filet knives and their sheaths are constantly exposed to moisture, fish offal, and other icky stuff (outboard motor fuel, oil, grease, you name it). There have been times that the bottom of my tackle box contained a mixture of insect repellant, mashed up salmon eggs, dead nightcrawlers, and some other stuff that doesn't fit any acceptable verbal expression (my kids think the tackle box is common property)—need I say anymore? The last time the filet knife saw the light of day, I found it right in the middle of the mess. It didn't seem to matter, because a thorough dousing with soap and water cleaned it up really good. The molded sheath even had a hole in the bottom so all the water drained right out.

I also like a molded sheath on a knife designed specifically for emergency work (police, fire, disaster, etc.). Likewise, knives for military and survival applications mate well with thermoplastic carrying containment. Since this type of knife is often a multipurpose tool, it follows that the sheath should be designed for alternative mounting (in a vehicle, as part of webbed gear, or on a harness). Molded thermoplastic sheaths work well in these applications.

Jennifer Thomsen-Connell

Here are three different styles of handmade leather knife sheaths, each made from a single piece of leather with integral keepers.

The option to screw, snap, or clip the sheath to an object is more readily available with this type of material. As much as I like leather, molded synthetics are often superior sheath materials.

When you purchase a new knife, don't overlook the sheath. Safe containment, ready access, and loss prevention are the main features of concern. Does the sheath hold the knife securely? To ascertain this feature, insert the knife in the sheath and

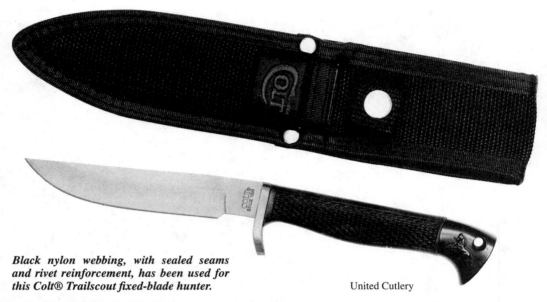

Black nylon webbing, with sealed seams and rivet reinforcement, has been used for this Colt® Trailscout fixed-blade hunter.

United Cutlery

see if you can shake it free. Then check to see if the knife still remains in place if the sheath is held upside-down. Next, can you grasp the knife and remove it from the sheath easily? Knife removal and return from carrying containment shouldn't take rocket science. If you have to read a set of instructions just to remove the knife from the sheath, then you're in *deep* soy sauce. Even more important, retainment of the knife within the sheath should be engineered so that release must be manual. There's nothing quite so exasperating as hiking through heavy brush, then realizing that the retainment strap on your sheath has come loose and the knife is nowhere to be found. Furthermore, some sheaths use a spring steel clothing clip for sheath retention. This is a great way to attach a knife at the edge of nearly anything (pants, boots, or pack). However, make sure there's enough clip tension to keep the knife where you put it. If it's a little difficult to clip the sheath on, you can be sure that it's going to be just as difficult to pull it loose.

Retaining straps and flaps need to fit and provide adequate closure. If the strap or flap is too long, the knife can bounce around and make a lot of noise. Noise is something most hunters want to avoid. I once blew a stalk on a nice buck because my knife clattered around in its sheath like a rattlesnake on the warpath. Brass snaps are traditional on knife sheaths, but Velcro® works as well and looks good on fabric or webbing. For many years, Puma knives were secured by a leather thong looped through a hole in the handle. I believe that many of the knives that company makes are still secured in a similar manner. Simple and effective, the thong worked as well as any other type of fastener. The only problem was that some knife owners didn't always remember to use it.

Beyond these considerations, carrying comfort is something that must also be taken into account. If the sheath rides too low on the hip, the knife will flop around like a fish out of water. If it rides too high, then expect to quickly realize just where your kidneys are located. The compact Bill Moran Lightweight Hunter fixed-blade, designed for Spyderco, comes with a sheath that provides for alternative belt positioning. This allows the user to find the exact carryingposition that best suits their own needs. And Spyderco isn't the only manufacturer that has engineered such a feature into a knife sheath. Some large folders even come in belt cases that allow for vertical or horizontal positioning. One of the best belt-carry designs that I've ever seen allowed for a right hip belt carry, with the sheath inserted into the rear pocket of a pair of

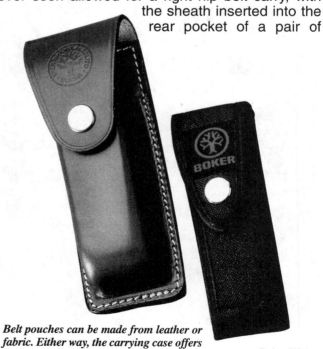

Belt pouches can be made from leather or fabric. Either way, the carrying case offers solid knife security.

Boker USA

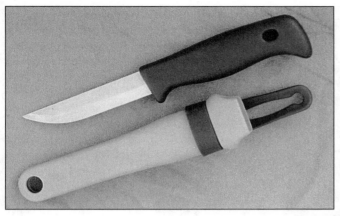

Kellam Knives

A form-fitting, molded plastic sheath contains this Finnish-designed utility knife.

If you use your knife in the outdoors, the sheath or carrying case is going to get dirty. A few scratches, a ding or two, and a little grime can be passed off as character. A major league application of mud (my last elk hunt), is just really nasty. Add some bloody fingerprints, a streak of fatty grease, some horse sweat and you have something more than a sheath with character. A small amount of dirt and debris can be removed with a damp cloth, or a scrub brush and a little warm water. If you clean leather, saddle soap works best. Don't forget to replenish the leather with a preservative after cleaning. Sheaths and carrying cases made out of webbing or fabric can be washed by hand with mild detergent and warm water. Thoroughly rinse, dry, and you're in business again.

When deciding on a particular knife, look at the sheath as well as the knife. If the sheath appears

jeans. In this manner, a sizeable fixed-blade knife and an accompanying sharpening stone could be carried without becoming cumbersome.

One of the worst cases of sheath carrying discomfort happened to me on a back-country deer hunt. About three or four miles into the hunt, the knife began to dig into my waistline to the point that a raw spot was developed. Upon further investigation, I discovered that the knife wasn't the culprit. A ridge of leather on the back of the sheath where the retaining strap was attached was to blame. Right then and there, the knife went into my pack. At the first opportunity, I gave that knife away to an associate—sure enough, he had a similar problem with the sheath!

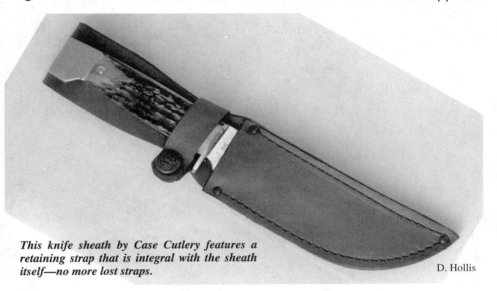

This knife sheath by Case Cutlery features a retaining strap that is integral with the sheath itself—no more lost straps.

D. Hollis

to be just another sheath—slapped together without much design consideration—it often provides insight into the knife's construction. A knife sheath can say more about the knife than the knife itself! On the other hand, if the sheath has all the attributes of premier materials and quality construction, then you can be sure that the knife deserves it!

In the words of Damascus forger and custom knifemaker Loyd Thomsen, both the knife and its sheath "should compliment each other." And that my friend is the conclusion of the whole matter.

Spyderco

The Kydex™ belt sheath designed by Spyderco for their Bill Moran Featherweight fixed-blade can be worn in a variety of positions, including lengthwise on the belt.

D. Hollis

From a bar of 440C stainless steel to a finished knife is a complicated process that includes in part, forging (two-step drop-forging shown), profiling, heat treatment, handle attachment, polishing, and final sharpening.

Chapter 5
Put It All Together

Whether it's baking or making, all manufacturing shares a common thread.

When I was a child, watching my mother and grandmother bake was a real treat. When obtaining ingredients, quality was always essential. Making a knife isn't all that different from baking. Whether it's a custom maker or a cutlery factory, the steps are extremely similar. Like the baker, the cutler uses raw materials and transforms them into the finished product—a knife. Individual bakers may use different recipes and methods. Likewise, different knifemakers may utilize divergent methodologies to accomplish the same task.

A knife begins life conceptually on a sketch-pad, drawing board, or as the product of specialized computer graphic software. The advent of computer technology into cutlery design and development has eliminated much of the trial and error prototype evolution. Well before a design is ever built, most, if not all, the problems with the interaction of various knife components (locks, springs, etc.) are all worked out through computer three-dimensional visualization. Once the design specifications are finalized and the materials decided upon, then working prototypes are produced. Prototype knives are evaluated by marketing experts and sales projections developed. Individual makers certainly don't have the luxury of all of these assets. However, the uniqueness of their designs, materials used, and professional standing may be enough to successfully launch a new design.

A knife blade can be produced using many different methods. If we exclude stone chipping as a practical production method, then hand forging is the oldest blade production technology. This technique traces its history to the early metal smiths of the copper, bronze, and iron ages. Hand-forging a knife blade is accomplished with a heat source (the forge), hand-held hammer, and anvil.

Forging a blade by hand is a tough job. For this reason, many knifemakers use a power hammer. The basics of hand forging involve heating a length of steel (bar, billet, or cylindrical ball bearing) until the forger is able to manipulate (move) the metal with the hammer. Repeated hammer strikes on the heated steel are used to form the raw steel into the desired shape.

The efficacy of forging a piece of raw steel into a knife blade has always been the subject of debate. The forger claims that the repetitive pounding of the hammer compresses the steel, compacting the molecular matrix and enhancing the internal grain structure. On the other side of the discussion, there are those that suggest that the only significant change in internal structure comes about through heat-treating and quenching. These same critics also suggested that the forger only elastically moves the heated steel with the hammer, and little, if any, compression of the molecular structure takes place.

Further complicating the issue are those that advocate the investment casting (pouring molten metal into a mold) of knife blades. While this has been used successfully, a cast blade generally lacks the tensile strength of a forged blade. All of the elements within the steel may not successfully bond, which can inhibit the overall grain structure within the steel. While such blades may be incredibly hard, they often lack the ductility necessary to perform adequately.

The process of casting or injection-molding a blade reportedly produces a stable, internal network of completely bonded, large, hard carbide molecules within the steel. Furthermore, cast blades reportedly offer enhanced cutting aggressiveness. This ability, advocates of this technology claim, is the result of tiny tooth-like projections that "pop" out of the steel when the blade edge is sharpened. Not unlike the microscopic serrations in a Damascus steel blade edge, these teeth (serrations) provide extended cutting life. Likewise, powdered ceramic can also be used to produce a knife blade. And like cast and molded metal, it has the same problems with tensile strength and ductility.

A blade can also be formed by using a drop-forge. This process consists of placing a heated length of steel into a form, upon which an extremely heavy die (hammer) is dropped. The drop-hammer's impact on the heated metal results in an elastic movement of the steel. This movement conforms to whatever shape has been cut or molded into the cavity created by the coming together of the form and die. Depending on the thickness and configuration of the steel, this process may go through more than a single heating and hammer impact. The end product is a rough, oversize blade blank. Drop-forging is an older method of cutlery production that was once widely used here in the United States. However, safety considerations and limited production output have made drop-hammer use obsolete in this country. Throughout Europe, Asia, and Latin America, drop-hammer forging is still in widespread use.

Blades can also be fine blanked from rolled steel of a predetermined thickness. This is the standard production process used in most of the larger cutlery factories. Production stock with an annealed surface shell comes from the steel mill in large rolls. This rolled steel is fed directly into a mechanical straightener that removes retained roll memory. From the straightener, the steel strip is guided into a multiple ton blanking press. This computer-controlled machine uses a precision die to punch out a blade "blank." Similar to cutting cookies out of fresh dough, the blank is

Buck Knives

Rolls of stainless steel are being fed into the fine blanking press at the Buck Knife factory.

sheared from the steel strip. The annealing of the steel surface shell at the steel mill allows this process to occur without placing undue stress on the cutting die. To maintain die integrity, this procedure has a limited number of production cycles, after which the dies are replaced. In some large cutlery factories there are internal die and tool shops in which dies are made, repaired, and reworked.

Small knife production facilities may not have the luxury of a fine blanking press, or heat treatment and tempering facilities. The installation of such a unit takes special zoning, flooring, ventilation, inspection, and other requirements that may be beyond the facility's means or location. Also, the actual number of knives produced may not necessitate such an investment. In this case, a laser, high-pressure water jet, or wire EDM (electrical discharge machining) cutter is used to cut the blade blanks out of sheets of steel. This process will also be used in a major factory with stainless steels like ATS-34, ATS-55, and 154CM. These steels have a surface hardness that prevents the use of a fine blanking press. Despite all of the advertising hyperbole that small firms use to tout the superiority of laser-cutting, with some steels, all production facilities (large or small), must use this type of technology. Even with such sophisticated processes, the edge of the steel will be chemically deformed. Whether a blade is fine blanked from roll stock, or cut out of sheet steel, the necessity of grinding to acceptable tolerances cannot be eliminated. Similarly, the heat treating and tempering processes may be contracted to an outside facility.

In many parts of the world entire communities, each with a specialized cutlery function, are used to forge, heat-treat, temper, assemble, and finish knives. The greater community becomes, in fact, an extended production cutlery facility. For example, in Solingen, Germany, a blade may be drop-forged at one location, heat-treated and tempered at another, shaped and profiled in a 19th Century grinding cottage with a water-driven grinding wheel, and assembled and finished in the actual knife factory. The same thing is true in Japan where the entire village participates in the knifemaking process, with oversight coming from a central facility. Since there are many ways to make a knife, total containment of the entire process in one production facility is a relatively recent development.

After the blade has been blanked, all of the necessary physical attributes—swedge, choil, shoulder profile, and blade grind—are all imparted to the blank. In the most technologically sophisticated manufacturing facilities, robotic tools are used for these processes. This provides production consistency that is not possible with hand grinding. During this stage of the knifemaking procedure, holes for the attachment of the handle, a pommel, guards, bolsters, etc. are also drilled in the blade blank.

After grinding and drilling, some manufacturers place the blade blank in a large vibrating vat containing a deburring and polishing medium. This process is similar, but on a larger scale, to the procedure a hand loader uses when cleaning brass cartridge cases. Instead of tumbling the blade blanks, which could cause damage to their surfaces, the vibration of the vat circulates the polishing medium along the entire surface of the blades. This removes most of the burrs, scratches, and other surface imperfections that remain after blanking, grinding and drilling.

The most important step in the creation of the knife blade is the heat treatment and tempering process. While the steel stock arrives at the plant in an annealed form, during the blanking and grinding process a certain level of work hardness is imparted to the blade. To remove this internal stress, prior to heat-treatment, the blade is subjected to low heat. This provides a consistent internal matrix that responds to high heat in a more predictable manner.

Next, the blade is subjected to extreme heat, in the gas-fired forge, for a precise amount of time. Large cutlery plants heat-treat their blades in a computer-controlled forge that can handle a large number of blades simultaneously. Both small production facilities and individual knifemakers may contract this procedure to an out-

Images Group/Schrade

In the production cutlery factory (Imperial-Schrade plant pictured), individual knife component parts are blanked out on large presses.

Swiss Army Brands

Lined up in a row, these high-tech machines are all involved in the manufacture of Swiss Army Knife components.

side shop. The actual time in the forge, or "soak time," allows the heat to completely penetrate the blade. This results in a blade that is hardened all the way to the core. What actually occurs during heat-treatment is the conversion of the internal large grain austenite structure to fine grain martensite. If the blade enters the forge with internal stress, work-hardened surfaces, or is not allowed to "soak" long enough, the conversion process will be inconsistent.

After heat treatment, the blade is quenched. This quenching process further produces a fine internal steel lattice structure. Carbon steel blades are generally subjected to a warm oil quench. Stainless steel blades, however, must be placed in a cryogenic environment (freezer) at a sub-zero temperature to complete the austenite-to-martensite conversion process. This sub-zero quenching must occur before any retained austenite has time to become stabilized. To prevent this from happening, the blades are transferred from the forge to the freezer shortly after the completion of heat treatment. If the blades are left out to completely air-cool, the steel matrix will become fixed and resist further internal conversion.

Blade tempering occurs after quenching and is simply a low heat process that "draws" off some of the hardness after heat treatment. This is necessary to impart a measure of ductility to the blade. If this isn't done, the blade will be extremely hard and very brittle. If it is dropped or subjected to lateral stress, the blade can fracture and chip. The terms, "double-draw" and "triple-draw" refer to the number of times that the tempering process is repeated.

While the blade is involved in its own creative process, the various handle components are also being produced. In some instances, bolsters, guards, and pommels are die-cast, or stamped with the same kind of press that's used to make coins. In a similar manner, the assorted connective pins are mechanically extruded or cut from wire stock. Additionally, handle scales are cut to size or punched out of sheet stock.

Knife assembly refers to the process of bonding the various component knife parts (handle, bolsters, guard, pommel, etc.). While the process lends itself to machine work, there is still considerable human handwork required. This is especially true when assembling folding knives. Folding knife blades must undergo an annealing process in the tang section, so that the hardness is harmonious with the hardness of the spring. This prevents the uneven wear that will result if steels of incompatible hardness come into contact. The blades are threaded onto the main pin(s) and placed into the framework of the knife.

Opinel (Fontana+Thomasset Photographers)

Knife fabrication includes precise fitting of all parts.

Frame liners, springs, bolster(s), and handle scales are all connected. At every step of the assembly process human hands are involved. This includes adjusting the fit and movement of the blade(s), as well as the working of the lock mechanism (if a lock-blade folder).

A fixed-blade knife must also have its handle, guard, and a pommel fitted and securely attached to the blade tang. If the handle is a thermoplastic material, it will be molded directly onto the tang after the blade is heat treated and tempered. While a fixed-blade knife has fewer components than a folder, nevertheless, handwork is still necessary to bring the handle elements together into "oneness" with the blade.

Polishing the knife is necessary to blend the various components into a single unit. This makes a knife truly saleable. Surprisingly, far more time is spent on the outward appearance of the knife, than one would imagine. This is the "silent salesman" that is part of the knife's retail presence.

Finally, the knife is sharpened. While hollow grinding and other edge profiling is done by

Even in a production cutlery factory (Imperial-Schrade plant pictured), knives are assembled one at a time.

Kershaw kai Cutlery

machine prior to heat treatment, most sharpening is performed by the human hand. The edge is carefully brought to its full cutting potential by hand on a machine-operated grinding belt of appropriate grit. As an alternative, some manufacturers use a production sharpening machine. No matter the exact process, knife sharpening still takes human involvement.

The knife receives its final touch-up to remove any surface blemishes and a final inspection is conducted. While quality control measures and inspections are conducted at various steps during the knife manufacturing process, and only a small percentage of all finished knives are rejected at the final inspection. Rejected knives have minor blemishes and will be reworked to bring them up to the desired quality level. Occasionally, a knife will manifest a major defect. When this is found, the knife will be torn-apart and the flawed component(s) replaced. Quality and consistency are the benchmarks of a production cutlery facility.

Some knifemakers take shortcuts in the knife fabrication process. A blade blank can easily be cut out of sheet steel with a metal bandsaw. This eliminates the need for most of the expensive machinery involved in knifemaking. Design features can be applied to the blank through a process called stock removal. Not unlike an artist

carving in steel, the knifemaker removes all of the unnecessary material through abrasion (grinding). This can be done in a small shop with very simple tools (hand files, a belt grinder, etc.), eliminating the need for expensive machinery. After the blade is appropriately profiled, it is then sent to an outside facility for heat-treating and tempering. Upon return, the blade receives a handle, final polishing, and sharpening.

Of course, there are those knifemakers who purchase precut, heat-treated and tempered blades and do nothing more than attach a handle, grind, polish, sharpen and call it good! Knifemaking prejudice being what it is, many knifemakers and blade enthusiasts may give such work little regard. I have, however, seen good knives at affordable prices that were produced in this manner.

To make the whole process of knife fabrication more understandable, the description of the various production steps has been greatly simplified. This has been done to help the reader more clearly visualize the transition from raw steel to a finished knife. In reality, there are dozens of steps within each major process. Furthermore, production cutlery manufacturers install quality control measures at every point in knife fabrication. This ensures that the final edged product meets the

D. Hollis

Hand assembly is still part of modern knife production. In the German Puma knife factory, this knifemaker is pinning the handle scales to a folding knife.

manufacturer's demand for quality before it hits the marketplace.

Some cutlery factories may have their own in-house packaging production facility. In the Schrade plant, for example, all of their packaging, plastic product containment, injection molding, and screen printing are all accomplished within the factory. This is also true with many other larger cutlery facilities. Smaller firms may contract this process to an outside vendor. The larger the factory, the more likely it will be that the total knife-making and packaging processes will be conducted at a single location. Conversely, the smaller the production facility, the greater likelihood that many functions, including packaging, may take place outside of the factory. In some instances, domestic "factories" may do nothing more than remove products from foreign shipping containment, insert them in individual boxes, and forward those products to wholesale or retail dealers.

When selecting a knife, much of what went into the production of that knife cannot be seen. The knife buyer must rest on the reputation of the knifemaker or manufacturer. If a maker or cutlery firm has been in business for a number of years, then their standing with the consumer has been dependent on the quality of their products. Simply put, they can't afford lesser quality material

Opinel

Blade grinding in the older Opinel factory at Cognin, France.

D. Hollis

Knife manufacturers spend as much time making their cutlery products look good, as they do in all the rest of the manufacturing process.

and inferior craftsmanship. Never forget that below a certain point in pricing, neither a knifemaker, nor a manufacturer can provide both quality materials and workmanship. If the border between production costs and the retail price indicates an inadequate profit, then either the quality of materials or product workmanship becomes jeopardized.

When selecting an edged product, look beyond the advertising hyperbole and fancy packaging. Unsubstantial advertisements, wild claims, or an attempt to camouflage the materials used in their products (440A stainless steel disguised as "400 series" stainless), is, in my humble opinion, suspect.

Certainly, knifemaking has entered a new realm of sophisticated technology. Even so, there is still room for the individual knifemaker. While those that work by hand may lack the luxury of computer-controlled machinery and robotic engineering, nevertheless, there is no substitute for the blood, sweat and tears that often go into a handmade knife. Conversely, factory-made knives offer a level of quality and consistency that is often questionable in a handmade product. More importantly, knife factories have made quality knives more affordable for the average person.

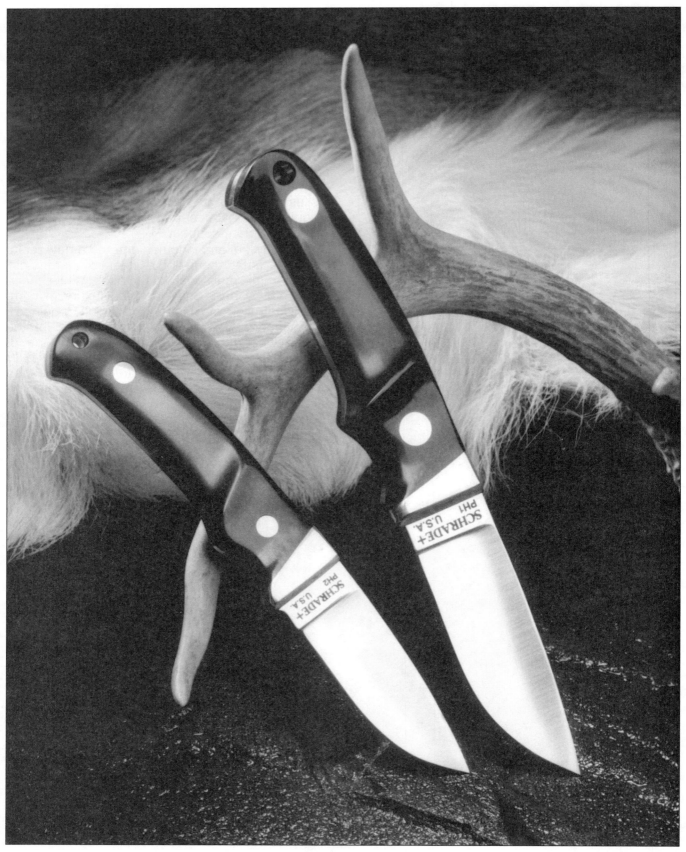

Images Group/Schrade

The Schrade Mini Pro Hunter (left), and its larger sibling the Pro Hunter (right), both feature ergonomic handles that allow for ease of movement and positioning when field-dressing, skinning, and butchering game.

Chapter 6
The Straight Stuff

It all began with a fixed-blade knife and in the new millennium this design is often still the choice of knowledgeable outdoors folk.

Knives are made in two basic configurations—fixed-blade and folding. Of the two, the fixed-blade knife design is by far the oldest. The term "fixed," means that the blade position never moves. Undoubtedly, the first knives used by man were of this design. Whether it is a stone shard, a purposefully-chipped cutting implement, or an early copper, bronze or iron-forged knife, each one of these cutting tools shares the same descriptive term—fixed blade.

A fixed-blade knife edge is always exposed. Since this could present a danger to the user during knife transport, the knife must be secured in an outer sheath or cover to prevent accidental injury. This covering imparted its own terminology, "a sheath knife," to the fixed-blade design. Even today, knives of this design are still commonly referred to by this jargon.

The forte of the fixed-blade or sheath knife design is manifest in its inherent strength, easy access and as a medium of personal artistic expression. No folding knife can ever equal the structural integrity of a fixed-blade. Subject a folder to lateral blade stress and you're bound to learn about knife failure. A folding knife blade is secured to the frame by the main or Tommy pin. Using the blade to pry or twist will put stress on the knife frame at the pin. That abuse can result in damage to the knife frame at the point of blade tang attachment, as well as blade fracture. Since most fixed-blade designs feature a tang insertion more than half way, if not all the way through the length of the handle, this is something that rarely occurs in this knife configuration.

Another negative characteristic of a folding knife is the mechanism by which the blade opens

H. Rexroat Photography

Gary Biggers used outer layer (bark) mammoth ivory on this tapered-tang, drop-point hunter.

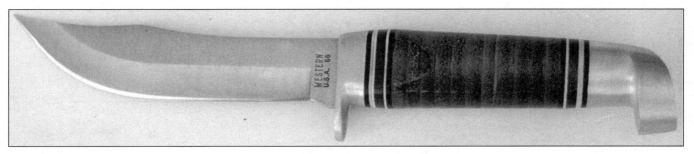

D. Hollis

This stainless Western sheath knife features a single guard, leather washer grip and stainless steel blade. Perfect for primary big game field care, this cutlery brand has been a favorite of outdoors folk for many generations.

and closes. It only takes a small amount of debris, hair, animal fat, or crusted blood to inhibit the blade pathway. This can occur either within the knife frame, or at the blade locking point. If the blade tang is unable to push its way through this material, it will not fully open or close. Should the knife feature a blade lock or brace, the mechanism cannot engage properly. If a back spring lock or inner liner brace doesn't engage fully, it will fail at an inopportune moment. Such failure can result in personal injury (read that as a serious laceration with a need for medical attention). A folding knife must be kept clean to function properly. In the field, a thorough cleaning may not always be possible. Even with the best of care, a folding knife will collect grit, grime, and foreign material and can become an accident waiting to happen.

Over time, all folding knives will manifest wear. (Absent some way of tightening the knife frame.) This can also impact tool use and safety. Some cutlery manufacturers do make provisions for adjusting blade tang tension (Benchmade Knives incorporates this feature in many of their edge products). This, however, is the exception, rather than common manufacturing practice. If you've never had this problem, then you haven't used your knife very much. Believe me. It gets really serious when a loose blade overrides the locking mechanism. Obviously, there are potential problems with folders. You may never encounter any of these situations, but such events do happen.

Since a fixed-blade knife has no moving parts, issues like those mentioned in the two preceding paragraphs have no impact on this design. Lateral blade flexibility in a fixed-blade design is far greater than any folder. One of the tests often performed on a fixed-blade depends on blade ductility. The blade is secured in a vise and a pipe is slipped over the knife handle. Then the blade is laterally bent 90-degrees from its normal position. After this, the blade is expected to return to its original position. Try that with a folder!

When it comes to cleanliness, a fixed-blade knife never needs a bath or thorough scrubbing to function properly. Clean or dirty, this knife design will provide adequate service each and every time. The knife's sharpness was the most important consideration. A knife might not look so good, but it still does the job.

In its purest expression, a fixed-blade knife features a blade tang that runs the full-length and width of the handle. The tang is simply a rearward extension of the blade itself. This provides a structure upon which the handle is attached. Other tang configurations exist—rattail, single narrow and double narrow—each allowing a particular type of guard, handle and pommel attachment. However, the full-length, full-width tang is the strongest design.

A fixed-blade knife can be of any size, length, or blade pattern configuration. A sword, a dagger, and a sheath knife are all of the fixed-blade design (ever see a folding sword?). Some blade patterns, like the trailing-point and broad skinning shapes are difficult to engineer into a folding knife design. Consequently, these patterns are generally found only in fixed-blade knives. Likewise, if the blade length exceeds a length comfortably carried in the pocket (about a maximum of 4-inches) when folded, it will seldom be found on a folder. While most fixed-blades feature longer blade lengths, this isn't always true. Ka-bar has a new line of Dan Harrison designed fixed blades that feature abbreviated blades. The overall sheath length of the new Ka-bar *Precision Hunters* is comparable to the size of a folding-knife belt case.

For years, a fixed-blade knife was thought to be the quintessential "hunting knife." This all changed in the early 1960s with the introduction of the Buck *Folding Hunter.* This Buck offering was a folding knife that featured a locking blade. Hunters and outdoors folk of every description took to this new concept "like a duck to water." Subsequently,

Ka-bar Knives

In the sheath, any one of this trio of Ka-bar fixed-blade Precision Hunters is no larger than a folder in a belt case. With the introduction of these tiny wonders, it would seem that the fixed-blade knife has entered a new era of acceptability.

sales of fixed-blades exhibited a marked decline. While there have been, and will always be fixed-blade enthusiasts, because of their carrying convenience current outdoor cutlery consumers prefer folders by a wide margin.

In truth, a fixed-blade is not all that convenient to tote on your belt. If the knife doesn't *jab* you in the kidneys, it *slaps* you on the leg. Even worse, trying to get into and out of a vehicle wearing a sheath knife can be a challenge. And if you do

much sitting in the field (glassing, in a blind, on a stand), a fixed-blade can ride up on your hip and dig into your side. Small fixed-blade knives are generally not a problem, but an overall length of about 6-inch is about the maximum.

Not all fixed-blade knife users want to carry a small knife. No doubt, you heard it stated that "only someone new to the outdoors would carry a big fixed-blade knife." Well, I can tell you—*it isn't true*. Pioneers, mountain men, and others who opened this country all carried fixed-blade knives of more than ample proportions. Petty criminals, gamblers, and whorehouse bouncers may have used push-daggers and pearl-handled toothpick knives, but the thought of carrying a small knife, or a folder (if such knives were obtainable at that time) would have marked the owner as "dandy," or worse.

Men of the outdoors (women too) were often faced with *hostiles*, grizzly bears, and a whole host of game-care chores. Those who depended on a firearm and a knife for survival often carried what amounted to a large butcher knife (lamb splitter). Certainly, Jim Bowie didn't earn his reputation with a folding knife. And historical figures, like Daniel Boone, Grizzly Adams, Kit Carson, Jim Bridger, and all the rest carried full-size, fixed-blade sheath knives.

Even today, many hunters, guides, outfitters and outdoor scribes prefer the fixed blade design. One of my friends, Zieb Stetler, is a sheath knife fan. An easterner by birth, Zieb has resided in

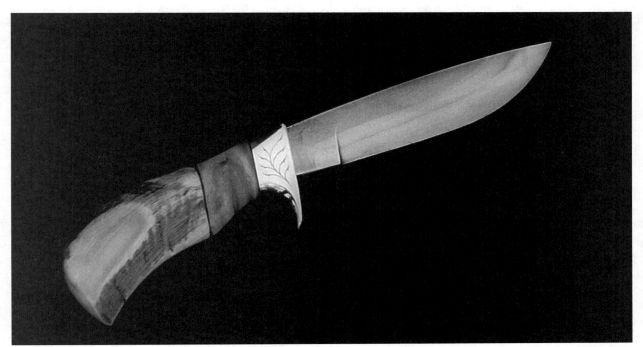

Ed Fowler

Ed Fowler has a reputation for making "hell for stout" fixed-blade knives. Certainly, this model with its sheep horn handle, engraved brass single guard, and drop-point blade pattern is all that and then some!

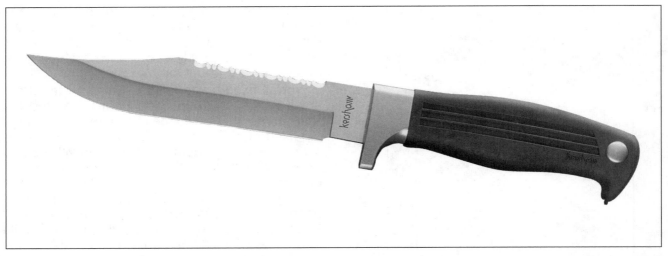

Kershaw kai Cutlery

The serrated sawback on this Kershaw fixed-blade offering works because the blade is housed in a belt sheath. With a folder this type of blade back treatment isn't possible.

Wyoming for a number of years. Among his many interests, he enjoys hunting on horseback. If you know anything about saddle stock, then you realize that there are times that things can go awry. This is particularly true if you're trailing a string of pack mules. When either mules or pack horses get their dander up, it's time to cut the string loose. Zieb's preference for this all-too-frequent cutting chore is a large fixed-blade knife.

"When I have to cut a pack string loose, there's generally no time to dismount, secure my horse and untie a knot. I just whip out my sheath knife, reach back and whack the lead rope or twine. If I had to fool around with a pocket knife, a sheath knife with a short blade, or even a lock-blade folder things could get out of hand. Before I know it, my own horse would be involved in the mess. Then it's only a matter of seconds before everything goes to pieces," Zieb said.

Zieb Stetler isn't the only outdoorsman I know that likes a big fixed-blade knife. Outdoor writer, Jim Zumbo, collaborated with the Schrade Knife folks to produce what he felt was the ultimate elk blade. The fixed-blade *Zumbo Elk Knife* is a sizeable field blade. This *keen* cutter combines a 6" Schrade+Stainless steel blade, with a guthook and saw back features. And the ergonomically-designed, molded handle provides plenty of blade control. Jim Zumbo has lots of experience hunting elk. If anybody knows what kind of knife it takes to handle a big bull, then he does!—and lots of other big-game hunters agree with him.

Knife handle shape is another plus for the fixed-blade design. No matter how a folding knife handle is designed, there is always going to be a certain amount of angularity present. A fixed-blade knife handle configured in the preferred oval shape easily fits the grip-pocket of the hand. With many cutlery manufacturers, the knife handle is an afterthought. Without consideration to the principles of gravity and leverage, many folding knives have handles that are short on blade control and any prolonged use will result in hand fatigue. Combine failing light and muscle fatigue with knife use and the doorway to accidental injury is wide open. If you don't think that such ergonomic considerations are important, then spend some time using both a fixed-blade and a folder and you'll quickly realize the superiority of the fixed-blade handle design.

Design simplicity is another fixed-blade asset. A fixed-blade knife can have as few major components as two individual pieces—a full tang blade and a molded thermoplastic handle. It just doesn't get simpler than that! Even a more sophisticated design, with a full-length tang, guard and paired handle scales, will only have five major elements. Add a couple handle spacers, a pommel or end cap and you still have fewer components than a folding knife.

Generally, a fixed-blade knife is a better value than a comparable folder (several popular and deeply-discounted folders are the exception). This is related to the time it takes to produce individual knife parts, put the knife together, fit and finish a folder. Building a folding knife takes more time and effort than putting together a similar fixed-blade. I can recall watching cutlers in the Boker knife factory in Solingen, Germany spend an inordinate amount of time tweaking a folder to give it a perfectly smooth blade walk and talk (movement of the blade tang along the back spring and a crisp locking action). Every Boker folding knife I ever handled felt the same. The blade tang move-

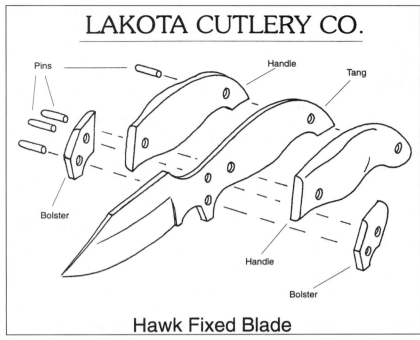

LAKOTA CUTLERY CO.

Pins

Handle

Tang

Bolster

Handle

Bolster

Hawk Fixed Blade

Line Art: Jon Cox

This exploded line drawing of a Lakota Hawk sheath knife graphically illustrates the simplicity of the fixed-blade design.

full-length tang, offer superior structural integrity. Any attempt at chopping with, or pounding on a folding knife blade can result in knife failure. While the same thing could happen to a fixed-blade knife, a thicker full-tang blade provides enhanced tool strength. Greater blade strength is the single factor that decreases the potential for knife failure. Even an overly-large main pin blade attachment cannot equal the strength of a fixed-blade rigid tang extension. There is simply no comparison!

It has already been stated that current sales trends put folding knives way ahead of sheath knives by a wide margin. This is only true with those products that we generally term "using" knives. These knives are the edged tools selected for everyday use in the outdoors. In spite of all of this, most handmade and custom knives are all fixed-blades.

I just returned from a knife show in southern California. With few exceptions, most makers exhibited fixed-blade pieces. Maybe this was true because the fixed-blade configuration offers a larger steel "canvas" upon which the knifemaker can demonstrate his prowess. And it

ment is so characteristic that with my eyes closed I can tell a Boker folder from the rest of the pack. However, quality of that level takes time—lots of it.

Furthermore, most fixed-blade knives have thicker blades, which, when combined with the

Buck Knives

Buck Knives makes a wide range of full-tang, fixed-blade models, including this Mentor (Model 470BK) with its rugged thermoplastic handle. This type of handle material guarantees a firm, non-slip grip even when wet.

could be that the simplicity of the fixed-blade design takes less of the maker's time. While this may be true for those using stock-removal methodology, a forger can spend countless hours on a fixed-blade knife. The sales disparity between fixed-blade and folding knives seems to be reversed in the handmade, custom, collectable and fantasy knife categories. Even with my own knife purchases (yes, writers do occasionally spend their own money on a knife), I can just salivate over the lines of a handmade fixed-blade knife. Yet, it takes something special to get my juices churned up over a folder.

Don't get me wrong. I like folders—a lot. This is especially true when the knife's blade movement is smooth. It's just that there seems to be so much more character in a fixed-blade design. Whatever the reasons, within the pages of any knife magazine, or at knife shows, you'll see far more fixed-blade offerings than folders.

How can the quality of a fixed-blade knife be determined? There are a few indicators that can provide a measure of insight. First of all, you should inspect a knife for perfect bilateral symmetry. That is to say, one side of the knife should mirror the other. Hold the knife up to the light and check for grind continuity on either side of the blade. While you're at it, look for "comet tails" that are sure indicators the knifemaker didn't polish the blade properly. Examine the guard, handle, and pommel (end cap) carefully to see if there are any gaps or uneven surfaces. The handle should look like it grew on the blade tang, rather than just being attached.

You should know specifically what kind of materials went into the manufacture of the knife. Buzz words like, "surgical" steel (surgical instruments are generally made out of the cheapest stainless steel possible), "high-carbon" steel, or "rust-free" steel are generally meaningless. What you want to know is the type (carbon or stainless) and number indicator (440A, 440C, 154CM, ATS-34, etc.) of the steel. Then you can know the composition of the steel formulation.

Additionally, you'll need to know the Rockwell test measurement of the blade steel. Any skilled knifemaker should be able to temper a blade to a precise degree. If the maker doesn't heat treat and temper his own knives, then the firm providing that service should be able to control the final Rockwell measurement. If the test range is wider than about two points, I would think twice about the purchase. Finally, information on all of the other knife components, including the attachment pins/screws, guard,

pommel (end cap), including handle material, and any other parts should be readily available.

When you're finished looking at the knife, give the sheath a thorough examination. I stated in a previous chapter that the quality of the sheath is a good tip-off to what you can expect in the knife—you better believe it! Only after a thorough inspection of the knife, its sheath and the material specifications does the final price have any meaning.

What will you pay for a fixed-blade knife? The sky is the limit. However, I would suggest a quality factory fixed-blade can be had for less than $100. It won't be fancy, but it will offer quality materials and craftsmanship. Handmade fixed-blades can be purchased for somewhere between $200-$500. I like to shop knife shows for new makers that don't think they're *all that* quite yet. These folks generally price their knives more competitively and are often willing to bargain. Knives made by stock removal will definitely be less expense then those that are hand-forged from scratch. You'll find a better bargain in some factory custom collaborations than if you go directly to the custom maker. And exotic blade and handle materials can push the price of any knife well beyond $1000, or more. Finally, expect art and fantasy fixed-blades to be priced for those with lots of disposable income.

In the final analysis of an outdoor knife, ask yourself which kind—fixed-blade or folding—would you like to carry in a survival situation. I had an acquaintance that won a Medal of Honor during World War II in the battle for Iwo Jima. He used his fixed-blade Ka-bar knife for everything, including opening canned rations, digging a fox hole, and defending his life. He strongly feels that there is no way a folding knife could have done the job. He's a Marine and that kind of sentiment is to be expected, but he certainly knows the difference between a fixed-blade and a folder.

For my part, I've always liked fixed-blade knives. Maybe it's because I began my outdoor career with one on my belt. Even with that preference, however, I still carry a folder for most deer, antelope, wild boar, small game, waterfowl and upland bird hunting. For bigger animals like elk, moose, caribou, most African game and camp work, a sheath knife is my idea of a serious edged tool. It's all a matter of personal taste and preference. But there is something about a sheath knife that I can't explain. And the farther away from camp I find myself, the more security there seems to be with a fixed-blade knife on my hip.

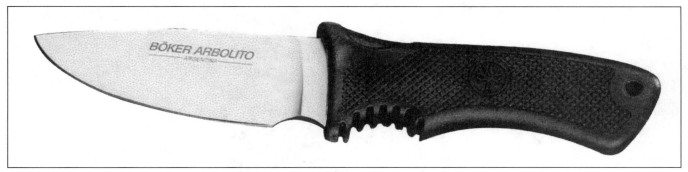

Made in Boker's South American cutlery factory and featuring a full-tang stainless blade and molded handle, this drop-point pattern Arbolito sheath knife is a fine all-around edged game and camp tool.

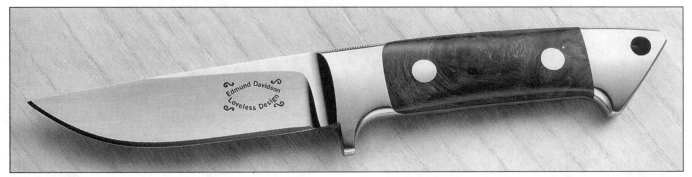

Here's a Bob Loveless design by knifemaker Edmund Davidson. Featuring a hollow-ground BG-42 blade, with hand-rubbed desert ironwood handle scales and stainless steel guard and pommel, this is a serious fixed-blade field knife.

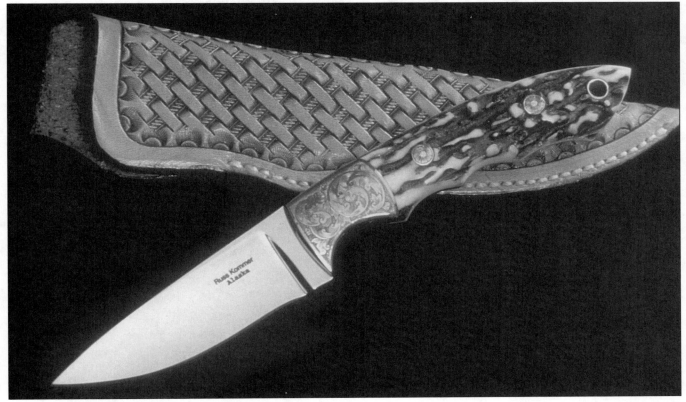

This full-length tang, drop-point hunter with a recessed choil is the work of Russ Kommer. This sleek beauty, named "The Packer," features a 2-3/4" blade of mirror-polished ATS-34. Bolster and fittings are 416 stainless with engraving by Jim White. The handle scales are presentation grade India stag. This is truly a distinctive one-of-a-kind piece.

Ka-bar

The lockblade folder (often carried in a belt case) with its clip-point blade, brass or stainless steel bolsters and wood handle scales has become part of many blue-collar professional's daily attire.

Chapter 7
Fold it Up!

Either in the pocket or on the belt it's all about carrying convenience.

About the time it became unacceptable to wear a sword or a knife openly in polite society, the folding (or pocket) knife made its emergence. Of course, men's pants had to acquire pockets first, but that was also an inevitable development. Over the years, this more compact knife configuration has become the choice of four out five knife owners.

The selection of a folder is usually stimulated by many things, not the least of which is public perception. It's a sad commentary on the state of modern society, but carrying a fixed-blade knife anywhere is sure to arouse the suspicion of the general public—law enforcement included.

Once, during the course of a fall deer hunt, I took an extra day at the end of the trip to visit a remote ghost town. Miles from anywhere resembling a populated area, an assemblage of old western buildings had been well preserved by the arid environment of the high plains. Fortunately, the state had the forethought (something that political entities are often short on) to make the area an historic site.

It was October and the usual crowd of summer visitors had diminished to less than a handful. I didn't think that a pair of jeans, plaid shirt, boots, and openly carried sheath knife was all that out of place—especially during deer season. However, some concerned citizen also visiting the ghost town felt differently. The local county sheriff's department received a call about an "armed and threatening-looking man" at the historic site. I guess my week-old growth of whiskers provided the threatening look and the sheath knife on my belt apparently put me in the "armed" category.

About the time I was wandering through the ghost town graveyard, a deputy sheriff approached me with a heightened level of caution. After a tense few moments, the deputy realized that I was about as threatening as a dry wind and my openly carried sheath knife didn't quite put me in the criminal category.

"Folks just don't like to see anyone carrying a knife, especially not a sheath knife. A few years ago, no one would have thought anything about it. Now, the attitude of the public has taken a sharp turn to the left," the deputy said. He apologized for the confrontation, but told me that it might be prudent to put the knife in my truck.

If the knife had been a folder in a closed belt case, it would have probably not have raised suspicion.

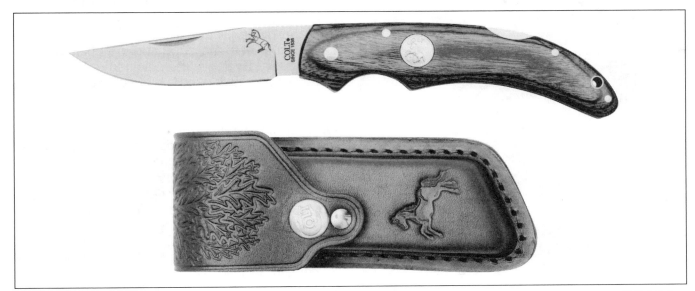

United Cutlery

Hidden from view in an embossed belt carrying case, this Colt® lockblade folder from United Cutlery draws little concern from onlookers.

Folding knives, either out-of-sight in the pocket or encased in a belt sheath are the daily attire of many blue-collar Americans. I doubt seriously that a truck driver, repair person, construction worker, or service maintenance person would ever be questioned about a folding knife worn on the belt.

I have a friend, Dave Long, who is a contractor. His belt carries a tape measure and a folding knife every single day. During the course of business, he visits the homes of the rich and not-so-famous and no one has been put-off by the presence of the folding knife on his belt. If the knife was a fixed-blade, however, I am sure that the perception of his prospective clients would be entirely different. How would you feel if a contractor showed up at your home wearing a sheath knife? And what about the power or gas company meter reader who could be trudging around the neighborhood toting a fixed-blade knife, or the postal person, or anybody else? I know that it would raise my level of anxiety, and you're probably no different. You see, we've all become indoctrinated with the fear of an openly-worn fixed-blade knife, especially anywhere outside of hunting camp.

The folding knife has gained a certain level of acceptance in society. Pocket folders are unseen, so nobody is alerted to their presence. Unless you whip out a pocketknife and start cleaning your nails during a parent-teacher conference at your child's school, or in the security check line at the airport, the authorities probably won't get

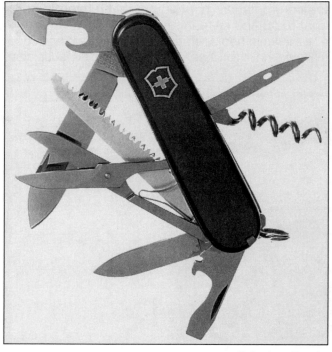

Despite a plethora of handy blades, any Swiss Army Knife model is hardly perceived as threatening by the citizenry at large.

involved. Wearing a folder in a belt case has even become acceptable in most venues. Since the introduction of the Buck lock-blade *Folding Hunter* in 1963, it, and other similar edged tools have been worn openly with impunity nearly everywhere but corporate offices. Even in the white-collar world, folders like several of the smaller Swiss Army Knife models, along with some of the tiny Spyderco offerings, don't seem to raise eyebrows. It's all about perception and in this arena the folding knife is a clear winner.

While image is a significant factor, carrying convenience is probably the biggest reason why folding knives predominate in the market. In the last chapter we discussed the pros and cons of fixed-blade knives. If you'll recall, I stated that a sheath knife can be a pain to carry.

Conversely, a folding knife carried in a belt case is virtually unnoticeable. There are some folding knife cases that can be located on the belt in either a vertical or horizontal position. This provides even more flexibility in positioning the knife where it's out of the way.

Furthermore, a folding knife belt case provides better carrying security than many fixed-blade sheath designs. There's never any worry about the knife inadvertently slipping out of the belt case when negotiating tough terrain, climbing in and out of a vehicle, or mounting and dismounting from a horse. Nothing is quite as embarrassing as swinging into the saddle and watching your sheath knife fly through the air. It gets worse when the point of the knife lands where it shouldn't. Companions don't like being on the receiving end of a loose knife, and neither do members of the equine family.

Safety is another consideration. A folder secured in a belt case isn't likely to inflict accidental injury. With the blade in the closed position, the cutting capability of both the edge and the point is totally suppressed. Even when contained, a fixed-blade knife is still capable of bailing out of sheath containment unanticipatedly. This can happen if you lose your footing and fall. During such an event there's no predicting whether or not the knife will stay in the sheath. The worse possible scenario can put you in a compromising situation.

A couple of drawbacks to the folding knife that haven't been mentioned yet are limitations of blade length and pattern design. Obviously, a folding knife blade can be no longer than the handle in which it is contained. Also, blade shape must conform to the size of the handle. A folder cannot easily contain a trailing-point or broad skinning blade pattern within its handle configuration. Even with these minor design boundaries, a folder is still an efficient edge tool in a wide range of outdoor appli-

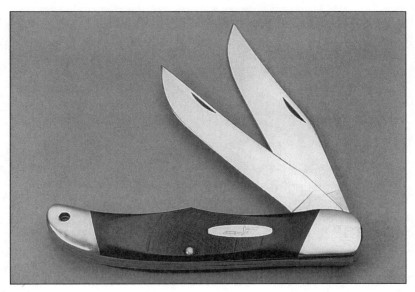

Buck Knives

Folded and enclosed within the confines of the knife handle, even the sizeable pair of blades on this Buck folder present no danger of accidental injury.

cations. And it is this efficiency that has propelled the design to the forefront of cutlery sales.

The seminal event that shifted the knife-buying public away from fixed-blade hunting knives to folders was the 1963 introduction of the Buck *Folding Hunter* (Model 110). This entry of a positive blade locking mechanism into the folding knife market saw every other cutlery manufacturer scrambling to catch up. If imitation is flattery, then lots of adulation was heaped on the Buck Knives. One after another, knife producers came out with

their own versions of what Buck had already made a reality. For sportsmen, it was a long awaited development, offering the best of both worlds—a rigid blade with carrying convenience. No longer was a fixed-blade knife the quintessential "hunting knife." The lock-blade folder made serious inroads in that market, and it has remained so ever since.

The Buck folding knife blade locking system wasn't the first knife blade lock ever made public. The cutlers of Sheffield, England, were producing and selling lock-back folders during the mid-1830s. The French wood-handled Opinel folder, introduced in the late 1890s, featured a moveable collar that rotated on a metal ferrule. When twisted into place, the ring-lock effectively secured the blade in an open position. This knife and the same blade-lock mechanism have been in continuous production ever since. In fact, the Opinel's many lifesaving feats have become as legendary as that of the famous Swiss Army Knife. The English and the French weren't the only lock-blade knife manufacturers. Reportedly, the Boker knife company, Solingen, Germany, produced a folder in 1903 that featured a front blade lock. As well, other foreign and domestic cutlery producers were making and selling lock-back folders well before Buck even conceived of the design.

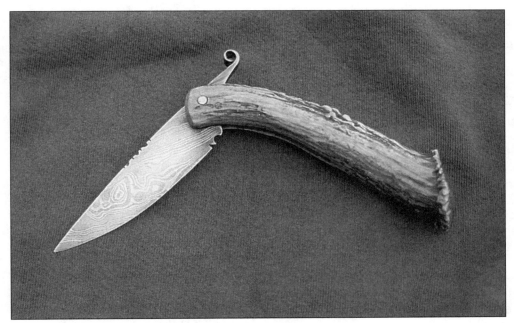

D. R. Good

Obviously, a folding knife blade can be no longer than the handle that contains it. The 3-1/2-inch, drop-point Damascus blade on this friction folder by D. R. Good is just a tad shorter than the white-tail deer antler handle.

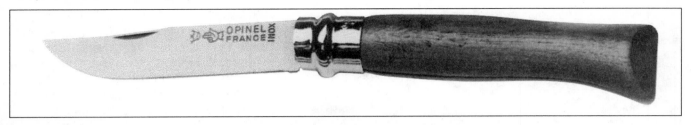

The French Opinel folder features a rotating metal collar that effectively locks the blade. This design dates to the late 19th Century.

The Buck creation, however, served as a catalyst for the expansion of blade locking systems to a wide range of folding knife designs—and it all made sense. Since the addition of a blade lock to a folding knife prevents the blade from inadvertently closing on the user's fingers, the safety factor alone made the concept a success. As a result, many leading edge developments in the cutlery industry during the 1970s-1990s—ceramic and titanium blades, thermoplastic handles, and innovative blade designs—found their genesis in lock-blade folders. The tidal wave of lock-blade folding knives that swept through the cutlery industry has continued to build momentum.

The Buck back spring lock, along with all of the rest of its imitators, uses a latch on the spring's front that fits, "locks," into a notch at the blade tang's rear. This effectively secures the blade in an open position. For a more visual explanation, refer to the exploded line drawing of the Buck *Duke* folder in this chapter. To close the blade, the user depresses the lock release which can be positioned in the rear, middle, or even the front of the back spring. When the lock release is depressed, it lifts the latch out of its "locking" notch, allowing the blade to fold and close. Lock failure can occur if the "locking" latch isn't seated securely in its corresponding tang notch. This is usually the result of an accumulation of foreign debris in the lock mechanism. Keeping a lock-blade folder clean just means an occasional bath, scrub, rinse and oiling. It's as simple at that!

In the 1990s, another change was seen in folding knife development with the introduction of the liner lock. At the time, liner locks may have seemed revolutionary. However, an inner-frame lock mechanism was the direct descendent of the earlier inner-frame blade brace (essentially a liner lock). When compared with a back spring lock, the forte of the liner lock was enhanced to ease the blade release. It didn't take Herculean strength to release the blade, something that many knife users with back spring locking folders had complained about. All of sudden other blade locking mechanisms were seen as dated.

To be sure, many other blade locking systems have been developed (Walter "Blackie" Collins and Michael Collins probably hold patents on the vast majority), and some have even seen the light of commercial production. In the early 1980s, Bench-Mark produced the unique *Rolox* knife. Another "Blackie" Collins creation, this folding knife really didn't fold at all—it rolled! To bring the blade into play, the rear of the blade was depressed and with the thumb it was pushed forward along a track until it locked open.

Another unusual blade lock was the Gerber *Paul Knife*. Designed by Paul Poehlmann, it opened by depressing a key button on the forward bolster and using your thumb to turn the axial-locking mechanism 180-degrees until the blade locked open. To close the blade, you simply reversed the process. Gerber also produced a *Bolt-Action* lock-blade folder that used a sliding "bolt" that fit into a corresponding slot in the blade tang to inhibit blade closure.

To be sure, there were many other blade locking mechanisms that hit the market. Some were very expensive to produce. Others just never caught on with the knife-buying public and none have had the longevity of the back spring blade locking system. However, with the advent of the inner-frame liner lock, it looks like we might just "have a new sheriff in town."

The positive blade locking mechanism, introduced by Buck Knives in 1963, can be seen in similar products by most other major cutlery producers. This Puma Prince has a comparable blade locking system.

The Kershaw folding field knife (Model 1050) combines strength, performance, and durability in a great hunting knife design.

The Marbles fixed-blade (left), as well as the Knives of Alaska folder (right) are both solid choices when it comes to putting venison in the skillet.

Buck's series of high-tech folders are great field knives for hunters, anglers, and backpackers.

Three outstanding edged hunting tools, from top to bottom,
Buck Knives, Loyd Thomsen, and Kershaw.

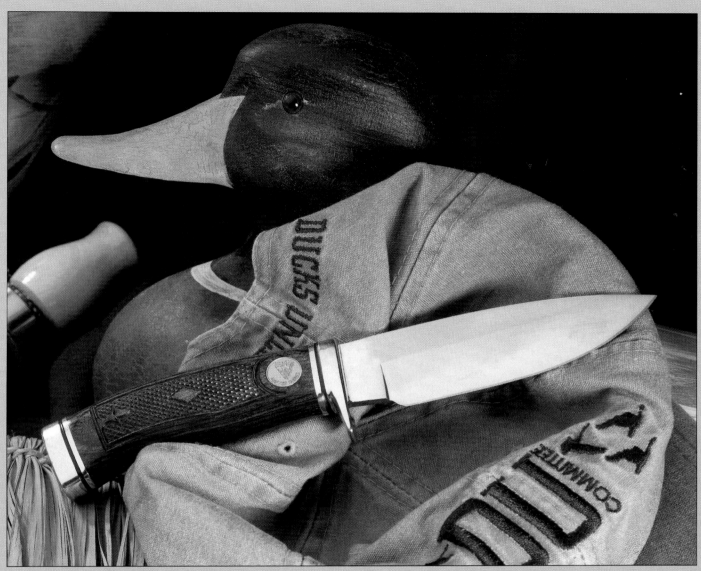

Buck fixed-blade hunters are traditionally shaped,
yet with high-tech blade and handle materials.

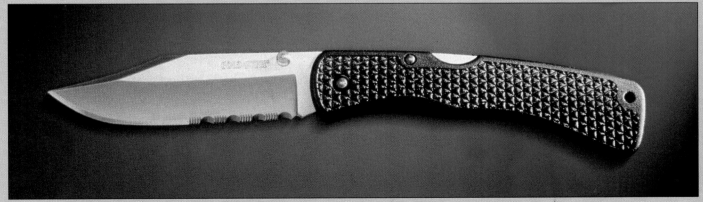

Cold Steel offers lockbacks in varying blade shapes,
including a modified clip-point pattern that most hunters prefer.

Ron Gaston's full-tang, stag-handled hunter
is built rugged enough to handle any game-care chore.

The Case Hobo folder is compact and a great travelling companion.

This double guard Bowie by Gary Biggers is great for camp chores.

Buck Knives' Big Sky™ model has the solid feel of a fixed blade in a folder.

A magnificent Damascus steel knife in a wave mosaic pattern by Lloyd Thomsen.

Blade versatility is another folding knife strong suit. A folding knife frame allows the inclusion of an infinite number of both cutting and tool blades. Both the Wenger and Victorinox Swiss Army Knife companies manufacture folders that contain so many blades that they're too thick to carry comfortably in a pocket. Devotees of these oversize multi-blade folders have to resort to carrying them in a belt case. In my experience, however, most folks seem to like their folding knives with far fewer blades.

Folders designed for hunting and fishing often have one, or two pairs of blades combined in a single frame. Companion blades can offer features like gutting, skinning, or sawing. A prime example is the Browning F.D.T.™ (Field Dressing Tool) line that offers a knife with differing assortments of blades depending on the application. Every knife in the line features AUS-8A stainless steel blades, Zytel® handle scales with checkered rubber inlays, and a rugged Ballistic Cloth® sheath. *The Angler* (Model 620) combines a partially serrated chisel-point main blade with a small plier/nipper blade and a scaler/hook removal blade. The *Wing Shooter* (Model 630) offers a hollow-ground clip-pattern main blade, entrails hook and a fine-tooth saw/gutting tool that can handle most waterfowl and upland-bird field chores. And the *Kodiak* (Models 600, 607, 608, 609 and 645) is a great steel sidekick for any big-game hunter, and is available in two and three-blade combinations that feature gutting blades, saws, or different cutting shapes.

There is a wide variety of other multi-blade outdoor folding knife patterns produced by factory and handmade cutlery manufacturers alike. A favorite folder that nearly everyone makes is the *Trapper*. This two-blade knife combines a clip-pattern main blade with a spey blade. The main blade works well for general field-dressing chores and the rounded tip of the spey blade easily handles skinning chores. A knife of this pattern is nearly perfect for small- or large-game field chores.

Specialized, multiple-blade folders for bird hunters are made by many manufacturers. Usually, such designs feature an elongated clip (Turkish clip)

main blade and entrails hook. Remington has taken this design one step farther in their *Waterfowl* and *Upland* knives by including a choke tool and pin punch in the frame, making it a four-blade knife. Handy with everything from basic small game and fowl evisceration, to field firearm maintenance, either one of these Remington offerings is sure to be a favorite with shotgunners.

Anglers also have their own share of the multi-blade folding knife market. Many cutlery manufacturers produce two-blade folders for fishermen that combine a slender clip-point blade with a hook/scale removal tool blade. Some models even have a hook sharpening stone on one side of the handle. When it comes to fish filleting, there's a selection of folding knives to handle this demanding assignment. There are also compact folders that include a main blade, scissors, screwdriver blades, hook/scaler and a host of other handy angling tools in a single folding knife frame. On the lake, stream, or even surf fishing along an ocean shore, a folding angling knife is a handy accessory.

In recent years, there has been a proliferation of what is called a pliers/knife tool. This design is centered around a set of pliers with folding handles, or a retractable plier head. Several different tool blades, including one or more knife blades, are contained within the paired handles. Such a configuration is really a set of pliers; however, the addition of the knife blades provides some direct relationship to a folding knife. Most major production knife factories—Buck, Gerber, Kershaw, Schrade, and others—all manufacture these handy tools. The Wenger Swiss Army Knife Company takes a different approach to this design.

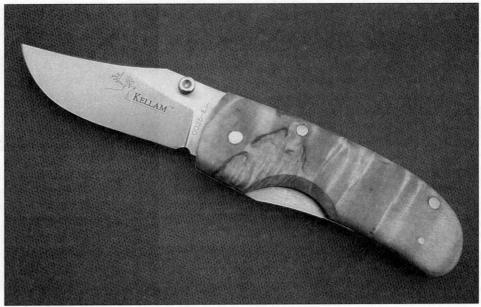

Kellam Knives

Here's an example of a Nordic designed liner-lock folder from Kellam Knives, that combines a broad 440A stainless steel clip-point blade, with curly birch handle scales.

Images Group/Schrade

A longtime favorite of hunters, this Schrade Old Timer® Bearhead Trapper features both clip- and spey-pattern blades for enhanced field versatility.

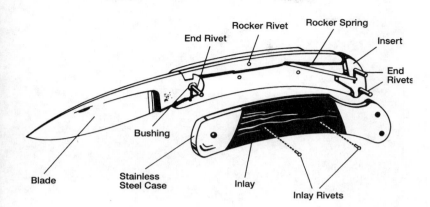

Spyderco

Spyderco eschews the traditional nail nick for blade opening and places an "opening hole" in the back of the blade which can be engaged by the thumb to more easily open the blade.

Buck Knives

This exploded drawing of a Buck Duke folder illustrates how the lockback work off of the spring, snaps into a notch in the tang, locking the blade in place.

What they have done is to include a plier head and handles in a folding knife frame, resulting in a knife/pliers tool.

Opening a folding knife has always been somewhat problematic. Traditionally, folders are opened by means of a nail nick in the blade. This curved slot allows the use of a thumbnail to lever the blade open. The problem is that some people have short nails, long nails, weak nails, or no nails at all. Any attempt at knife blade movement can result in a chipped or broken nail. Moreover, in cold weather, it's virtually impossible to engage the nail nick with gloves on. And if age, or infirmity (arthritis), has inhibited manual dexterity, then it can be impossible to open a folder.

This all changed in 1981 with the introduction of Spyderco's first CLIPIT folding knife model. This design featured a large "opening hole" in the back of the blade. The actual wording of the patent covered any depression (a hole is just two depressions on either side of the blade that merges in the middle) in the blade meant to be engaged by the thumb to facilitate blade opening. The hole in the blade solved the problem of needing two hands to open a knife. Since the *Clipit* was a lock-blade folder, the audible sound of the blade lock engaging also eliminated the need to visually check to see if the knife blade was fully open. Knife deployment was markedly streamlined by these features—particularly the one-hand opening capability.

While the Spyderco's patent prevented other makers from copying the design, it didn't prevent the development of alternative blade opening methodologies. It was evident that the Spyderco opening hole had to be exposed above the knife

frame to provide adequate thumb engagement. This is the reason for the characteristic "hump" in Spyderco folding knife blades. A stud or set of studs (one on each side) screwed into the blade back worked just as well and didn't demand any change to the blade shape. In short order, knife manufacturers began inserting "opening studs" into the back of many of their folders.

Knifemaker, Ken Onion, combined a torsion bar assist with an opening stud to produce a nearly self-opening folder. The opening stud provides leverage to lift the blade from the frame. Then the torsion bar assist takes over and pushes the blade completely open. The first time I handled a Ken Onion folder, it nearly *jumped* out of my hand. After a couple of careful dry runs, I quickly mastered the blade opening technique. In my experience, no folder opens any easier than an Onion design. Working in collaboration with Kershaw Knives, this custom maker's innovative folding knives are available at a very attractive price point.

For the outdoors person, a folding knife is often the tool of choice for fishing, hunting, camping and other chores. Field dressing fish and game, making gear repairs, even handling food preparation is well within the realm of possibilities for a folder. For the urban dweller, a knife also plays an important role in many facets of daily life. Whether it's opening cardboard cartons, trimming the tops off of carrots, or self-defense, a knife is as important in the confines of steel and concrete as it is beyond the city limits. Never threatening, easily carried, quickly brought into play, and with the option of a blade locking device, a folding knife has become the *right* choice for most who need a cutting edge.

Kershaw kai Cutlery

Hunters will find more than adequate cutting satisfaction with one of the many forms of clip- or drop-point blade patterns.

Chapter 8
The Shape of Things

Form follows function.

Walk into any hardware store and you'll find a vast assortment of hand tools. Within each tool category there is even more diversity. You can find sledgehammers, framing hammers, cabinet hammers and utility hammers. There are offset wrenches, metric wrenches, English standard wrenches, and a whole host of other wrenches and—don't even try to sort out all of the types of screwdrivers!

This same level of diversity is also manifest in edged tools—specifically knives. In addition to both fixed-blade and folding designs, each knife configuration can be purchased with several different blade shape options. Since the folding knife frame allows the incorporation of more than one blade in a single unit, blade pattern choice is enhanced even more.

Recently, I thumbed through both the Victorinox and Wenger Swiss Army Knife catalogs. Either firm produces a virtual plethora of knife models, each one with an abundance of blade choices. The largest knife models combine nearly 20 different blades in a single frame, with many of the blades offering multiple functions. Of course, most of these oversize cutters can wear a hole in your pants pocket. However, they're unequaled for blade shape diversity.

Despite the plethora of possible blade choices, for most outdoor cutting assignments, these five—spear-point, clip-point, drop-point, trailing-point, and guthook—are probably the most useful. A description of these blade shapes, as well as commentary on use, will assist readers in understanding their functional applications.

Spear-Point: This blade pattern reminds one of an ancient spearhead, hence the nomenclature. The blade pattern is formed by the meeting of the cutting edge and the blade back, in identical curves, at the blade point. The blade formation suggests that someone designed half of the blade, then flipped it over and repeated the configuration to form the remaining half. A classic example of this blade pattern is the main cutting blade found on most Swiss Army Knife models. Europeans also seem to favor this blade shape on their hunting knives. The forte of this pattern is piercing

and slicing, which makes it ideal for general field dressing of fish and game. I've used this type of blade for detail trophy work and have found it to offer superior performance when cutting around antler butts, ears and eyes.

Clip-Point: The clip-point pattern is characterized by the back of the blade point being "clipped" away to join the cutting edge. Because it fits so compactly into the knife frame, clip-point blades are often found in folding models. However, many

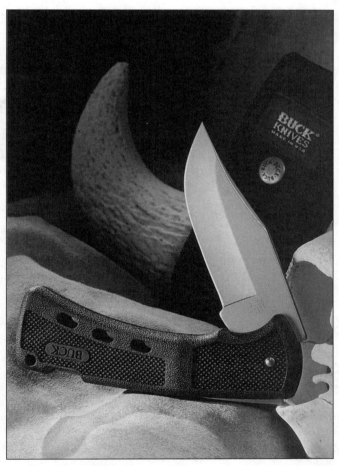

Buck Knives

The clip-point blade pattern has become overwhelmingly popular with hunters because of its combination of cutting features. This Goliath folder (Model 446) from Buck Knives is an excellent example of just how well this pattern blends both a fine blade point for general chores and a deep sweeping belly designed for skinning assignments.

77

fixed-blade knives also feature this pattern. The blade "clipping" can take several forms, from the abrupt spey pattern often found in some skinning blades, to the elongated Turkish-style clip that is common on so-called "bird knives." One of the more popular clip-point patterns is the saber clip. This pattern features a concave shape to the blade back, giving it the appearance of a miniature saber or cutlass. A prime example of this blade pattern is the Buck *Folding Hunter* (Model 110). Offering both a fine blade point for detail work and a deep blade belly for skinning, this pattern is a great all-around selection for a field knife. The only drawback found in the clip-point pattern is an inherent blade point weakness. Since there is a limited amount of support at the tip, lateral (side-to-side) stress can fracture the blade at this point. Most of the clip-point knives that are returned to cutlery factories for repair have been damaged at the blade tip.

Drop-Point: This pattern features a convex curve on the blade back that effectively "drops" the point away from the direct line of the cutting force. I've never seen a drop-point pattern blade with a broken tip. However, such an occurrence is commonplace with a clip-point blade. Offering more metal at the blade point, this pattern provides enhanced resistance to breakage at that critical location. Combining superior blade strength, enhanced cutting utility, and the broad sweeping blade belly of a skinner, the drop-point pattern is often the choice of veteran big game hunters. The archetypical drop-point blade is seen on the Gerber *Gator* (Model 06064) folder. As well, other cutlery manufacturers feature drop-point pattern blades in many of the knife models they produce. While the drop-point doesn't fit into a folding knife frame quite as compactly as a clip-point blade, it can be easily adapted to this design. As an all-around field pattern, the drop-point lacks the clip's precise cutting capability for detail work like head skin cape removal. Nevertheless, the broad blade belly and sweeping cutting curve of drop-point are superior to the clip-point when it comes to skinning assignments. A solid choice for field-dressing and skinning chores, the drop-point blade pattern is one of my favorites.

D. Hollis

This fixed-blade Muela drop-point model shows how the convex curve of the blade spine near the tip provides great strength in this critical area.

Trailing-Point: The opposite of a drop-point, the trailing-point positions the blade tip above the blade back. The strength of this blade pattern is the extremely long radius of the cutting edge. This sweeping curve is just right for hide removal and inhibits slicing into the underlying muscle tissue.

Two different basic versions—broad and narrow—of this blade pattern are often seen. The broad trailing-point is characterized by the famous Russel-Harrington skinning knives that figured so predominately in the buffalo trade. Since the blade is very wide at the tip, its use is restricted solely to hide removal activities. An alternative trailing-point configuration features a narrow blade with a slender point. The trailing-point is a pattern that I've used successfully on a wide range of big game animals. However, my preference is the narrow blade version of this pattern.

Guthook: The guthook is as much a tool as it is a cutting implement. Seen in many forms, a guthook can either be engineered into the back of a blade, or exist as a completely separate blade. In either instance, the inside curve of the "hook" serves as the cutting path. The hook may be pointed enough to slice into the hide, or dull and rounded so that a small slit must be cut first to allow entry. Once entry has been accomplished, the guthook is pulled like a zipper, effectively slitting the hide without compromising underlying muscle tissue. Examples of the blade back guthook design on fixed-blade models are the following: Buck fixed-blade *Zipper* (Model 191/691), Schrade *Sharpfinger Guthook Skinner* (Model 1580T), and the guthook blade in Kershaw *Alaskan Blade Trader* exchange-blade knife (Model 1098AK). Freestanding guthook blades can be found on the Remington *Grizzly* lockback folder, Buck *CrossLock*

care applications, both clip- and drop-point blade patterns offer the greatest cutting versatility. It's possible to field dress, skin, cape, and bone a deer carcass, or any other game mammal, with either type of blade. This is the most compelling reason why the Buck *Folding Hunter* (Model 110), Schrade *Bear Paw* (Model LB7), Gerber *Gator* (Model 06064), and similar folders are so widely popular. All three: clip-, drop-, and spear-point blade designs are solid choices for big game hunters.

Handling large game animals—caribou, elk, moose, and some bears—can demand extensive time in skinning activities. I often select a narrow trailing-point pattern blade with a slender tip for such assignments. My rationale centers on the trailing-point design's greater strength as a skinning blade. Most skinning patterns are too broad at the tip to function well in primary game care. A narrow trailing-point blade with a pointed tip, however, can handle this chore as well as a drop-, clip-, or spear-point pattern.

My approach to any field-dressing situation is to ask for someone to "show me a better way." The first time I saw another hunter put a guthook to use, it was a better *pitch* for that particular blade pattern than any cutlery salesperson could ever make. Watching my companion slit open a deer, both during the initial gutting phase and in preparation for skinning, was amazing. The cutting action of the guthook blade was like pulling a zipper—the hide just opened up! Furthermore, there were no cuts in the internal organs. As well, the muscle tissue underlying the hide wasn't compromised. Some hunters might ask,

The trailing-point design of this Charlton/Damascus USA fixed-blade knife places the blade tip well above the line of the blade spine. This provides a longer cutting radius for skinning and prevents accidental slicing into the underlying tissues.

3-Function Hunter (Model 180D3), and Browning *Kodiak F.D.T.* folder (Models 600,608, and 645). The guthook is a functional blade design that offers invaluable assistance when field dressing and skinning.

In actual field situations, I've used every one of the aforementioned blade patterns. For most game

"What's the big deal about cutting into the meat?" In my experience, every time you accidentally slice into the meat unintentionally it opens a pathway for insect intrusion. Flies will lay their eggs anywhere moisture is present. Once a carcass is glazed-over, moisture dissipates quickly. External bullet or broadhead damage, as well as knife cuts in the

Buck Knives combines both a drop-point blade, and an adaptation of the guthook pattern for cutting seat belt material, in their Cross-Lock folder designed for law enforcement work.

meat, will weep fluid and attract flies. If fly eggs are deposited on these surfaces, they will become a perfect environment for maggots. The bottom line in this discussion is simply that the use of a gut-hook when making hide incisions can prevent collateral blade edge damage.

Of course, there are other blade designs—skinner, sheepsfoot, Wharncliff, straight and European-style gutting blades—that can be useful. Some of these blade patterns may be unfamiliar to readers, so I suggest that you refer to line art illustration contained within this chapter for enhanced visualization.

Skinner: Skinning knives can be based on clip-, drop-, or trailing-point blade patterns. The two main features of a skinner are a broad blade belly and a sweeping cutting edge radius. The Buck *Skinner* (Model 103) is a clip-point blade that features a straight, abruptly angled clipping of the blade. Basically, this knife resembles a rather broad spey blade. One of the two blades in all folding *Trapper* knife models is a spey blade. While the spey blade is rather narrow, nevertheless, the blunt clipped point and rounded tip

makes it ideal for skinning chores. And the *Pro Guide* (Model UC1203) fixed-blade knife, designed by Gil Hibben and marketed by United Cutlery, incorporates an overstated cutting edge radius in a basic drop-point pattern.

European-style Gutting Blade: Long before guthook blades emerged, European cutlers were producing a specialized gutting blade. The cutting edge of the blade is situated behind the rounded, blunt blade point. To use this blade, the rounded blade tip is inserted into a small slit in the animal's hide. The skin rides up and over the blunt tip of the blade and comes into contact with the sharpened edge. As the blade is pushed forward, the hide is opened without damaging the underlying tissue. Usually offered as a companion blade in a folder, this blade pattern can be found on many knives of European origin.

Equally as efficient as the guthook, the European-style gutting blade has really never caught on in this country. For a time, Buck Knives offered this design as an option in their exchange blade folder. Presently, however, no domestic cutlery manufacturer offers this blade pattern.

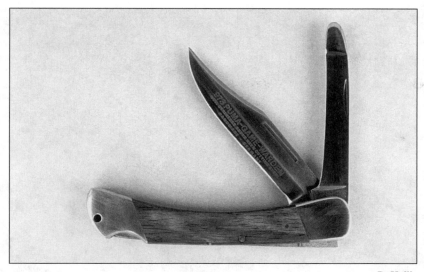

D. Hollis

In addition to its main saber clip-point pattern blade, this Puma folder also carries a blunt nose European-style gutting blade.

Wharncliff: This blade pattern is similar to the sheepsfoot, but the blade is much narrower and the curve of the back of the blade occurs over a longer radius. A very precise cutting tool that's more useful than the sheepsfoot with caping and other delicate chores, the Wharncliff can be found on the tiny *Precision Engineered Compact Knife* P.E.C.K. (Model 2400, 2410) knives, designed by Ed Halligan, and made by Columbia River Knife and Tool Company.

Straight: This pattern is distinguished by the linear line of the blade back that never deviates from horizontal. The cutting edge tapers ever so slightly nearly the entire length of the blade, until it makes a final curving upsweep over an extended radius to meet the tip. This blade pattern is typical of filet and boning knives.

Sheepsfoot: The sheepsfoot blade pattern looks very much like the curve on a sheep's hoof. The cutting edge is completely straight and the back of the blade curves abruptly to meet the edge. Since the back curve is convex, the pattern fits into the drop-point category. However, the design is unique enough to deserve its own nomenclature. Featuring a very blunt tip, the sheepsfoot is quite useful in making precise cuts.

In use, this design allows the user to impart added downward force to the cutting edge. When working on birds and small game, a sheepsfoot blade is great for cutting through leg and wing joints. Many manufacturers add serrations to the cutting edge to enhance blade performance when slicing through tendons and bone joints.

Entrails Hook: An entrails hook is often paired with a Turkish clip blade in a "bird" knife configuration. Traditionally, the main blade and the entrails' hook are positioned at either end of the folding knife frame. After the body cavity of a fowl has

been opened with the point of the blade, the hook is inserted into the bird, twisted to engage the entrails, and then withdrawn pulling the viscera out of the body cavity. Once the internal organs are removed, the hook can be detached and returned to its place of rest in the knife frame. The main blade can then be used to sever any connections that exist between the vitals and the interior of the body. While the use of this blade is not widespread, it does offer distinct advantages. Certainly, it facilitates handling all kinds of wild fowl in a manner that keeps the mess to a minimum.

As much as I enjoy using "do-it-all" blade patterns, there are times that the strength of a specialized cutting tool can be advantageous. Nothing beats a skinning knife when it comes to hide removal. I generally carry a skinner in my pack or saddlebags on big game hunts. When the need arises, then it's time to bring that particular knife into play. Furthermore, a European-style gutting blade offers performance not unlike that of a guthook. Paired with a clip- or drop-point blade in a folding knife frame, a gutting blade extends the functional versatility of that cutting implement.

While we're on the of subject game care, the straight blade pattern of a specialized boning knife is without peer for butchering in the field. Likewise a straight blade cannot be bettered for fish fileting chores. The long, slender, straight filet blade has the ability to execute precise slices over an extended distance, something that is unequaled by other blade motifs. The Warncliff blade, with its ability to make precise and controlled incisions, makes it a fantastic tool for trophy work. And big game hunters probably won't appreciate the advantage of a sheepsfoot blade or an entrails hook, but waterfowlers and upland shotgunners certainly will.

Case Cutlery

The straight blade pattern is typical of the design most often encountered on fillet knives. These three Case fillet models show how this works on blades of differing lengths.

There are some other knife blade patterns that are tools, rather than primarily cutting implements. At times, both sawtooth and screwdriver blades can be of paramount importance to outdoor folk. Some knifemakers add these tools as a companion to the main cutting blade, or as one of several tool blades. A look at these two blade patterns will assist readers in understanding the role of each as choices in a folding knife frame.

Saw: In the outdoors, there are cutting chores that necessitate more than just a knife blade. In this realm, the knife-contained saw blade can work wonders. The Schrade *Buzz Saw Trapper* (Model 970T) is just one of many such folders that includes a saw blade as an additional cutting resource. The Buck *3-Function Hunter* (Model 180D3) folder takes a different approach by placing a saw-tooth edge on the back of a guthook

CRKT

This Columbia River Knife & Tool Company (CRKT) Cattleman (Model 6320) pairs both a plain edge clip-point and serrated sheepsfoot blade in the same folding knife frame.

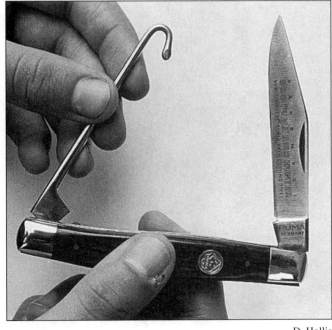

D. Hollis

Paired with a Turkish clip-point pattern blade, the entrails hook is designed as an aid for field dressing game birds.

Images Group/Schrade

A saw blade, like the one on this Schrade Buzz Saw Trapper (Model 97OT) is a very advantageous addition to a hunting folder.

companion blade in this handy combination. This knife is also available with Buck's Ionfusion (ziconium nitrate) coating on the 420HC stainless steel blade that pushes the Rockwell value to Rc 80. More than a serrated blade, and less than a hand-saw, a sawtooth cutting edge is a great asset when field dressing big game (cutting through rib and pelvic structures). Likewise, a saw blade can come in handy when cutting small branches (opening a shooting path for arrow flight), brush removal (establishing a camp site), or similar chores. I've even used a knife-contained saw blade for simple household chores (cutting through PVC pipe). A saw is a great addition to any folding outdoor knife, especially for game care chores.

Screwdriver Blades: The humble screwdriver is often a little-appreciated tool. Should the need arise for such an implement, a hardware store or your toolbox is generally a long way from camp. And if you're deep in the backcountry, tool acquisition is even more impossible. The usefulness of both a standard and Phillip's head screwdriver blade in a folding knife frame cannot be over-stated. When it comes to minor repairs, both driver head configurations are needful. Several knives have incorporated these tool blades into their design. All of the plier/knife tools have screwdrivers in their tool package. Likewise, several

Swiss Army Knife models also feature one or more screwdriver blades.

In the outdoors, my dad was always in need of a screwdriver. He ruined the tips of many knife blades using them in that capacity. In front of his two sons, such events were generally referred to as "field modifications." Despite his tendency too accidentally *reconfigure* a perfectly good blade pattern, I am sure my father would have been able to appreciate a knife with one or more screwdriver blades.

Cutting satisfaction in most venues can be found in a clip- or drop-point blade. It is their ability to handle many chores, without necessarily gaining the specialized mastery of any single assignment, that has endeared both blade patterns to generations of outdoors enthusiasts. Like a family physician, knives featuring clip- or drop-point blades are often the first, and sometimes the only cutting tool that can handle the job at hand. There are times, however, that a specialist is needed to handle more unique tasks. Blade shapes designed for such applications are without peer when it comes to their own cutting specialty. Furthermore, tool blades have proven their worth as a knife component. If a loose screw, a bothersome thorn, or a branch stands between you and the accomplishment of a task, then the importance of these blade designs will quickly become manifest.

H. Rexroat Photography

Gary Biggers combined a 4" drop-point blade of ATS-34 stainless, with 416 stainless bolsters, and stabilized walnut burl handle scales.

This discussion has only opened the door to knife blade shape diversity. There are far more blade patterns and functions than those that have been covered in this chapter. Like so many avenues in life, blade shape diversity is all about choice. The choices you make can alter the outcome of future events. If it wasn't so, then man-kind would still be field dressing game and fish with nothing more than a chip of volcanic obsidian glass. If need is the wellspring of invention, then the creation of new and exciting designs will continue to evolve. Quite obviously, need dictates function, and functional application is what the "shape of things" is all about.

BASIC BLADE SHAPES

Clip — The length and angle of the concave curve on the non-cutting portion of the point determines whether a clip blade is just a "clip" (short, pronounced curve), a "California" clip (longer, gentler curve) or a so-called "Turkish" Clip (very elongated).

Modified Clip — A recent design development that has proved popular on high-tech, one-hand knives. Exact shapes vary.

Drop-Point — This blade has a gentle, sloping convex curve to the point, less abrupt than the spear blade, and without the concave curve of the clip blade.

Serrated — By adding serrations, we give your Buck blade greater cutting power. Available on several models.

Gutting & Skinning — Buck's own creation, available on Zipper and CrossLock models. Makes it a cinch to field dress game.

Sheepsfoot — Got its name from the shape of the point resembling the hoof of a sheep. With its distinctive flat, straight-line cutting edge and rounded point, it's well suited to clean cuts of such things as rope, tubing or insulated wire.

Spey — As the name indicates, this blade was originally developed to castrate animals. Rather blunt point and overall blade configuration make the spey function well for skinning.

Pen or Spear — This is a smaller version of the larger "spear point" blade. Spear points are more popular in Europe, while in America the clip blade is the preferred option. Pen blades are usually on pocket knives as a handy, all purpose blade. It was originally developed to trim quill pens, and that name has stuck through the years.

Coping — A narrow blade with a sharp, angular point, designed to be used for cutting in tight spots or curved patterns, much as you would with a coping saw – only without the teeth.

-Courtesy Buck Knives

The carbon steel Schrade Sharpfinger Guthook Skinner combines the sweeping edge of a drop-point blade pattern with a functional gut-hook feature.

Chapter 9

What's the Hook?

Guthook and gutting blades do more than just catch attention.

When a salesperson asks a product manufacturer, "What's the hook," the question refers to a particular product feature that can grab the consumer's attention. Many years ago, a particular knife feature caught my notice and it has been with me ever since.

The deer season for riflemen along California's central coast begins in early August. The daytime temperatures run in the triple-digits and things don't cool off very much at night. If you're fortunate enough to kill a buck, then meat care is a prime concern. In the mountains during the fall, a successful deer hunter can leave the skin on a deer for an extended period of time. In fact, this will keep the venison from drying out in the thin, high-altitude air. Along the central California coast, it isn't so easy. The hot weather dictates that not only must the deer be immediately field dressed, but the hide should also be removed to further cool the carcass.

Field dressing and skinning a deer isn't difficult. However, opening the abdominal cavity without cutting into the underlying viscera, or making incisions in the hide in preparation for skinning, can be challenging assignments. If, during the evisceration process, you accidentally slice open the stomach or intestines, the contents thereof can taint the meat. This is something you absolutely will want to avoid. Furthermore, should you nick or gash the muscle tissue while making cuts in the skin to facilitate skinning, these cuts will weep moisture that in turn can attract insects. Flies will lay their eggs on these moist areas. In warm weather, the eggs will turn into maggots overnight. Without further description, I am sure you have already guessed where this discussion will lead.

On opening day of the California coastal deer season, I managed to score on a nice forked-horn buck just after daybreak. Those of you who are venison *connoisseurs* understand the succulent and tender quality of the meat from a young deer. With scorching heat in the forecast, the immediacy of game care couldn't be underestimated. My hunting companion helped me drag the buck into the shade where we could undertake the chores of field dressing and skinning.

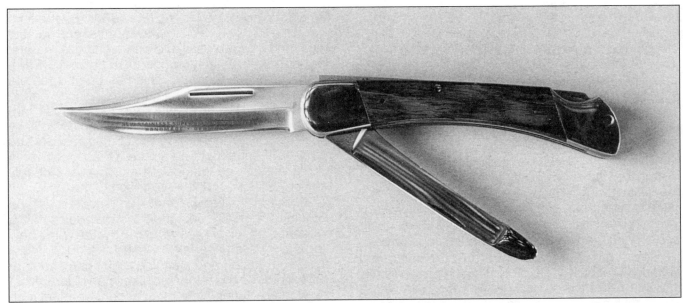

D. Hollis

One of the most efficient big-game knife designs ever conceived, this Puma Folding Skinner features a clip-point main blade and the traditional blunt-point European gutting blade.

The deer's stomach was full of oak mast and he was as fat as a barnyard pig. Trying to be careful, I used the point of my knife to cut open the abdominal cavity. Right away, the stomach and intestines billowed out through the initial incision. I tried to avoid the entire mess, but the knife blade accidentally nicked the stomach. The next event can only be described as distasteful at best. Stomach juice, acorns, partially chewed twigs and leaves all boiled out like crabs out of a bucket. It was a nasty mess!

Quickly, my hunting companion came to my rescue. He pulled out his folding knife, whipped out one of the weirdest blades I'd ever seen, and opened the deer up without any problem. Stepping out of the way, he let me continue with my field-dressing efforts. All the time, I couldn't get my mind off of the strange-looking blade that my companion had used.

After field dressing the buck, we decided to skin the deer, cover it with a cloth bag, and leave it to cool in the shade. To skin a deer, it is necessary to cut open the hide in a number of places. Undaunted by my earlier failure, I moved to the animal's rear and started to make an incision in the hide. My knife blade hadn't gone three inches when it cut into the muscle tissue beneath the hide. I adjusted the cutting angle and continued the procedure. Sure enough, the same thing happened again. At that point, my buddy pushed me aside and said, "I'll handle this."

Once again, the funny-shaped folding knife blade came into play. He slipped the dull tip of the blade under the hide and the skin opened up like the Red Sea before Moses. After he finished with one leg, he moved onto the other three. In less than a minute, he had made all of the skinning incisions, all without a nick on the underlying musculature.

"Whatever kind of knife blade that is, it works just like a zipper," I said.

My hunting companion took the time to explain that the blade was a European-style gutting blade. The tip of the blade was thick, rounded and completely blunt. However, just behind the tip, a sharpened edge ran the entire length of the blade. Once the tip of the blade was inserted into a tiny opening in the hide, the skin slipped up and over the tip onto the blade edge. The sharp edge sliced the hide open better than anything I'd ever seen before. Even better, the blunt point and dull blade back never once made a nick in the underlying viscera.

After that hunt, I really didn't give the matter any serious thought. That is, until the next season when my old friend showed up in camp with a fixed-blade knife that looked like he'd somehow taken a slice out of the back of the blade near the tip.

"What happened to your knife blade?" I inquired.

I guess the world record for asking stupid questions is mine alone, because the use of a sharpened notch on the back of his knife blade was readily apparent. I guess keeping my mouth shut and waiting for the explanation to come all by itself isn't one of my strong suits.

"It's a guthook," he explained in reply.

Okay, I'll bite, I thought to myself. Maybe if I don't say anything else, he'll explain what a guthook is all about.

Like most hunters, if they have a nifty piece of gear, they are eager to show it off. My friend wasn't any different. He handed me the knife and explained that the hook-like notch on the back of the blade was designed to cut open the hide without compromising whatever might lie beneath the skin. And before that trip was over, I watched him use the guthook on a couple deer. That knife feature worked even better than the European-style gutting blade he had first shown me. If you held the blade upside-down and angled hook's tip in the right position, it "hooked" into the hide without making any other slits into the skin. After engaging the hide, all that was necessary was holding the knife parallel with the skin and pulling. Once again, it was just like having a built-in zipper in the hide.

This time, the concept of opening up a big game animal, without all of the trouble associated with using a regular knife blade, caught a hold of me (I was hooked!). At my first opportunity, I acquired both a fixed-blade and folding knife with that particular feature as part of their functional package. Interestingly, the guthook was a completely separate blade within the folding knife frame. And it looked just like a hook.

My first exposure to both the gutting blade and the guthook occurred in the late 1960s. By the time the mid-1970s were in full swing, several factory knife models were available with a guthook feature. The origin of the gutting blade is definitely European—probably German. This has been a feature found on Solingen-made folders since before World War II. While I have seen the guthook feature on several Scandinavian knives, particularly those used by Laplanders for gutting moose and reindeer, it appears to be a recent blade feature. In all likelihood, the guthook feature was probably borrowed from our domestic cutlery industry.

Sources indicated that knifemaker, Merle Sequine, originally designed the guthook to lift a coffeepot off of a hot campfire by the wire bail. Reportedly, Sequine later refined the hook into a big-game gutting and skinning tool. I can't confirm the validity of this story, so like many tales from the world of cutlery, one must accept or reject it on its face value.

No matter the exact point of origin, the proliferation of guthook blades (both as a blade feature, and as a separate blade) cannot be denied. Most major knife factories feature at least one knife model with this feature. It can also be found in the offerings of some custom makers. A look at what's available from a selection of the major knife producers is sure to whet the appetite of any big-game hunter who's looking for a "better way to go."

A. G. Russell: Instead of a clumsy, hard-to-use blade spine guthook feature, the *Gut Hook Trapper* in this firm's mail-order catalog combines a specially-designed 2-1/2-inch guthook blade, with a 3-1/2-inch spey blade in the same folding knife frame. Both blades are made from AUS-8A stainless steel, and the frame features brass liners with nickel-silver bolsters and caps. This is a well-designed guthook, which faces in the correct direction, and can slit open a hide with ease.

Boker USA: While Boker doesn't make a specific guthook knife model, they do provide a drop-point pattern guthook blade (item 9013) for their *Optima* interchangeable blade folder. The 3-1/8-inch blade is crafted from mirror-polished 440C stainless steel, easily interchanges with all of the other blade types, and fully locks when in place. The *Optima* knife handle features nickel-silver bolster and is available with either gray bone or black Delrin® handle scales. The knife comes in a black Cordura® nylon case for a secure belt attachment. When it comes to blade choice, Boker definitely has the edge!

Browning: The folks at Browning have embraced the guthook/gutting blade principle in a big way. In their year 2000 catalog, this firm lists five folders and three fixed-blade knife models that all have either a guthook feature, or the unique Browning push/pull hide cutter blade. On both the Michael Collins designed *Featherweight™ Composite Skinner* (Model 819), and the *Sambar Stag Skinner* (Model 519), a generous guthook is featured on the blade spine near the tip. Either knife features a 4-inch blade, crafted from AUS-8A stainless steel. The main difference between these skinners is the handle treatment. The *Featherweight™ Composite* model employs a Zytel® with a laminated wood insert for good looks and a light weight. The Sambar Stag model uses handle scale of genuine stag accented with a brass guard. Even more unique, the *Swivel-Lok Hunter* (Model 614) also features a similar guthook feature. In their folding knife lineup, Browning offers the *Kodiak F.D.T.™* (Field Dressing Tool) in two distinct versions (Models 600, 608) that feature a guthook blade in combination with a drop-point main blade, or a drop-point main blade and a saw blade. Both knives have AUS-8A stainless steel blades. The Zytel® molded handle features checkered rubber inlays for a non-slip grip. A third

version (Model 645) incorporates a guthook feature in the drop-point main blade and includes a bone saw as a companion blade. Similar to the other folders in this series, instead of a black-colored handle it features Mossy Oak® Break-Up™ camo on the grip. Finally, Browning offers a triple-blade folder, in the *Featherweight™ Composite* and *Sambar Stag* models. Either knife features a clip-point main blade, bone saw blade, and a push/pull hide-cutter blade. With the widest selection of gutting blades and guthook features, Browning knives have a lot to offer.

Buck Knives: The Buck *Zipper™*, and the *Zipper-R™* fixed-blade knives both feature similar guthook features. The only differences between these two models are the type of handle and sheath. The *Zipper™* (Model 191) features a laminated wood handle with a leather sheath, and the *Zipper-R™* (Model 691) comes with a rubberized handle and Cordura® nylon sheath. Both knives have 4-1/4-inch, hollow-ground, satin finished, 420HC stainless steel blades based on a drop-point pattern. The guthook is situated on the blade spine, just behind the tip. A brass guard and pommel (Model 191 also has black spacers) complete the package. This is a terrific fixed-blade design that, with the addition of the guthook feature, extends its functional versatility for the big game hunter. In addition to these two fixed-blade models, Buck also makes a great folding knife with a guthook feature. The *CrossLock® 3-Function Hunter* (Model 180D3) lockblade folder combines a 3-1/4-inch, drop-point pattern main blade with a similar length guthook/saw blade. Both blades are crafted from 420HC stainless steel and feature easy-opening thumb studs. The blades lock open by means of an inner-frame line-lock system. The patented rollover action allows for instant blade opening/closing with just one hand. The tapered handle features a metal clothing clip and is available in Advantage Classic® Camo. With one of the best-engineered guthooks on the market, Buck has gone a long way to give big game hunters what they need.

Camillus Cutlery: In their Cartridge Shield folding knife lineup, Camillus offers the *Sportsman 2-Blade LockBack* (Model C3) that features a clip pattern main blade paired with a blunt-nose gutting blade. Both 3-3/8-inch blades are crafted from stainless steel and are secured when open by means of a double offset locking mechanism. The handle scales are a Delrin® plastic in a simulated staghorn pattern, with a .30-06 Springfield cartridge case head shield and nickel-silver bolsters. As part of the Camillus' Western knife line, the fixed-blade *Guthook Hunter* (Model WR18) offers a 3-7/8-inch, high-carbon stainless steel, clip-pattern blade with a guthook feature on the blade spine just behind the tip. The knife has a non-slip Kraton® handle with molded finger grooves for a superior grip. Big-game hunters can't do any better than either of these edged game-care tools.

Cold Steel: The Cold Steel fixed-blade *Master Hunter Plus* incorporates a guthook feature into the blade spine of the original drop-point design. Crafted from Carbon V® carbon steel, the thick (3/16-inch), broad blade is flat ground extra thin, with a distinct distal taper for greater cutting power. The well-designed grip is heavily checkered Kraton®, which has been molded directly onto the full-tang. The knife comes with a Concealex™ sheath that allows for a variety of secure carrying options. A fine working knife that offers superior performance, the addition of the guthook feature makes it even better.

Columbia River Knife & Tool: The *Wind River* (Model 2001) fixed-blade, part of CRKT's Big Sky knife series, features a 4-3/4-inch, drop-point pattern blade with an integral guthook feature. The blade is crafted from AUS-6M stainless steel and is just the right size for field care on all types of big game. The handle material is a molded thermoplastic for soft, comfortable and secure hand-to-knife contact. The knife is supplied with an extra-tough 9-ounce leather scabbard with rivet and lockstitch sewn construction. A fine knife packed with lots of features, this guthook skinner is hard to beat.

Gutmann Cutlery: As part of their Jungle knife line, Gutmann offers four different knife models that have guthook features. The *Baby Hook Cleaver* (Model K02002) features a 4-inch blade crafted from AUS-8A stainless steel. This little cleaver has an exaggerated cutting edge radius, built-in finger hole, thumb rest serrations and a large guthook on the blade spine. The Kraton® handle grip allows for complete blade control when skinning or chopping through heavy gristle, cartilage or bone. The *Alaskan Hook Cleaver* (Model K02001) features a larger 5-7/8-inch chopping blade of AUS-8A stainless. This cleaver is designed for heavy-duty work and combines a straight cutting edge with the rounded tip of the Eskimo Ulu knife. The built-in finger hole, Kraton® handle grip, and thumb rest serrations on the blade spine enhance blade control in all cutting situations. Best of all, the extra large guthook feature works on all big game animals, from the smallest deer to the largest moose. Gutmann has also collaborated with a Japanese custom knifemaker, Tak Fukuta, to produce two fine skinners (Models K02027, K02028) that offer oversize guthooks. These are magnificent knives that combine AUS-8A stainless steel blades with Sambar stag handle scales, nickel-silver guards, with prominent thumb stops and generously-profiled guthooks situated on the spine of these functionally-design blades. When it comes to serious field butchering, Gutmann has it going on!

Ka-bar: This well-recognized cutlery firm recently introduced their Precision Hunter series of bantam-sized fixed-blade hunters. The *Game Hook* (Model 1441) features a 2-2/8-inch long, drop-point pattern blade crafted from 440A stainless steel, which has a guthook engineered into the blade spine near the tip. The Kraton G® thermoplastic elastomer handle offers a non-slip grip and maximum control during all phases of game care. This is a great knife whose functional abilities are enhanced by the addition of the guthook feature. Bigger isn't always better and this little Ka-bar offering proves it!

D. Hollis

The Wind River fixed-blade knife from Columbia River Knife & Tool Company has an integral guthook feature on the blade spine, near the tip.

Ka-bar

Part of Ka-bar's new series of small fixed-blade knife models, the Game Hook features a blade just a tad over 2-inches in length, with a guthook on the back edge.

Kershaw: The *Elk Skinner* (Model 1014), and the *Elk Skinner II* (Model 2014) are fixed-blade models that feature clip-pattern, AUS-6A stainless steel blades, with integral guthooks and comfortable synthetic handles. The Kershaw *Alaskan Blade Trader* (Model 1098 AK) combines a clip-pattern main blade, saw blade, and a very large and open guthook with an exchangeable handle. The blades are made from AUS-6A stainless steel and this exchangeable-blade set comes in a harness leather belt sheath that encases all components. Extremely versatile, this is a serious cutlery set for the serious hunter. Kershaw also markets a pair of *Sportsman's Shears* (Model 1130) that feature both a skinning blade and a guthook on one of the scissors blades. Made from AUS-6A stainless steel, with a comfortable molded pair of handles, this keen cutter does a lot more than just perform like a heavy-duty scissors. Obviously, the folks at Kershaw like guthooks well enough to provide lots of choice in that area.

Knives of Alaska: The "Light Hunter" *Mini Skinner/Cleaver* made by this firm is designed for those who need more blade power to cut through medium-size bones, as well as assistance with hide removal. The blade is crafted from double-drawn and cryogenically-treated D-2 tool steel. A deeply-recessed choil and grooved thumb rest provide enhanced blade control. The guthook feature on the blade spine near the tip is large enough so that the thick hair of sheep, mountain

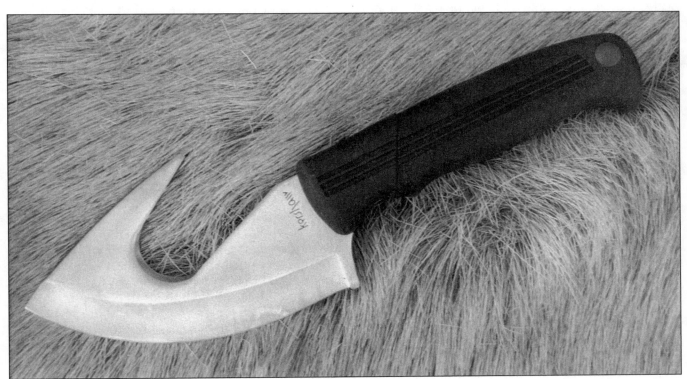

D. Hollis

Kershaw's Alaskan Blade Trader exchange-blade knife features a clip-point utility blade, a saw blade and a very large, open guthook skinning blade.

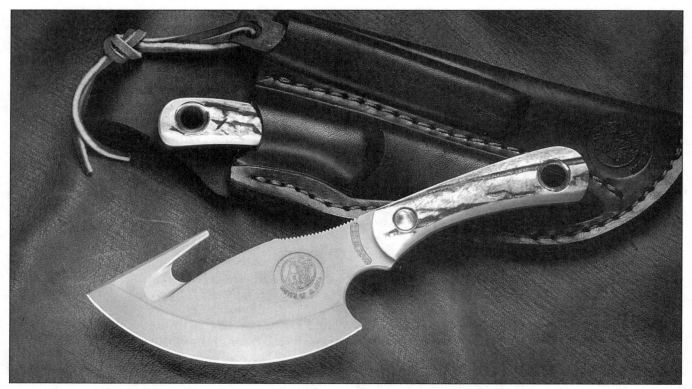

Knives of Alaska

The Mini Skinner/Cleaver from Knives of Alaska has all of the design features, including a well-thought-out guthook, to make it a solid choice for big-game field care.

goats, elk, moose, and northern whitetail deer won't "ball up" and inhibit the cutting action. A brass-ferruled lanyard hole is situated at the end of the handle. Available with either black rubberized, or genuine Sambar stag handle scales, this is an excellent heavy-duty cutting tool when you need to keep weight at a minimum.

Outdoor Edge: All of the award-winning T-handle *Whitetail Game Skinners* (Models GS100, GS100S, WT-10, and WT-10S) produced by this firm feature guthooks on their AUS-8A stainless steel blades. Winner of *Blade* magazine's 1988 Most Innovative Import Design award, the knives in this series are the ultimate in fixed-blade skinners. Also, Outdoor Edge makes the *Kodi-Skinner* (Model KS-10), a guthook skinning knife that is part of their *Kodi-Pak* game care combination set. This fixed-blade knife offers a 4-3/8-inch blade crafted from AUS-8A stainless steel, with a guthook that is raised well above the blade spine to facilitate easy hide insertion. One of best adaptations of a guthook to a fixed blade knife that I've seen, this is one skinner that can be counted on to do the job—and do it well.

Puma: Distributed by Coast Cutlery, this fine line of German-made cutlery has earned the respect of hunters worldwide. Newly introduced is a *Pro Hunter* (Model 116800) fixed-blade that includes a guthook feature on a narrow drop-point

blade pattern. This stainless steel, full-tang knife also has Sambar stag handle scales adding a touch of class to a field knife. Lightweight and fully capable of handling both field dressing, hide slitting, and skinning chores, this is an excellent choice for the single-knife hunter who packs light and hunts hard.

Schrade: As part of their Old Timer knife line, Schrade makes two different fixed-blade knives that have guthook features. The *Sharpfinger Guthook Skinner* (Model 158OT) features a full-tang blade made from easily-sharpened carbon steel. The blade design provides a long sweeping curve, with a guthook feature on the spine at the tip. Handle scales are saw-cut Delrin® that's practically indestructible. And the knife comes in a form-fitting leather belt sheath. The *Blade Runner* (Model 143OT) fixed-blade model combines a Schrade+Stainless (420HC) steel blade, with a TPR (thermoplastic rubber) molded handle. With both a guthook feature on the blade spine and a handle that allows a superior grip, wet or dry, this hunter is at the top of its game. Schrade has put more knives in the hands of outdoors enthusiasts than any other American knife company. The innovative design and superior craftsmanship of these two guthook models reflect the quality and economy that this nearly 100-year-old firm has built their reputation with.

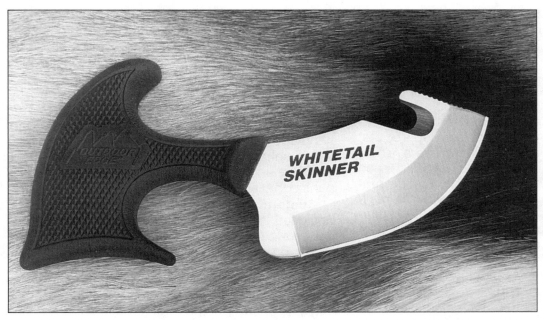

Here's a sleek little gut-hook design from Outdoor Edge. The T-handle cuts down on user fatigue and the guthook works just like having a zipper in the hide.

Outdoor Edge

The 3-3/4-inch stainless steel blade on this Puma Pro Hunter features an integral guthook and the curved stag handle grip provides a superior gripping surface.

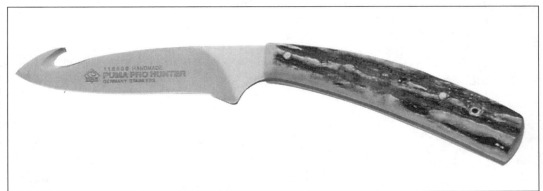

Coast Cutlery

The Schrade Blade Runner, with its integral guthook feature, is one of the newest members of the Old Timer® Safe-T-Grip knife series.

Images Group/Schrade

Remington: With four folders and one fixed-blade model, Remington has embraced the guthook concept in a big way. In the new Rattlesnake™ "One-Hander" series, there is a two-blade folder that features a broad drop-point pattern main blade and a sawblade/guthook companion blade. The black molded nylon handle and one-hand opening features are both user-friendly features that any hunter will be able to appreciate. The Grizzly™ line of unique folders has a single lockback, and two double-lockback models, each of which incorporate a guthook feature. The rugged RemGrip™ on these knives provides a resilient and non-slip grip for any field-care assignment. Though compact when folded, any of these model's locks open to offer the size and strength of a fixed-blade. Great design features combined with superior craftsmanship, this series of folders has it "going on." A single fixed-blade knife, with a guthook on the blade spine near the tip, rounds out Remington's guthook offerings. The full-tang, drop-point pattern blade is crafted of 440A stainless steel. The molded handle thermoplastic rubberized handles provide exceptional hand-to-knife contact and are finger-grooved for enhanced blade control. A study design with exceptional features, this knife can meet any game care need.

United Cutlery: This firm carries the *Game Zipper* (Model RG82), handy little tool for serious big game hunters. This keen cutter features a blade made from 420-J2 stainless steel that is just 2-7/8-inches in length, with a raised guthook on the blade spine. The handle is molded black rubber that fully encapsulates the blade tang. The special double-finger grip engineered into the handle reduces hand and wrist fatigue, while providing enhanced cutting control. A great little field dressing and skinning tool, this is one steel companion that's right on the mark.

Custom Guthook: No matter how it's designed, the insertion of a guthook edge on the spine of a blade tends to detract from the design. The words, "really ugly," come to mind when someone mentions a guthook knife. This may be the reason why few custom makers produce guthook models. However, at least a couple that I know have entered the arena.

Specializing in Damascus steel, knifemaker Loyd Thomson makes one of the finest looking guthook skinners I've ever laid my eyes on. With its bold Damascus blade pattern and desert ironwood handle, this is a striking integration of a guthook feature within a drop-point pattern design.

Canadian, Dan McCormick makes a fixed-blade

D. Hollis

This Remington Grizzly double lockblade folder features a clip-point main blade, and a guthook/saw combination companion blade.

Jennifer Thomsen-Connell

Built by knifemaker Loyd Thomsen, this Damascus guthook knife features a stabilized redwood handle and "mosaic" pins.

guthook, which completely eliminates hair from clogging the cutting surface, a problem common to all of this style blade. Made from CPM 10V carbon steel, the knife is handled with stone sheep horn scales and features a stainless steel bolster. A unique design that really works, this concept is definitely a departure from the ordinary.

Not everyone appreciates what a guthook or gutting blade brings to the game. I am sure that this lack of understanding is centered in a shortage of game care exposure. Once a hunter is able to see these cutlery assets in action, the advantages they hold are clearly manifest. For my part, I long ago embraced both features. From start to finish, a guthook or a gutting blade can turn game-care drudgery into a simple assignment. It's just as easy as that!

Weyer of Toledo

Dan McCormick made this pair: the upper knife is a trailing-point skinner, the lower one a unique gutting tool.

Buck Knives

Plain edge or combination (plain/serrated)—now knife users have a choice (Buck Protégé Lockblade folder pictured). For tough jobs, partial serration at the bottom of the blade edge can save the tip for more delicate work.

Chapter 10
The Ragged Edge

Serrate: [Latin: serratus] having saw-like notches along the edge. Serration: 1. The condition of being serrated. Webster's New World Dictionary, 3rd College Edition, Newfieldt, V. ed., Simon & Schuster, Inc. 1988, 1991, 1994.

Knife blade edge serration is nothing new. Cheap steak knives, found in equally as tawdry eating establishments, have offered this feature for years. Restaurant utensils take some rough handling. Dumped into a dishwasher and jostled around with other tableware isn't my idea of favorable treatment. Even worse, cutting against a hard ceramic surface (the dinner plate) is sure to turn the best edge. And no restaurant manager or waiter wants an irate guest to have access to a sharp knife. The serrated steak knife was the resolution to all of these problems. Even if the edge got banged around a bit, it didn't matter. Contact with a hard surface didn't seem to inhibit satisfactory performance. And with a rounded tip, a serrated steak knife is about as threatening as a dull butter knife. The serrations' irregular nature does offer enhanced cutting ability, and their performance is seemingly unaffected by rough handling and misuse.

Most of the earlier serrated edges were nothing more than a series of alternating pointed teeth, with a gap in between each tooth of consistent size and depth. While this seemed to work, the cutting action was rough and the edge had a tendency

inexpensive serrated culinary cutters of the past and some produced in the present.

Under magnification, any edge is noticeably irregular. Then, the descriptive terms—plain and serrated edge—would refer to perception without visual amplification. At this level of acuity, the character of a plain edge appears completely smooth, and a serrated edge looks highly asymmetrical. Point of fact, however, is that both are irregular. The unevenness of a plain edge is only visible under magnification. The coarse appearance of a serrated edge is readily apparent without optical enlargement.

Just how does a serrated edge work? A plain edge has extremely fine irregularities. In use, these tiny teeth spread the cutting force across a wide microscopic plane. Conversely, a serrated edge is extremely asymmetrical, with large highly irregular teeth which concentrate applied force at the specific point of penetration in the particular cutting medium. The teeth pierce and hold the material to be cut, while the concave scalloped edges situated behind these penetration points actually perform the cutting movement. The concave edge of every scallop, when compared to a plain edge, extends the length of the sharpened

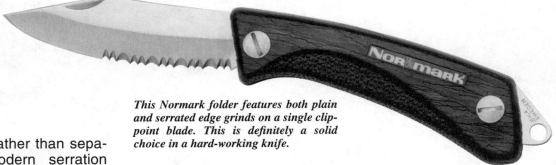

This Normark folder features both plain and serrated edge grinds on a single clip-point blade. This is definitely a solid choice in a hard-working knife.

Normark

to tear rather than separate. Modern serration patterns usually combine teeth and recessed cutting scallops in a much broader pattern, with both small and large recessed curves. This is more effective in rotating the sharp concave edges around the medium to be cut. Moreover, modern steels and heat-treating processes combine hardness and toughness to enable enhanced edge retention. This is a far cry from

edge resulting in a longer cutting radius in a shorter blade. This focuses the cutting pressure, which is realized in enhanced performance. Due to the recessed nature of the sharpened surfaces, they are protected from primary contact erosion. In turn, not only is performance intensified, the edge life of each concaved cutting edge is extended.

Interestingly, the forging process serrates the edge of a Damascus knife. If you look at the edge under magnification, you will notice that the multiple layers of steel come to an irregular apex. These ultra-fine irregularities give Damascus the cutting edge over many other steels. And this is true for all of the same reasons that a more formalized serrated pattern also offers extended edge performance.

Understanding the amplified cutting power of a serrated edge, you'd have thought that it would be found in venues beyond the confines of kitchen cutlery. For whatever reasons, knife users initially didn't seriously consider the serrated edge as useful in any other setting. No doubt, some of this had to do with the perceptual attachment to the kitchen. Possibly the conceptual leap from using a blade that could efficiently slice salad tomatoes to field dressing big game, wild fowl and fish was a notion born before its time. Whatever the reasons, a discussion of a serrated outdoor knife blade is enough to bring a skeptical look from many quarters.

More significant to the lack of general acceptance was the fact that no one was making a sharpener for the serrated blade. I think most knife users realized that despite the extended usefulness of a serrated edge, there would come a point in time when the need for knife sharpening couldn't be put off. Faced without a mechanism to reestablish that edge, the serrated blade was condemned to isolation in a culinary prison.

Since edge serration is applied only to one side of the blade, cutlery manufacturers initially recommended that the blade be sharpened on the side opposite of the serrations. This was a satisfactory recommendation for temporary edge reestablishment. Smoothing out the opposite side of the edge only cleaned up the turned, or wire edge on one side of the blade. The tiny recessed edges benefited little from such an attempt, and edge life wasn't really improved a great deal. In time, however, sharpeners for serrated edge knives were developed. Now, it's possible to keep a serrated edge as keenly honed as any plain edge blade. Considering the fact that a serrated edge will cut much longer than a plain edge, time spent in edge restoration efforts is greatly reduced.

More than anyone else, Sal Glesser, and his firm, Spyderco, can be credited with the creation, promotion, and public acceptance of the serrated edge. The *Mariner* (Model C02) was the first Spyderco knife model that carried what was termed the "SpyderEdge." This knife, introduced in 1982, featured a sheepsfoot style blade and was specifically designed to cut line and rope. Since a serrated edge offers superior performance over a plain edge when cutting fibrous medium, the new SpyderEdge made a big hit.

Where does the serration edge fit into the cutlery market? Edged cutting tools to deal with twine, line, rope, rubber hose, plastic pipe and cardboard are common to any urban setting. Furthermore, outdoors enthusiasts can benefit from a more aggressive knife edge as well. Big-game hunters use their knives for cutting through gristle, cartilage, and

Jennifer Thomsen-Connell

If you look at the edge of a Damascus blade under magnification, a noticeable line of fine serrations will be seen. This is why the steel cuts so well.

This Gerber Gator® lockblade folder is available with a plain or partially serrated edge.

Gerber Legendary Blades

across hair. Likewise, small game hunters, water-fowlers and uplanders need a rugged edge to sever bone at various joints, and to cut through feathers and fur. Anglers also require something more than a plain edge to deal with fish bone and skin. Since serrations provide exceptional cutting power, with strengthened edge life, it is the edge of choice for all applications—and more.

While the serrated edge provides distinct advantages, it is not the answer for every cutting situation. It has already been stated that a serrated blade is the cutting edge of choice for use on fibrous materials. For cutting meat and the preparation of food, however, the plain edge is often a better choice. The reason for this is the difference between the resultant cut. A serrated edge provides an extremely aggressive, but less controllable blade movement. On the other hand, a plain edge produces a finer cut with more manageable and smoother cutting action.

Understanding the difference between the serrated and plain edge, cutlery manufacturers began to produce a blade edge that offered the best of both worlds—a combination of both features. Realizing that the lower 40%-50% of the blade receives little use, it was here that the application of edge serration seemed to be most advantageous. For precise cutting action, the leading plain edge could be brought into play. The rear-serrated portion of the blade could be used for all of the rough work. Hunters and anglers took to this concept quickly. In fact, using the serrated portion of the combination edge saved the leading blade edge from premature contact erosion.

An alternative approach was to include both plain and serrated blades in a multiple blade folding knife configuration. Just after the Coleman Corporation purchased Western Knife Company in the early 1980s, they introduced a folder that featured just such a combination of blades. Sadly, Western Knife is no more, but other cutlery manufacturers have continued this theme.

Most big-game hunters aren't fans of blade edge serration. I believe that this is because they are only involved in basic field dressing. When it comes to game evisceration, skinning and boning, a plain edge is the right choice. If quartering a game carcass in the field is the job at hand, then the forte of the serrated edge will come to the forefront. Cutting across wire-like hair, or slicing through cartilage can wreak havoc on a plain edge. However, a serrated edge can handle either chore with equal aplomb. I am a real fan of either the combination edge, or a companion blade with a serrated edge. So equipped, it's possible to handle every field dressing and skinning chore—including butchering—without stopping to sharpen my knife.

I am fortunate enough to live in a state that has a burgeoning population of wild hogs. There is no season or bag limit on these surly 2beasts, so this provides ample opportunity to hone my cutlery field skills. On a recent hunt, I shot a sizeable boar hog. Unfortunately, there was no vehicular access and it was miles back to my truck. Faced with the insurmountable job of dragging a near 200-pound animal out of the woods, I chose to reduce the carcass to boned meat and a set of trophy tusks. In a pack, such a load weighs less than half the weight of the animal on the hoof.

Remington

This handy Remington pocketfolder has a main clip-point, plain edge blade, as well as a drop-point serrated edge secondary blade.

In my experience nothing is harder on a knife edge than a wild hog. Boar hair resembles wire-like bristles, and it's often crusted over with mud. Cutting through that stuff will give a whole new meaning to the words, "edge retention." Just as bad are the tough sinew strands and thick hide. Anyone who thinks field dressing, skinning and butchering a wild hog is easy, then they haven't had the experience. If it wasn't for the sweet, succulent flavor of lean wild pork, I don't think you could ever convince me to hunt wild boar again.

Beginning the field-dressing process, I cut around the terminal end of the digestive system (isn't that a nice way of putting it?). Then, moving forward, I opened the abdominal cavity from the top of the pelvis, to the bottom of the ribcage. Since I wasn't going to mount the head skin, cutting through the ribcage cartilage offered easy access to the heart/lung cavity. Using the lower serrated portion of my fixed-blade knife's combination edge, the old boar's chest came open without a problem. It was a simple matter to remove the viscera using the leading plain portion of the knife blade edge. In preparation for skinning, I once again used the serration portion of the blade edge to remove all four

hocks and opened the hide along each leg. The plain edge (along with some discreet hide manipulation) handled all the rest of the skinning chores. When the job was over, I hadn't needed to sharpen my knife at all.

Likewise, if you use a knife on small game and birds, a serrated blade edge is really handy. If you use a plain edge to remove wings and feet, you'll need to resharpen your knife before the next cutting assignment can be undertaken. Fur and feathers can be tough on a blade. The worst part of handling birds and small game is that a plain edge has a tendency to slip across, rather than cutting through pliant skin. A serrated blade, however, can slice through gristle, joints, and tough skin hide without an impediment or impacting its cutting ability.

Just last season, I watched as a friend of mine struggled to field dress, skin and prepare a limit of quail for the barbeque. We'd spent the morning having one of the best quail hunts of our lives. After the initial flush, a covey of more than two dozen birds scattered in some knee-high grass. One-by-one, the little buzz bombs took to the air, affording some of the finest upland shooting we'd ever experienced. After we returned to the ranch headquarters, it was decided that a taste of quail would go well with wild rice and a green salad at lunch. While I cleaned the shotguns and watered the dogs, my friend volunteered to field dress and fix the birds for the fire. By the time the chore was finished, he had stopped to sharpen his plain edge knife more times that I could remember. I don't know about you, but I'd rather spend time hunting than in blade edge restoration activities. The use of a combination edge (50% plain/50% serrated) could have saved him a lot of trouble. In some cutting situations, a serrated edge can't be beat (removing game bird wings and feet are a good example). And that, my friend, is a simple fact!

Backpackers and hikers are faced with more varied cutting challenges than any other group of outdoor folks. During the course of an excursion in the wild, a knife may be called on to clean a limit of fish, whittle a new tent peg, open packets of freeze-dried food, or a dozen other chores. In this

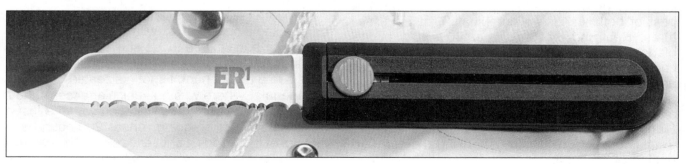

Cold Steel

This Cold Steel Emergency Rescue retractable blade knife, designed for law enforcement, paramedic, and emergency response teams, has a serrated sheepsfoot blade for cutting through seat belts, rope, and cord.

venue, the serrated edge is right at home. You see, functional versatility, combined with low tool maintenance, is what such an asymmetrical edge knife is all about.

Anglers also can benefit from the use of a serrated edge. Someone gave me a filet knife that had a short section of serrations right at the blade tip. I thought that the tip of a filet knife was a dumb place to put a serrated edge, however, I learned a new lesson. Filleting a pile of freshly caught fish can be wearisome. The real problem is initially cutting into the skin. Well, the serrated blade tip on my filet knife solved that problem. Heavy scales, tough skin, neither one was a problem for that slender filet wonder. Indeed, this old worm dabbler now has a new way to go.

In addition to hunters, anglers, backpackers, and other outdoor folk, urban dwellers can also benefit from blade edge serration. Most of the cutting chores encountered in a concrete and steel environment are more easily maneuvered with a serrated blade. Dealing with pressboard, rope, and plastic strapping is no challenge for a serrated edge. However, most plain edge knives would struggle with these cutting mediums. Opening boxes, cutting through seat belting, and a whole host of other assignments are children's play to the serrated edge. For this reason, most paramedics, fire fighters, and law enforcement officers carry knives with just such an edge. Likewise, you're likely to find a serrated blade knife in the pocket or on the belt of most tradesmen, contractors, and even skilled professionals. The basic fact is that most people don't know a thing about sharpening knives. A serrated edge will keep on cutting long after a plain edge has taken a beating. It's a simple matter of economics. Time is money and knife sharpening is not only bothersome, it's time consumptive. A serrated edge saves both time and money!

Combining his experience in development of blade sharpening tools, with deeper involvement in the knives, Glesser perfected his SpyderEdge. For a time, the cutlery industry was slow to realize the potential importance of Sal Glesser's re-introduction of an old theme. By the late 1980s, however, the impact of the serrated edge on the cutlery market was as monumental as the 1963 introduction of the Buck lockblade *Folding Hunter* (Model 110). Buck Knives brought the carrying convenience of a folding knife and the safe use of a lockable blade to the cutlery industry. This was something that the knife buying public embraced with enthusiasm. In fact, the lockblade folding knife is a modern cutlery phenomena. Equally as dominating was Spyderco's introduction of blade edge serration as a practical cutlery reality. Today nearly every production knife factory offers one or more knife models that feature full- or partial-edge serration.

Not all serrated patterns are as effectively designed or rendered on the blade edge with the same proficiency as Glesser's original design. Nevertheless, most adaptations can take ruthless use—even abuse—and still keep on cutting. Blade edge serration was a concept whose time had come, and Sal Glesser was just the innovator to make it happen. Others have picked up that baton and have attempted to run the race. However, the SpyderEdge is still hard to beat.

Spyderco isn't the only firm offering knife models with serrated edges. Most, if not all, of the production knifemakers have embraced this theme, and rightfully so. For a using knife, edge serration can be extremely advantageous. This is especially true for use in resistant, rough surfaced, or fibrous materials. Even if the sharp serrated points are eroded through use, the recessed edges keep on cutting. It takes a lot to dull a serrated edge and that alone is a great asset.

Kershaw kai Cutlery

Here's a great combination of blade edges in a single folding knife. The plain edge for light to medium duty assignments, and the serrated edge for all the tough stuff.

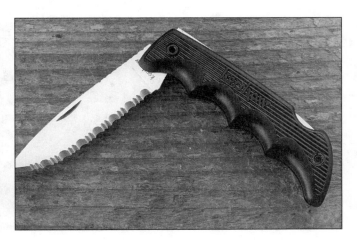

Kershaw kai Cutlery

If it gets any more aggressive than this serrated edge, then it would have to be a saw blade.

D. Hollis

Even with snow on the ground, it's important to field dress big game immediately to prevent premature spoilage.

Chapter 11
Big-Game Blades

The single largest group of outdoor knife users are big-game hunters. Those selecting a blade for field dressing, skinning, and butchering harvested game have a sizable array of edged tools from which to pick.

The single largest group of outdoor knife users are big game hunters. Those selecting a blade for field dressing, skinning and butchering harvested game have a sizable-array of edged tools from which to pick.

No matter how uncomfortable hunting camp might be, or physically demanding the terrain, the pursuit of big game is still a grand experience. Despite our individual levels of enjoyment, at the moment the ball, bullet or broadhead has reduced pursuit to game possession, the fun ends and new chores are just beginning. In this realm, the knife and related edged tools are the defining components of the hunt.

Big-game hunters have a wide range of cutlery from which to select. Most choose a single knife with blade shape versatility. Europeans favor the

spear-point blade, but it finds few followers in this country. The majority of American hunters like clip-pattern blades, with some endorsing drop-point designs. The argument for either design is functional versatility. With nothing more than a single clip- or drop-point blade you can field skin, cape and butcher most big-game animals.

If you become very involved with field care of big game, the need for other blade patterns, types of knives, and cutting tools will become manifest. Skinning goes easier with a skinning knife—just ask the buffalo skinners of old. Without a blade shaped somewhat like a scalpel, caping can be a real chore. Field and home butchering also demand specialized cutlery.

In my mind, a hunting knife not only has to perform, it also must possess certain attributes. Chief

Benchmade

A collaboration between the Benchmade Knife Co. and custom knifemaker, Mel Pardue, produced this outstanding knife. Featuring an AXIS® locking mechanism, ATS-34 clip-point pattern stainless blade and a machined aircraft aluminum handle with clothing clip, this folder has all the makings of a great edged tool.

among these qualities is design symmetry, blade configuration and user comfort. Like everyone else, I have my own preferences based on experience and perception. This chapter provides the opportunity to share with you some of those choices from both production and custom knifemakers.

Benchmade: Always on the leading edge of cutlery development, this firm's products are some of the best. One of Benchmade's newest folders has a host of features any hunter can appreciate. The combination of a clip-point pattern, ATS-34 stainless steel blade, and the Benchmade exclusive AXIS® locking mechanism, has resulted in one of the toughest lockblade folders available. The machined aluminum handle scales have a handy clothing clip attached on one side. This collaborative effort with knifemaker, Mel Pardue, is pack full of high-tech properties that can make any hunter a proud knife owner.

Boker USA: The clip-pattern, fixed-blade Arbolito hunter (Model 517), made at the Boker plant in Argentina, is one of my favorite elk knives. This game care tool features a 420HC stainless steel blade, with a recessed choil, that measures 4-7/8-inch in length. An ergonomically-correct thermoplastic handle encapsulates the full tang and offers a non-slip grip. Supplied with a top-grain black leather sheath, this is an affordable and well-made piece of cutlery.

Browning: The two-blade Kodiak lockblade folder (Model 609) features both a drop-point and a clip-point blade in the same folding knife frame. Both of the 3-1/2-inch blades are made from AUS-8A stainless steel. For amplified force, when cutting through cartilage and gristle, the lower portion of the clip-point blade is serrated. The impact-resistant handle is made from tough Zytel® and features a checkered rubber insert for exceptional hand-to-knife contact. The rugged Ballistic Cloth® sheath provides out-of-the-way carrying ease. Designed by Michael Collins, this is a big game hunting tool that can offer peerless performance with every phase of field care.

Buck Knives: A Buck model that I've used extensively is the Woodsman (Model 102) fixed blade. This handy little knife features a 4-inch clip-pattern blade, made from 420HC stainless steel. The blade length is just about the right size for fish and small game, as well as deer, wild hogs and antelope. Handle, guard and pommel choices are either black phenolic with aluminum fittings (black sheath), or a laminated cocobolo wood handle with brass guard and pommel (brown sheath). The sheath, designed with an offset snap fastener to prevent it from catching on brush, affords a secure belt carry. Small enough to ride comfortably on your hip, this knife is big on game-care performance.

Case Cutlery: A couple of years ago Case brought out a new fixed-blade model in two different blade lengths (3-1/2 inch and 5 inch). Instead of the typical rounded shape, the handle scales on these knives were somewhat flattened. Correspondingly, the knife earned the name Slab-Side Hunter. Crafted from Tru-Sharp® steel, the blades feature a clip-pattern configuration with a wide fuller. Depending on the model selected, handle scale choice includes: stag, rosewood and chestnut pick-bone. Case has always been at the top of their game with an extensive line of folders. While the introduction of a new fixed blade is a departure from that motif, it certainly is a welcome addition to their cutlery line.

Camillus Cutlery: A few years ago, Camillus acquired the famous Western Cutlery line. In addition to manufacturing several knife models under that name, they also produced private label selected designs for other firms. The fixed-blade hunter (Model WR12) in the Western line is a sturdy and affordable field knife (a similar model is also available from Remington). This edged tool combines a clip-point, 4-1/4-inch, high-carbon stainless steel blade, with a finger-grooved, non-

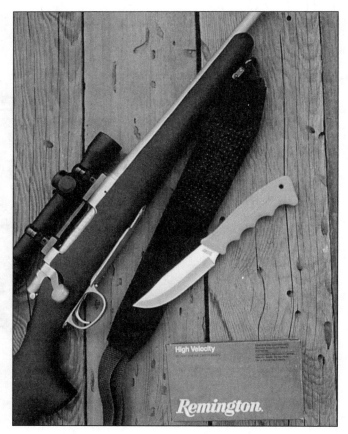

D. Hollis

While private labeled for Remington, this fixed-blade is no different than a similar model in the Western Knife fixed-blade line-up. With its drop-point stainless steel blade and finger-grooved thermoplastic handle, it's definitely a serious big-game knife.

slip Kraton® handle (black-WR12, orange-WRO12). A straightforward design, able to handle a wide range of game-care chores, this sheath knife is a reliable choice in an edged tool.

Cold Steel: This firm makes a terrific hunting knife in their Master Hunter fixed-blade offering. The 4-1/2-inch, drop-point pattern (also available with a guthook feature) blade is 3/16-inch thick and won't give up no matter what the challenge. Available in either Carbon V®, or 8A stainless steel, the blade has been flat ground with a distal taper for an enhanced combination of cutting ability and edge retention. The checkered Kraton® handle grip has been molded directly on the full-length blade tang. Field-tested extensively in Africa, Australia and throughout this country, this knife is one of the finest-edged working tools anywhere.

Columbia River Knife & Tool Co. (CRKT): A relatively new player in the cutlery market, CRKT's affordable, innovative products have been the choice of many. In their hunting knife line, the fixed-blade Bridger (Model 2002) is my idea of a good thing. The 3-3/4-inch drop-point pattern blade is made from AUS-6M stainless steel, taper-ground for a superior edge, and featuring a grooved spine for added blade control. The molded thermoplastic handle and ribbed guard fully encapsulated the full-length blade tang. A black leather carrying sheath is part of the package. A proven blade design, high-tech materials and very affordable, this is one CRKT product that's hard to resist.

Gerber Legendary Blades: This Pacific Northwest cutlery firm is always on the leading edge of innovation. This was certainly true when they first brought out their Gator"® folder a few years ago. Now, this great knife comes with an ATS-34 stainless steel blade for heightened edge retention. The Kraton® thermoplastic handle material is solidly affixed to a nylon inner core and highly-texturized for non-slip hand-to-knife contact. Supplied with a Ballistic® cloth sheath, this is one serious game-care tool.

Grohman Cutlery: This Canadian manufacturer produces the famous D. H. Russell Belt Knives. For big game work, I like the original design (Model R1S). The 4-inch, elliptical (spearpoint) blade is available in either carbon or high-carbon stainless steel. Standard handle material is hand-burnished rosewood in a user-friendly design. A brass-lined lanyard hole, fitted with a nylon wrist thong, and an oil-tanner leather sheath completes the package. With a blade rugged enough to split wood, yet still capable of delicate trophy work, it's easy to understand why this knife has been a favorite of Canadian hunters for more than four decades.

Gutmann Cutlery: This firm markets a line of innovative hunting knives designed by Japanese knife maker, Tak Fukuta. The Tak Fukuta Fixed-

This Gerber Gator® lockblade folder is available with a plain or partially serrated edge.

Gerber Legendary Blades

D. Hollis

Kershaw's collaboration with knifemaker Ken Onion has resulted in a number of superb liner lockblade folders. The Serrated Ricochet model is an excellent choice for hunting duties.

Blade Hunter (Model K02026) features a very narrow drop-point (almost straight) blade. The blade itself is 4-1/8-inches in length and made from AUS-8 carbon-modified stainless steel. The handle scales are Sambar stag and impart an uncommon level of beauty to this field tool. A trademark braided leather lanyard is attached to the end of the knife handle, adding to the striking appearance of this fine knife. Ideal for field dressing and trophy work, this game-care tool combines thoughtful design, quality materials, and excellence in manufacture.

Ka-bar: My fondness for small fixed-blades was reinforced when knifemaker, Dan Harrison, first introduced me to the Precision Hunter (Model 1443) drop-point pattern sheath knife. Featuring a 3-1/8-inch, hollow-ground blade made from 440A stainless steel, with a Kraton G® thermoplastic elastomer handle, this knife has everything you'd expected from a sheath knife. When carried on the belt, the knife and protective covering measures only 6-3/4-inches overall. Working in collaboration with the folks at Ka-bar, Dan Harrison has come up with a peerless fixed-blade game-care implement.

Kershaw: This cutlery manufacturer has been working with knifemaker, Ken Onion, to produce a series of innovative folders. The Serrated Ricochet (Model 1520ST) is just such a product. The knife features a 440V stainless steel blade, in a drop-point configuration, that's just 3-1/4-inches

long. The handle scales are made from the tough G-10 material, frame liners are titanium, and there's a pocket clip for carrying convenience. Best of all, the knife has the patented Onion "Speed Safe," torsion bar assisted opening. Just open the knife once and you'll be convinced that it's the easiest and fastest opening lockblade folder on the market.

Knives of Alaska: At the top of my cutlery creation "wish list" was for some manufacturer to make a folding knife for trophy work. Well, Charles Allen at Knives of Alaska has made that wish come true. The new Alaskan Super Cub places a 2-1/2-inch, slender drop-point blade, made from VG-10 stainless steel (Rc 59-61) in a narrow frame that's just 4-1/4-inches in length. Just behind the edge, a recessed choil and a corresponding thumb rest on the blade spine provides added control when cutting in tight quarters. Within the frame, a bearing-actuated liner lock mechanism provides "glass-smooth" blade opening and closing. Furthermore, a blade-mounted, thumb stud can be moved to either side of the blade for easy opening. Since trophy work can be really messy at times, the space between the liners has been left open to facilitate cleaning after use. Handle scales are available in your choice of

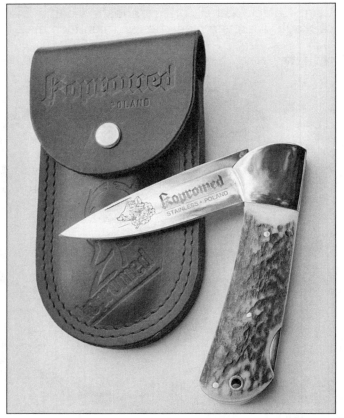

D. Hollis

Mirror-polished stainless steel, stag handle scales, and an oil-tanned leather belt pouch are all features any seasoned hunter can well appreciate.

rubberized "Suregrip," carbon fiber, of the toughest G-10 materials. A handle-mounted clothing clip allows for a variety of carrying styles. When it comes to caping knives, this little number is a real "stand out."

Kopromed: While this Polish cutlery manufacturer has been making knives for many years, their products have only recently been made available in this country. There is definitely an Old World design flair to these knives. If you like stag-handled knives as much as this writer, then you'll find Kropromed's products to your liking. My own personal selection would be Model 23. This is a lockblade folder that features a mirror-polished, 440C stainless steel (Rc 56-58), drop-point pattern blade. The bolsters appear to be stainless steel, and the handle scales are European red stag. The knife is supplied with an oil-finished leather belt pouch. Crafted by cutlers who are steeped in tradition, this folder has "hunting" written all over it.

Marbles: In 1892, Webster Marble started in the cutlery business with his famous "Safety Axe." After many periods of change, in 1997 this firm resumed the full-time manufacture of the famous Marbles® fixed-blade hunting knives. My "pick of the litter" is the new Fieldcraft™ model. The blade is 3-3/4-inches long and crafted from 52100 carbon steel. The final Rockwell rating of Rc 59-60 offers the best possible combination of incredible strength and maximum edge retention. The clip-pattern blade is an interesting departure from the tradition configuration. This combines both an extremely fine point and a sweeping blade belly. Incredibly sharp, the blade edge is convex ground. The guard is brass and the pommel is aluminum. The handle options are stacked leather washers, tigerwood, and Michigan maple. A limited number of knives will be available with Sambar stag handles and stag or aluminum pommels. Supplied with a guide-style wraparound leather sheath, this knife certainly reestablishes the cutlery design leadership of this more than a century old firm. Webster Marble would be proud!

Normark: The American Hunter™ (Model 420) is a very economically priced lockblade folder. Featuring a 3-1/2-inch, stainless steel, clip pattern blade, with a lock release situated at the rear of the handle, this knife takes and holds a solid edge. The textured soft grip handle is designed for maximum leverage and control. Best of all, the handle scales can be removed for complete knife cleaning. Available with, or without a black leather sheath, this is a fantastic value in a quality piece of game care cutlery.

Outdoor Edge: A game care knife doesn't have to be overly large to get the job done. I can recall my father using a three-blade stockman pocket-knife to field dress everything from quail to geese, and squirrels to deer. The fixed-blade, Wedge II (Model WG-2), by Outdoor Edge possesses a blade that is just 3-inches in length, yet is quite capable of handling most routine hunting needs. The drop-point pattern blade is crafted from 6M stainless steel and is contained within a molded sheath that, by means of a swivel clip and/or cord loop, can be worn in a variety of positions (on the belt, clipped to a loop, or even around the neck). The sheath has a quick finger release mechanism that provides both carrying safety and ready access. The knife handle is molded directly onto the blade tang and fea-

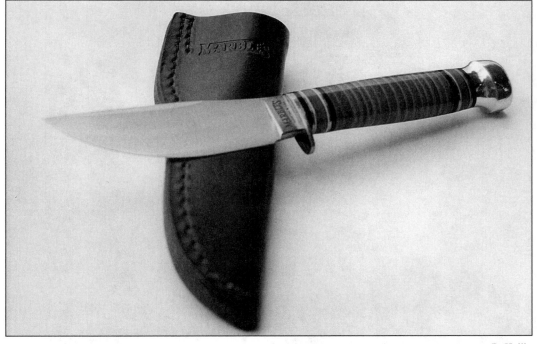

D. Hollis

The reintroduction of Marbles hunting knives was a welcome event by many. This Marbles fixed-blade Fieldcraft™ model features an alloy carbon steel blade, brass guard, aluminum pommel and stacked leather washer handle.

tures gripping ridges for improved control of the cutting force. This little knife is so light, accessible and handy, you'll wonder why you ever thought that something more was needed.

Puma: This Solingen, Germany-based cutlery manufacturer has always had a strong hunting knife presence. Their fixed-blade White Hunter II can handle every species of big game, from tiny African antelope to Canadian moose and anything in between. Featuring a functionally-designed stainless steel blade, with an integral thumb rest on the spine, brass single guard, and riveted stag handle scales, this knife is a fine-edged primary field-dressing and skinning tool. Supplied with a loss-proof leather belt scabbard, this Puma is one big cat that can really hunt.

Coast Cutlery

When you're in the thick of it, there's no better companion than a Puma White Hunter II fixed-blade.

108

Spyder Co.

The Alaska Department of Fish and Game, Hunter Information and Training Program selected the Spyderco Wegner CLIPIT lockblade folder for their hunter education clinics. Need I say anymore?

Schrade: If there's one knife design that incorporates everything a big game hunter needs, then it can be found in Schrade's Sharpfinger (Model 152OT) fixed-blade design. The carbon steel blade combines the sweeping belly of a skinner, with the sharp and narrow point of a clip, in what resembles a trailing-point pattern at first glance. Handles are saw cut Delrin® and are rivet-attached to the full-length blade tang. The top grain leather sheath is molded to fit the knife like a second skin. An absolutely unrivaled design that can "do it all," and with clear superiority!

Spyderco: The folks at this forward-thinking cutlery firm have collaborated with knifemaker, Tim Wegner, to produce the Wegner CLIPIT (Model C48) folding lockblade hunter that is "tough enough for Alaska!" Featuring a hollow-ground, 3-5/8-inch blade made from ATS-34 stainless steel in a drop-point design, this is one fantastic folder. On the blade spine, above the one-hand opening hole, a textured thumb rest provides added cutting power. The famous Walker inner-frame liner locking mechanism secures the blade when opened. Both plain and combination (plain/serrated) blade edge models are available. Everything about this folder is tough, including the G-10 laminate handle scales and stainless steel fittings. Lastly, there's an easy access pocket clip for attachment to the belt, pocket or the edge of anything. This folder is used exclusively by the Alaska Department of Fish and Game Hunter Information and Training Program in their field dressing and meat care clinics. I guess they know a good thing when they see it!

United Cutlery: The Hibben Pro Guide Hunter (Model UC1203) was the result of a collaboration between United and knifemaker, Gil Hibben. Designed to handle large big game animals, the knife is endorsed by the Alaskan Guide Association. The 440A stainless steel blade is 4-5/8-inches in length and manifests all of the strength of a drop-point design. Quite capable of handling everything from field dressing game to camp chores, this field tool is a great choice for those who hunt the wild places. The finger-grooved Micarta® handle scales provide a reinforced grip and are firmly affixed to the full-length blade tang with stainless steel pins. Carried afield in its black leather sheath, this is one rugged steel sidekick.

A Touch of Class

There's nothing wrong with taking a handmade knife to the woods. Just because you spent the better part of a month's wages on such a knife doesn't mean that you can't use it. There is a plethora of knifemakers and space prevents comment on all of these cutlery specialists. Moreover, there is a big difference between a knifemaker and one who also has first-hand knowledge of the field.

United Cutlery sought out the services of knifemaker Gil Hibben when this fixed-blade Pro Guide Hunter model was designed.

United Cutlery

Featuring a drop-point stainless steel Damascus blade, bolsters and liners of titanium, with sheep horn handle scales, this locking folder by Keith Coleman combines intricate beauty and functional design.

Keith Coleman

Some makers do, however, have the necessary game-care experience to understand what works best under demanding conditions. The following is a representative sampling of those individuals:

Keith Coleman makes a beautiful stainless steel Damascus folder. Featuring a drop-point blade, frame bolsters and liners of titanium, and sheep horn handle scales, this is one impressive outdoor knife. And there's nothing wrong with mixing beauty with function. Certainly, Keith Coleman knows his stuff!

Edmund Davidson has crafted a fixed-blade beauty that features a 4-inch, hollow-ground, drop-point pattern blade crafted from 440C stainless steel. A set of buffalo horn handle scales provides a solid grip platform. The final touch is provided by engraver Jere Davidson, who did the work on the guard and pommel. This is a simply wonderful knife that's sure to make a hit in deer camp.

Ed Fowler is an ABS Master Blade smith, hunter, and noted columnist for *Blade* magazine. When it comes to cutlery knowledge and game care, this

Talk about fancy, this drop-point, fixed-blade hunter by Edmund Davidson is all that, and then some. Featuring a 4-inch, hollow-ground, 440C stainless steel blade, buffalo horn scales, and engraved (Jere Davidson) guard and pommel laced with 24k gold lace, this is one hunter that looks good.

Point Seven Studios

Wyoming rancher has few peers. With a lifetime of outdoor experience under his belt, Ed Fowler understands the nature of game care and related cutlery needs. All of his knives are hand forged from 52100 carbon steel. His basic knife style is a full-tang drop-point blade, with a brass single guard and a sheephorn handle. Available in several blade lengths, Ed's knives all manifest a certain commonality. Not that he couldn't make other styles—he can! It's just that his knives incorporate all of the experience of a seasoned user, materials best suited to field applications, and proven hand-forged construction methodology. My pick of his knives would be the Bird & Trout model, because it also works well as a deer and antelope game-care tool. When you consider that if your knife ever fails to perform properly, it will be replaced free-of-charge. At any cost, this guarantee alone makes an Ed Fowler knife an unmatchable bargain.

Lynn Griffith makes a great drop-point fixed-blade with a 4-1/4-inch blade of ATS-34 stainless steel. The full-length blade tang is housed in black Micarta™ and shaped to fit the hand comfortably. The sheath is made from tough molded Kydex™ for safe containment and ready access. A fine edged game-care tool, this maker definitely has the hunter in mind.

Russ Krommer is an Alaskan knifemaker has been a hunting guide for more than two decades. His Caribou Hunter fixed blade features a 3-1/2-inch, drop-point pattern (nearly straight) blade of ATS-34. The bolsters and fittings are 416 stainless. And the handle scales are stabilized buckeye burl. Krommer wants his knives to do it all, including primary field-dressing, skinning and trophy work. Certainly, this model is a great example of first-hand experience combined with quality knife-making skills.

Jay Maines makes a couple of different styles, but my pick would be the small drop-point fixed-blade model (Models DZ-7302, 03, 05, 05) that's carried in a horizontal belt sheath, along with an aluminum body AAA Mini-Mag flashlight (optional ASP Tac Light available at extra cost). The steel used in this knife is 440C stainless (Rc 57-58).

And each blade is hollow ground with thumb rest serrations added on the spine. Bolster choices are stainless steel, nickel-silver or brass, and handles come in black Micarta® or soft neoprene. Jay Maines has spent a lot of time in the outdoors, and he has combined the two most important assets a big game hunter can carry in the field—knife and flashlight—in a single belt-carried package. This maker's knives are available by custom order through DeltaZ Knives, Inc.

Loyd Thomsen, a South Dakota rancher is a specialist in Damascus steel. Not only does he make some of the most magnificent looking knives I've ever seen, his blades also perform in the field. A Damascus steel knife isn't inexpensive and Loyd's work is no exception. Despite the cost, as well as the increased blade care necessary with a Damascus knife, many of his customers use their knives on game every year. I can tell you this, Loyd Thomsen's knives seem to keep on cutting long after many of the so-called "specialty steels" have given up their edge. Knowing this, it's readily apparent why his knives are found in hunting camps throughout the country.

There are many more knifemakers that could have been included in this chapter. Notwithstanding, I believe that those mentioned produce edged products that are prime examples of quality game-care tools, and all have spent enough time on the hunt and at the forge to be considered masters of both disciplines.

The Final Cut

Adequate field care of big game is both essential and ethical. A knowledgeable choice of edged tools for this assignment is paramount to the overall success of the hunt.

The knives you can select will make the difference between being just a hunter, or someone who is committed to the hunt. After the shot, it's the knife that brings consonance to the killing grounds. Without that primary tool, the hunt has little meaning and dubious substance.

C. Ward

When field dressing, skinning and quartering large animals like moose, elk, or caribou you need a sizeable blade. This drop-point Tracker knife by Lynn Griffith is certainly all that. The 4-1/4-inch, ATS-34 stainless steel blade is mated with black Micarta® handle scales and housed in a Kydex® sheath.

D. Hollis

Knifemaker, Jay Maines, is one of the best and his talent is demonstrated in this knife and flashlight combination.

Jennifer Thomsen-Connell

This Loyd Thomsen fixed-blade Damascus and impala horn offering will add a touch of class to any hunting camp.

Russ Kommer

Knifemaker, Russ Kommer, is a hunter himself. Expectedly, that interest is manifest in his exquisite fixed-blade designs.

Big-Game Field Dressing

After your shot has found its mark, the most important thing you can do is immediately field dress the animal. The effort you put into this activity will insure that the game meat that reaches your table is in prime condition. Field dressing is neither complicated, nor is it difficult. Just follow the simple steps outlined below:

Step One: Approach any downed animal cautiously.

D. Hollis

Step One: Approach any down animal cautiously. Once you're assured that all life signs have ceased, unload your firearm and place it in a safe location. Remove your coat or jacket, roll up your sleeves (protective gloves are a good idea), take off your watch and any other personal jewelry that might be damaged by contact with bodily fluids. Move the animal to a location where you can work on level ground—in the shade.

Once you're assured that all life signs have ceased, unload your firearm and place it in a safe location. Remove your coat or jacket, roll up your sleeves (protective gloves are a good idea), take off your watch and any other personal jewelry that might be damaged by contact with bodily fluids. Move the animal to a location where you can work on level ground—in the shade.

Step Two: Turn the animal on its back and cut around the terminal end of the digestive system. The incision should be deep enough to free the anus from the surrounding muscle tissue.

Step Three: Make a vertical incision into the abdominal cavity that runs from the top of the pelvis to the bottom of the sternum. Use caution when cutting and avoid puncturing the underlying viscera.

Step Four: Cut through the diaphragm on both sides, all the way down to the spine. Reach forward, past the heart and lungs, and locate the windpipe (a ribbed tube). Sever the windpipe and pull down and out of the chest cavity. The lungs, heart, stomach, and intestines should easily come free.

Step Five: Grasp the lower end of the intestines and pull it upward out of the abdominal cavity. You may have to do a little discreet cutting here and there, but the rest of the intestines, urine bladder, and rectum should come free.

Step Six: Elevate the carcass to allow any blood to drain out of the body cavity. Wipe out any remaining fluids, fecal material, or stomach contents with water from your canteen.

When you've finished with the chore, move the carcass into the shade. The final act in this scenario will take a pack frame, wheeled cart, or lots of muscle power.

Step Two: Turn the animal on its back and cut around the terminal end of the digestive system. The incision should be deep enough to free the anus from the surrounding tissue.

D. Hollis

D. Hollis

Step Three: Make a vertical incision into the abdominal cavity that runs from the top of the pelvis to the bottom of the sternum. Use caution when cutting to avoid puncturing the underlying viscera.

D. Hollis

Step Four: Cut through the diaphragm on both sides, all the way down to the spine. Reach forward, past the heart and lungs, and locate the windpipe (ribbed tube). Sever the windpipe and pull down and out of the chest cavity. The lungs, heart, stomach, and intestines should easily come free.

D. Hollis

Step Five: Grasp the lower end of the intestines and pull it upward out of the abdominal cavity. You may have to do a little discreet cutting here and there, but the rest of the intestines should easily come free.

D. Hollis

Step Six: Elevate the carcass to allow any blood to drain out of the body cavity. Wash out any remaining fluids, fecal material, or stomach contents with water from your canteen.

Just how far is it to the truck?

D. Hollis

Author Hollis, along with many other outdoor writers, spend more days in the field than the average hunter. This experience provides plenty of exposure to knife work.

Chapter 12
The Professional Edge

When it comes to knife work, few hunters have the experience of a professional guide or outdoor writer.

Most big-game hunters spend a few days, or maybe as much as a week each season, in pursuit of their favorite game species. The fortunate few may hunt in other states, provinces or countries, or participate in more than one type of hunting activity. While all of us would like to spend more time afield, it can be difficult to carve out time for hunting. This means that the average person receives only a minimal amount of knife use experience annually. A hunting guide or outdoor writer has many more opportunities to devote time to hunting and related activities. Clearly, these individuals are able to gain a wealth of experience with edged tools in a variety of outdoor chores.

A look at my own field experience reveals that during any given year I might hunt deer in two or three states, pursue elk, go after antelope and bear, shoot a pile of wild hogs, and travel to Africa for some plains game hunting. In each instance I'll use one, or more, of my knives to field dress, skin, and quarter every animal. Also, I might do a little caping and bone-out a ton of meat. When you total up all of that expenditure of energy, it's a lot of time with a knife in your hand. The same is true for most professional outdoors folk.

During my time afield, I've shared campfires and game trails with several guides and outdoor writers whose game-care cutlery experiences are not unlike my own. Whether they are working for a client (no room for error here), or dealing with their own hunting success, these individuals are truly some of the most knowledgeable knife users you could ever meet. They know what kind of edged tool it takes to get the job done. And most of all, they have an understanding of what works—and what doesn't! Let me share with you some of the thoughts on knives and game care cutlery several guides and outdoor writers have expressed over the years.

Duwane Adams is the owner and operator of Arizona Big Game Hunts. When I began my own quest for a Coues whitetail buck, Dwane was my first choice as a guide. Born and reared in Arizona, no one knows the rugged Southwest and the deer of that area any better. Dwane hunts mule deer, Coues deer, elk, javelina and upland

game. If Dwane can't get what you're looking for, it just can't be done.

In a recent conversation, Dwane shared with me his own personal cutlery likes and dislikes. "I don't like sheath knives because they dig into your hip and get hung-up on the brush when you're hunting," he said. "I carry a lock-blade folder and haven't ever found a better hunting knife design."

When I asked him about blade length, Dwane didn't hesitate. "I like a blade not much longer than my index finger. A big knife will simply wear you out long before the job is done. And caping an animal with a large knife is a real challenge,"

Duwane Adam

Duwane Adams (rear kneeling) is one of Arizona's most successful big-game guides. Here he's pictured with Dean Lippert and a huge mule deer that scored 212 Boone & Crockett points.

Buck Knives

Pictured here are two different-sized finger-grooved Buck lockblade folders. This is the style, blade shape and blade length that Duwane Adams prefers for field dressing, skinning, and big-game trophy work.

Dwane stated. "Any attempt at that is like trying to a saddle a mouse," he added.

When the conversation turned to blade shapes, Dwane was equally as resolute. "A clip-point blade, like the one on the Buck Folding Hunter (Model 110), is the best for everything. Drop points are great for skinning and will take a lot of abuse, but they're terrible for caping. You just can't get a drop-point blade tip into those tight crevices at the base of an antler or horn butts when you're working on a cape," he said.

The subject of steel came up in the discussion and Dwane said, "I like whatever steel stays sharp the longest. There is nothing worse than a dull knife!" He certainly didn't find any disagreement with me on that point.

When I asked Dwane about his preference in brand names, he said, "I've used knives made by Buck, Gerber, and Kershaw. They all worked for me and I really don't have any preference for one to the other."

Just before we finished our conversation,

Dwane made a point that I've heard before. "Most of my hunting clients carry custom knives, but I've never seen one put to use. Some guys say that they're afraid the knife might get scratched up. I can even recall one guy telling me that his knife cost too much to take a chance on breaking it," he commented. "The best excuse of all was the hunter that told me his wife gave him the knife as a present and he didn't think she would want him to get it bloody. Try to figure that one out."

Craig Boddington, the former editor of *Petersen's Hunting* magazine, is one of this nation's most widely-published and well-recognized worldwide big-game hunting authorities. Someone once said that Craig Boddington has shot every kind of big game animal that ever mattered. I won't disagree!

Several years ago, Craig and I entered into a discussion about knives for big game. I'd just settled into a chair in front of his desk, when he reached under some papers and picked up a Schrade Sharpfinger (Model 102OT) fixed-blade knife. Leaning back in his own chair, this veteran of more adventures afield than any dozen other hunters I know said, "Is there a better big game knife design than this? It has a decent piece of steel in it, as well as a thin point that's useful in everything from field dressing to caping. There's enough curve to the edge that it makes a great skinning knife; the full-width tang runs all the way through the handle; and the handle slabs are attached to the handle with brass rivets."

Before I could even comment, he went on to say, "And there's an oiled leather carrying sheath that's molded right to the shape of the blade. I think you can find this knife at any gun shop, sporting goods store, and every Wal-Mart across the country, and at a price anyone can afford. Now go on and tell me about exotic blade steels, stag handles, and totally useless blade shapes."

I couldn't have said it more clearly. Furthermore, he covered everything from knife steel to blade shape, handle material to sheath design. While it may have not had all the "bells and whistles" of more costly knives, that particular Schrade offering was just about everything you could ever ask for in a hunting knife. It's been awhile since Craig and I have spent some time together. If my association with him through the years has established anything, however, I know him to be one who doesn't change his mind easily. For that reason, I am betting he still uses the same knife.

C. T. Boddington

Craig Boddington is one of this country's most well-respected outdoor writers. Clearly, few have the broad-based experience of this seasoned professional.

Images Group/Schrade

Simple, straightforward and affordable, the Schrade Sharpfinger fixed-blade knife is, in the opinion of writer Craig Boddington, just about everything you could ever ask for in a hunting knife.

D. Hollis

Outfitter and guide, John Winter (standing) guided the author (left) and another client to a pair of 6x6 bull elk in Wyoming's Brider-Teton Wilderness.

John Winter is the owner and operator of Two-Ocean Pass Outfitting. Since he was a kid, John has outfitted and guided hunters in the Thorofare and Two-Ocean pass area of the Bridger-Teton Wilderness. His reputation for putting his hunters on game is unblemished and he knows how to care for meat and trophies.

On my first hunt with John, I was surprised to see him haul out an oversized Western Cutlery folder out of a belt sheath (the Western Cutlery Company was sold some years ago and their assets acquired by Camillus Cutlery). The knife had a large clip-pattern blade at one end, and an equally gigantic saw that folded out of the opposite end. Since we were field dressing and quartering a bull elk that I had just taken, the blade and the saw were about the right size. The knife blade and the saw were both made from carbon steel, but aside from dark patina resulting from years of use, neither blade had a speck of rust on them. The handle scales were made out of some sort of rugged thermoplastic and had enough texture to provide an adequate grip. It was, in fact, a fine choice (unfortunately, this particular knife model is no longer in production) for the job at hand.

I asked John about his preference in knives. "This Western knife has proven itself time and time again on everything, including elk, moose, deer, bear, sheep and mountain goats. I like the fact that

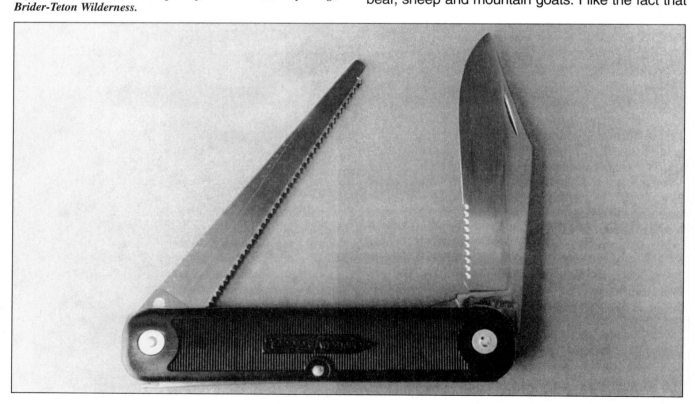

D. Hollis

This large Western Cutlery folder, with its clip-point main blade and companion saw blade, is John Winter's favorite big-game knife. Unfortunately, it's no longer in production.

120

the blade has enough point to handle even the most detailed field dressing and caping chores. The blade also has enough sweep to work as a skinning knife. And the saw blade comes in handy to cut through pelvic bones, chest cartilage, and leg hocks."

Pressing him further, I inquired about the issue of blade steel. "It doesn't make much difference to me what kind of steel is in a knife. The most important questions are: is it sharp?, can it be sharpened in the field?, and will it hold an edge?," John said. "Some clients carry custom knives that aren't very sharp to begin with. Even worse, the knives are so hard that it's nearly impossible to sharpen them in the field."

Over the years, I've hunted with John Winter on several occasions and that old Western folder is still at his side. Nothing fancy, it's just a plain knife that performs. What else can you ask for?

Bob Robb is a name that's familiar to most hunters. For years his byline has appeared in nearly every outdoor magazine published. He has been a newspaper and magazine editor, a columnist, book author, and more recently, a full-time freelance writer. Along the way, he serves as a consultant on hunting gear and has spoken at many seminars across the country. For the past ten years, Bob has made his home in Alaska. There, he has taken some of the finest trophies with rifle and bow the North Country can produce.

Because Alaska is such big country, it also holds serious consequence if you make the wrong choices. Bob is notoriously hard on gear, so he demands the best and toughest available. When

Bob Robb

From centerfire rifle to pistol to front-loader or bow, outdoor writer Bob Robb does it all. This fine 8-point whitetail buck demonstrates that this is one professional that knows whereof he speaks.

D. Hollis

Bob Robb likes fixed-blade knives and the Puma Skinner is one of his favorites.

asked about his selection in a knife, he replied, "I'll take a rugged fixed-blade design every time. Folders can give out when you least expect it. If you have an accident with a knife in Alaska, it's a long walk out to medical care."

Bob knows all about self-inflicted knife injuries. Working on a bear hide one season, he cut his hand badly with a knife. By the time he received proper medical attention, an infection set in. It took weeks of aggressive treatment and some surgery to save a couple of his fingers. A painful lesson, but one he hasn't forgotten.

When asked about blade steel, Bob stated, "Alaska is one big rain storm. If your knife isn't stainless, you'll end up with a visit from the rust Gods. All the argument about carbon steel and stainless steel is nothing but bull fodder. I use stainless knives and haven't had a problem with edge retention or resharpening with any one of them. My advice, buy good knives and learn to sharpen them."

Bob was equally as opinionated about blade shapes, edge grinds, and handle material. "For my money, a clip-point blade is just right for field dressing, skinning and caping. And you can forget about a serrated edge. The teeth don't cut cleanly when working in meat. The current trend in the cutlery industry is synthetic handle material. Kraton® and other similar resilient material offer a great gripping surface, but it's all nasty-looking stuff. I still like a solid piece of wood or stag on my knives."

Jim Matthews is another widely-published freelance outdoor writer. His syndicated newspaper column appears weekly in 10 metropolitan newspapers. And his work appears regularly in many of the major outdoor magazines. Jim lives in southern California, which just so happens to have a burgeoning population of wild boar. Consequently, most of his big-game hunting endeavors involve the pursuit of these surly animals.

When asked about his first choice in a big game knife, Jim replied, "I like multiple blade, stainless steel, locking folders. In my gear you'll find knives made by Browning, Buck, and Gerber that fall within those parameters. Everyone has a personal preference for one blade steel over another, with ATS-34 being the darling of the industry right now. After hunting wild hogs for years, I can tell you that gutting and skinning a boar is tough on blade steel. That being true, 440C stainless hasn't ever disappointed me on a pig."

Blade shape and handle materials were my next avenues of inquiry. "A clip-pattern blade works best for general game care, but a drop-point is a better skinning shape. When it comes to handle material, looks aren't important to me. I don't think there's any better knife handle material than Kraton®. It feels great in your hand, never slips when it's wet, and if you drop your knife it won't crack or break," Jim went on to say.

Jim Matthews

Big game or small, outdoor writer Jim Matthews just likes to hunt. His syndicated newspaper column appears weekly in 10 newspapers, and his byline has appeared in most major outdoor magazines.

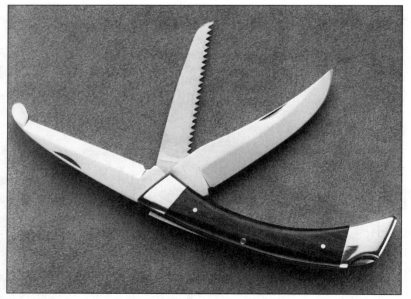

Browning

When it comes to big-game work, Jim Matthews really likes the blade diversity of this Browning lockblade folder. The clip-point main blade, blunt nose gutting blade, and the saw blade are all major assets when dealing with evisceration, skinning, and butchering in the field.

John Higley

For more than 30 years, John Higley's byline has appeared in most major outdoor magazines. While he has hunted many big-game species, at his heart he's a mule deer hunter.

Buck Knives

John Higley's favorite lockblade folder, the BuckLite now comes in two sizes (2-3/4" and 3" blade lengths), each with a lightweight thermoplastic handle and a detachable metal clothing clip.

John Higley has been an outdoor writer for more than thirty years. During his term at that assignment he has been a magazine columnist, book author, and a freelance writer. While he has taken a lot of different big game, at heart, he's a mule deer hunter. All of that cumulative hunting experience has given him the knowledge necessary to make an informed decision about the knives he includes in his gear.

"Hands-down, my favorite knife is a lightweight Buck lock-blade folder. Personally, I think a folding knife is far more convenient to carry than a fixed-blade model. And the addition of a blade locking mechanism to a folder makes it nearly as tough as a sheath knife. Given a choice, stainless is my first, last, and only selection in blade steel. It's easier to keep clean under field conditions, and it takes less effort to do so. I don't care much for blade serrations. My plain edge knife has done well by me for years. I don't think it's possible to make a dent in that kind of history," John said.

"If you can't hold on to your knife, then it's as dangerous as a loose cannon. Too much handle texture can be uncomfortable, but too little is even worse. Frankly, molded synthetics suit me just fine. I don't claim to be a knife expert, but I do like a drop-point blade. A clip-point can break off at the tip if you really work the blade. With a drop-point I find it easier to field dress and skin without worrying about ruining the knife. Now are we going hunting, or what? The afternoon is about gone and we don't have a lot of daylight left. I can always use another hog in the freezer," John remarked anxiously.

Peter Hathaway Capstick, the noted writer and author of several best sellers, and I, had a chance meeting several years ago during the annual Shooting, Hunting, and Outdoor Trade show. Over the years, we continued to run into each other at this event on a regular basis. Knowing that Peter maintained a residence in South Africa, I made it a point to get into contact with him during one of my hunting/business trips to that country. Always the consummate host, Peter invited me to have lunch with him and his wife. During the course of that meal, the conversation eventually came around to knives.

The first thing I asked Peter was what kind of knife he felt was best suited to game-care chores. While several different knives came to mind, he finally narrowed it down to a Randall fixed-blade model. "It (referring to the knife) has been my companion on more hunts than I care to remember. The 5-1/2" blade is a trailing-point design that offers both the skinning curve of the Green River pattern and enough blade point to be useful in gutting and caping."

I went on to inquire about the type of knife steel he preferred. "Damascus," he replied without hesitation. Continuing the thought, Peter said, "It is the best of all worlds. Damascus responds to sharpening quicker than any other steel I've used, yet it seemed to maintain that edge longer than one would expect. If you look at a Damascus edge under magnification, you can see tiny irregularities in the steel that offer significant protection against blade-edge contact erosion. Even though the edge may lose some of its performance ability, the recessed cutting surfaces still remain sharp, thus rendering extended life to the edge.

Of course, I immediately voiced my concern about the increased knife maintenance demanded by a carbon-steel Damascus blade. Peter disagreed. "If you own a quality knife, you will take care of that knife, no matter what circumstances you may find yourself involved in. Remember, just as cleaning a gun after a day afield is a privilege and a responsibility, so is caring for a fine knife," he stated.

The late Peter Hathaway Capstick, wrote several popular books on African big-game hunting. His extensive experience in the field gave him an in-depth understanding of knives and knife steel.

Paul Kimble

Jennifer Thomsen-Connell

Peter Capstick preferred Damascus steel to all others. He felt that it responded to sharpening faster than other steel, yet seemed to maintain edge integrity longer than one would expect. This cable Damascus drop-point model by Loyd Thomsen is representative of the kind of knife Capstick favored.

Capstick's most important comments were reserved for last. As we parted company, he stated, "Far more important than the kind of knife you use, is that it must be sharp. A blade edge does nothing more than separate molecules. If that edge is dull, the performance level of the knife will be severely impacted," he said.

I certainly agree with Capstick that a trailing-point knife with an adequate point can be an effective tool in all primary game care responsibilities. Also, a carbon steel Damascus knife with its microscopic edge serrations does seem to cut longer than one would expect. And Peter's opinions about

This fine Kershaw lockblade folder (Model 1050), with its AUS8A stainless steel, drop-point pattern blade, brass bolsters and finger-grooved phenolic handle has all the features that Doug Roth likes in a knife.

D. Hollis

Guide, Doug Roth (rear, pictured with the author and his wife, Anita Hollis), prefers a lockblade folder with a blade not much longer than his index finger.

knife upkeep and edge maintenance are right on target. Sadly, Peter Hathaway Capstick has passed away. His comments regarding knives, blade steel and knife maintenance, however, are timeless.

Doug Roth guides hunters on more than 50,000 acres of property on California's central coast. Annually, his clients take more than 300 wild hogs, a couple of dozen deer, and an assortment of turkey, pheasants, quail and rabbits. When it comes to game care, Doug is definitely an expert. He has used more different kinds of knives and blade steels that you could ever imagine.

"I use my binoculars a lot to search for game. If I am wearing a sheath knife, when I settle into position the blade gets in the way. And if you're moving into and out of a vehicle, a fixed-blade knife dangling on your hip is just a lot of trouble. In my opinion, a lock-blade folder is the way to go," Doug stated.

Blade length and shape are two other opinions that Doug has fully formed. "A big knife is alright on elk or caribou, but most of my field work is on wild hogs, deer and birds. I like a blade not much longer than 3-1/2-inches. While I have used several different drop-points for field dressing and skinning, a clip-point is better for trophy work," he commented.

"Stainless steel doesn't take a lot of effort to maintain. I wash my knives off and then wipe them off. Rust has never been a problem with stainless. It's true that most stainless blades are a little more difficult to sharpen than my dad's old carbon steel pocket knife. When you're working a wild hog, it can destroy most blade edges, stainless or carbon steel, in short order. Their hair is

like wire, the hide is tough, and then there's lots of dirt and grit to deal with. If the blade steel isn't hard enough, your knife edge will turn over like a flapjack. All things being equal, stainless steel works just fine and it's easier to keep clean," Doug went on to say.

The only negative comment Doug made was about knife handle material, "Some of the more high-tech looking knives have smooth handles. Get one of those numbers bloody, or wet, and it can be tough to hang onto. Give me a knife that won't slip out of my hand and I am a happy camper."

Tom McIntyre is a dedicated hunter. He has traveled over most of North America, Europe, Asia and Africa in pursuit of this passion. A noted author and current hunting editor for Sports Afield, Tom knows his stuff.

When asked about what type of knife he prefers, Tom stated, "If it folds shut and locks open, I like it! A fixed-blade knife just doesn't feel right on my hip. I think a folding knife is safer because the blade is completely covered, rather than exposed inside a sheath. If you fall when carrying a fixed-blade, the blade might punch right through the sheath." Clearly, Tom McIntyre is a lock-blade folder affectionado.

Tom also expressed a liking for stainless steel in his knives. "Not only do most stainless steel blades seem harder than carbon steel blades, they're also easier to keep clean," he stated. "After field dressing, I generally wash the blade off with water or wipe it clean on my jeans. Such treatment doesn't favor a carbon steel blade."

"I've used a Gerber Bolt-Action exchange-blade folder for a number of hunting

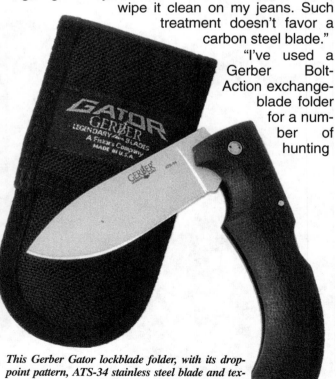

D. Hollis

Noted author and hunting editor of **Sports Afield** *magazine, Tom McIntyre, knows all about game care (pictured working on a wild boar carcass) and the kind of cutlery it takes to do the job right.*

This Gerber Gator lockblade folder, with its drop-point pattern, ATS-34 stainless steel blade and textured thermoplastic handle has all the features that Tom McIntyre prefers in a big-game blade.

D. Hollis

seasons. It's been a great knife, and the exchange-able saw blade comes in handy when cutting through bone and cartilage. I've used others, and the Gerber stainless blade tends to hold its edge a little longer. Like many, I have a hard time sharpen-ing a knife, so I think edge holding is far more important than ease of sharpening. I want a blade that can handle a couple of animals before it needs edge work," he said.

Blade shape is another subject that McIntyre couldn't resist commenting about. "A drop-point blade works best when field dressing. Since it's well below the line of the blade spine, you have more control of the point. With a clip-point blade you have to be extra careful or you'll punch into the stomach or intestines," he continued.

Like many other professionals, Tom doesn't like serrated knives. "My only comment about serra-tions is that we already have enough bells and whistles on knives. All the nonsense about how well a serrated blade cuts without constant sharp-ening is great for many applications, but when it comes to field dressing and skinning, a plain edge works best," he opined.

His final comments were regarding knife han-dles. "I like molded, synthetic knife handles. My interest in a nice-looking handle—like stag or wood—is minimal at best. Function is far more important than good looks," McIntyre stated.

Steve Comus is one of the most experienced writers in the country. He has worked as a newspa-

D. Hollis

Outdoor writer, book author, and the current editor of Safari Club publications, Steve Comus, likes fixed-blade knives because they're easier to bring into play than a folder.

perman, freelance writer, book author, magazine columnist and editor, and is currently employed as the editor of all Safari Club publications. Most of all, how-ever, Steve just likes to hunt.

Not only is Steve a southpaw, he also espouses a minority position with regards to his knife preference. "Folding knives have always given me trouble, especially in cold weather when my hands are numb. Just try opening and closing a folder that's gunked-up with the byproducts of field dressing in the dead of winter and you'll understand why I like a fixed-blade," he remarked.

"I don't like a serrated blade," Comus added. "The little teeth are hard to sharpen. I have enough trou ble sharpening a regular blade and the thought of working on all those tiny teeth seems to be the ultimate frustration."

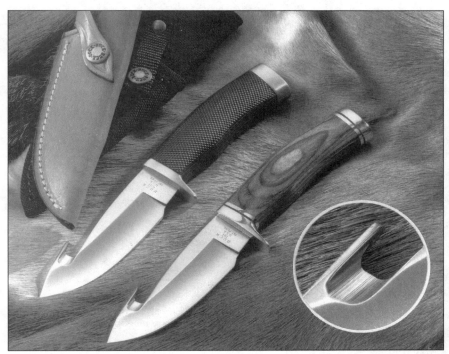

Buck Knives

Based on the Buck Knives Vanguard® fixed-blade design, these two models have the addition of a guthook feature on the blade spine, near the tip. No doubt Steve Comus would like this useful enhancement to his favorite edged field tool.

One thing Steve Comus expressed his like for was a Buck fixed-blade model. "While I've only been using it for a couple of seasons, the Buck Vanguard fixed blade is my favorite. I'm left-handed and many knives don't feel right in my hand, but this one was a winner from the outset. It's almost too big, but it fits my hand really well. In addition to being the right size and shape, it has a drop-point, stainless steel blade and a wonderful non-slip Kraton® handle," Steve said.

Dan Schmidt is a deer-hunting fanatic. Schmidt is the managing editor of *Deer & Deer Hunting* magazine, and he has spent the past 17 years hunting whitetails with his bow, rifle, shotgun and muzzleloader. Schmidt, a former associate editor of *Blade* magazine, is a big fan of today's factory knives. "For most hunters, one knife will do an adequate job from field dressing to skinning," Schmidt said. "Several knives are necessary, however, if you hunt more than just a few days each fall. Although I don't carry all of them at the same time, I think it takes no less than six knives to get me through one hunting season: a serrated Spyderco folder, a medium-size folder from Buck or Case, a Gerber utility knife, a Camillus belt hunter and boning and skinning knives like those from Knives of Alaska.

If he could only have just one knife, Schmidt said he would opt for the Camillus lockback with the ever-popular Buck 110 folder coming a close second. "Knives deer hunters carry on their belts probably can be attributed more to family tradition than anything else," he said. The Camillus is safe and durable, making it a great choice for a hunter who wants to pass it down to their son or daughter.

Daniel E. Schmidt

Buck Knives

Schmidt's favorite knife is the Camillus lockback. Both compact and reliable, it performs effectively in all settings.

Managing editor of **Deer & Deer Hunting** *magazine, and former associate editor of* **Blade** *magazine, Dan Schmidt is a big fan of today's factory knives.*

The Final Word

I find it difficult to express fault with any of the opinions shared by the guides or outdoor writers in this book. Like most hunting knife users, the majority of these professionals prefer lock-blade folders and for all of the right reasons—carrying convenience and safety. Those who liked fixed-blade models did so because they felt the design was stronger, more straightforward, and reliable. For my part of the discussion, I have a strong preference for fixed-blade knives. While a large sheath knife can be a hassle to carry, some of the newer designs take up no more room on your hip than a folder.

With the exception of Peter Capstick, everyone else expressed their liking for stainless as a blade steel. I am sure that knife maintenance had a great deal to do with this decision, but Capstick's opinion about caring for a fine knife can't be overlooked.

Blade edge serration didn't rate very high with either the guides or the outdoor writers. Personally, I like a blade with a short serrated section near the guard/bolster. The serrations don't interfere with the primary cutting ability of the plain edge, and they come in handy when removing leg hocks and cutting through rib cartilage.

This choice of knife handle material manifested a certain amount of disparity. Most of those questioned, however, choose function over looks. The resilient, slightly tacky feel of Kraton®, or one of the other molded synthetics, certainly is non-slip under the most demanding field conditions. No doubt about it, the rubbery stuff works but it's damn ugly! I'll take a piece of stag anytime.

Interestingly, most of the professionals used production knives. That speaks loudly about the current state of factory-produced cutlery. Some might argue that factory knives are more widely available and less costly than handmade cutlery. In many instances, that is certainly true. However, most professionals want gear that holds up regardless of availability or cost. With state-of-the-art technology, modern materials, and designs that often use the collaboration of a custom maker, it would seem that factory knives are often the right choice.

(Note: some of the interview material in this chapter originally appeared in the May 1997 issue of *Blade* magazine, Krause Publications, under the title, "Favorite Knives of The Outdoor Writers.")

With the right skinning knife design, even the toughest hide will peel off easily. Here, a successful hunter skins a Wyoming mule deer.

Chapter 13
Skin Game

*Hide removal with the wrong blade shape is like
spreading peanut butter with a knitting needle—lots of work, very little progress.*

On my first big-game hunt, I was only marginally prepared for field-dressing activities. When it came to skinning, any previous experience with small game provided little confidence. Fortunately, I was guided through the process by a hunting buddy that was an old hand at the game. As I watched him separate the hide from underlying tissue, there was little noticeable blade work. He seemed to pull and tug on the skin more than he used his knife. He did make several initial incisions along all four legs of the deer, but all the rest of his cutlery handiwork consisted of long sweeping strokes that really didn't seem to cut anything at all. When the hide was finally removed from the carcass, I noted that there wasn't so much as a nick in the musculature.

After covering the naked carcass with an insect-proof cloth bag, I thought we were finished with skinning. Not so, it seemed. Laying the deer hide out on a flat surface (hair side down), my friend carefully used his knife to remove any residual scraps of meat. It took him some time to completely "flesh" the underside of the hide, but when he was through it looked as clean as a white sheet. Interestingly, the manner in which he had removed the skin resulted in a nearly square hide. The final act in this scenario was salting down the skin to absorb any moisture. My companion explained to me that the salt also temporarily preserved the hide until he could get it to the tannery. At that moment all my school studies about the early American fur and buffalo hide trade came together.

One of the first things I learned about skinning game was that there are knives you can skin with, and then there are skinning knives. The difference between the two is centered in blade design. Traditionally, skinning is defined as the precise removal of an animal hide (skin) from a carcass. Since many hides have a future value as tanned leather, it is important to remove the skin in its most usable manner (as square as possible). Also, during the process of skinning, the knife should not compromise the integrity of the hide (no cuts, nicks, or slices). While it's possible to use any blade design to skin, flawless hide removal is best conducted with a knife designed especially for that activity.

The most salient feature of a skinning blade is the off-center shift of the cutting force from the point to the blade belly. This can be accomplished by a couple of design maneuvers. The trailing-point motif places the point of the knife above, or trailing behind, the blade spine. The position of the blade point effectively eliminates an accidental hide puncture.

An alternative to this concept is an abrupt clip which can be seen in the spey-point. Once again, the knife point is shifted away from the direct line of the spine, resulting in a cutting emphasis on the edge curve. Originally, the spey-point was used exclusively to neuter domestic animals. Since avoidance of an accidental puncture wound was necessary, the blade point was somewhat blunted and shifted away from the direct line of cutting force. Additionally, a skinning blade using this design is generally wider than a more traditional clip-point pattern. The spey blade in a folding trapper knife is designed for skinning furbearing animals. Since muskrat, mink, ermine, beaver, badger, coyote and fox are relatively small in size, this blade configuration works well in skinning chores.

A different tack on the spey concept can be seen in the Buck Skinner (Model 103). This is nothing more than a larger and wider (with more flare at the leading edge) version of the basic spey concept. Such a knife tends to be blade-heavy, allowing the edge to literally separate the hide from underlying tissue almost without effort. The classic Green River Skinner (see sidebar Russell Harrington Cutlery), which was the 19th century benchmark skinning knife for the buffalo trade, combined both a blade-heavy spey clip with a trailing-point design. This concept must have been an effective hide removal tool, since its rate of acceptance on the killing fields of the Great Plains was overwhelming.

What are the salient features in a skinning knife? Obviously, as cited in the preceding paragraph, blade design is paramount. The main features of any skinning blade should place the cutting focus completely on the edge curve. The blade belly should be wide and sweeping enough to facilitate forceful hide removal. In addition, a skinning knife should have a comfortable handle that provides for complete blade control through the entire skinning stroke. One of the problems that quickly manifests itself in this activity is wrist fatigue. For this reason, the straighter the gripping position, the less wrist and hand fatigue will result. The Outdoor Edge Game Skinner and Whitetail Skinner, with their T-shaped handles, resulted from the application of ergonomics in knife design to address the specific problem of hand and wrist fatigue when skinning.

Beyond these basics, a skinning knife is the simplest of edge tools. Used correctly, it can separate the connection between hide and underlying musculature with little effort. I've watched skinning activities in butchering facilities that were absolutely flawless in their execution. The knives were sharpened often, but it was the blade design alone that controlled and directed the cutting energy. Let's look at some selected handmade and production skinning knives and review the features that have made them popular.

Al Mar Knives: This well-respected firm makes a great skinning knife design, as demonstrated by their Gunstock V (Model 8505) fixed-blade offering. Crafted from 6A stainless steel, the 4-1/2-inch blade incorporates some trailing-point characteristics in a drop-point pattern. The serrated thumb rest on the blade spine provides a measure of added blade control. The laminated wood handle fits the hand without noticeable discomfort. For my money, it doesn't get any better than this.

Boker: In their cutlery manufacturing facility in Argentina, this firm produces a full-sized fixed-blade skinner. The clip-point blade pattern has a

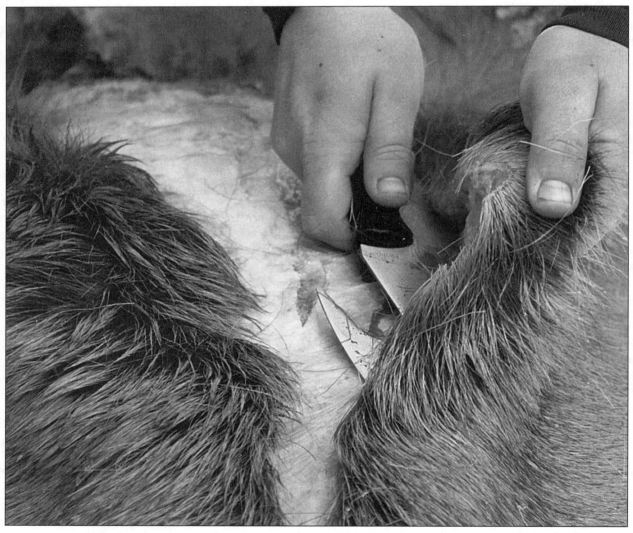

Kershaw Kai Cutlery

A combination of the right knife design and knowledgeable use can make any skinning assignment a simple matter.

slightly upswept point that serves to increase the edge radius. This added radius is a distinct advantage when separating hide from underlying muscle tissue. The molded thermoplastic handle is heavily textured for enhanced blade control and positive hand-to-knife contact. A snap-closed, top-grain leather sheath accompanies the knife and provides safe and secure transport containment.

ning of this chapter. Made from 420HC stainless steel, the broad blade and sweeping edge curve make this knife my kind of hide removal tool. Two different handle treatments are available: black phenolic with aluminum fittings, and laminated wood with brass guard and pommel. I like the look of the wood and brass, but your preference may be different. Either model, however, offers the same great skinning blade features. This was the first skinning knife I ever used, and it still remains my favorite.

The Boker Arbolito fixed-blade skinner mates a full-tang stainless steel blade with an ergonomically-designed molded handle.

D. Hollis

This is a clean design that has been well executed. While a bit on the large side, nevertheless, those who hunt large mammals will appreciate the size and the design.

Buck Knives: The Buck Skinner (Model 103) has already been briefly mentioned at the begin-

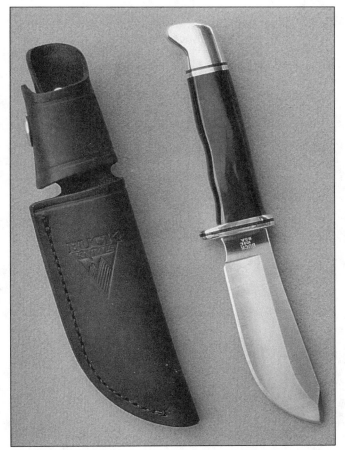

D. Hollis

This skinning design from Buck Knives is a larger and wider version of the basic spey pattern blade configuration.

Case Cutlery: The Case Ridgeback™ Hunter (Model 362/398) has one of the most dramatically upswept clip-point blade patterns I've seen lately. This blade layout puts the knife clearly into the hide removal cutlery category. The 3-1/2-inch blade is made from Case's Tru-Sharp® stainless steel and features both forefinger and thumb rest serrations on the spine. The handle choices are either molded Zytel® (Model 362), or rosewood (Model 398). Encased in its leather sheath, this edged tool is a superb choice for both skinning and other primary field-care assignments.

Columbia River Knife & Tool Company: The CRKT Partner (Model 2003) takes the drop-point concept and emphasizes the skinning functions of that design. The 4-3/4-inch, taper-ground blade in this model is made from AUS-6M stainless steel. The synthetic handle is molded directly onto the full-tang and configured for user comfort. A black leather sheath, with snap closure, provides safety and security when the knife is carried on the blade. Simple and straightforward, this skinner is everything one would expect in a quality product.

Gerber Legendary Blades: The Gerber Pro Guide™ Skinner (Model 04262) takes the hide separation process to a professional design level. The 3-1/2-inch, 400 series stainless steel blade has a slightly upswept look. The glass-filled nylon handle is textured for a solid grip and is triple-riveted onto the full-length tang. A Ballistic Cloth® belt sheath comes with the knife. Using input from professional guides and outfitters, Gerber has crafted one of the best factory skinners I've seen in a long time.

Grohmann Knives: After the successful introduction of the D. H. Russell Belt Knives, Grohmann produced their own line of specialized skinning knives. There are five models in this

Russell-Harrington Cutlery

The name John Russell could have easily disappeared from the pages of cutlery history had it not been for his development of the Green River knife. Truly an American original, it was designed especially for frontier duty. The knife itself featured an 8-3/4-inch, clip-pattern, carbon steel blade with a pair of wood handle slabs triple-riveted to the full length tang. More than just a knife, if demanded, this versatile tool could be used to chop and dig, as well as the more mundane game-care chores.

The demand from the new markets in the recently opened West was unrivaled. Between 1840 and 1860, some 720,000 Green River knives were sent beyond the banks of the Mississippi. Russell didn't stop here with a single knife pattern. Variants of the basic design concept eventually emerged. The Dadley, a spear-point fixed blade was favored by river boat gamblers, outlaws, lawmen, and frontiersmen. A serious self-defense and survival blade, it could also handle most primary game-care chores. The next and even more important edged tool in the Russell line was the famous Russell Buffalo Skinner. The broad sweeping blade belly, blunted point, and slightly trailing-point concept were a buffalo hunter's concept of what a skinning knife should be. Inexpensive, easily sharpened, and big enough to handle large animals, this was the quintessential American skinning knife.

John Russell was born on March 30, 1797, in Greenfield, Massachusetts. As a teenager, he followed his father's profession of working with gold and silver, and he mastered the art of engraving. Local business folk became aware of young Russell's business acumen. He was sent to Georgia as a representative of a group of Greenfield investors to look into developing a cotton industry in that state. Spending 12 years in the South, Russell made a sizeable fortune and retired at 33 years of age.

Returning to Greenfield, Russell eventually married and raised a family. Apparently, he just couldn't keep away from the business world. Sensing an opportunity, he established a cutlery factory on the banks of the Green River. Like all new ventures, the plant struggled at first, but then sales of Green River cutlery managed to move well ahead of foreign competition and became well established as the knife of choice for American hunters.

The Green River knife line is still being produced in Massachusetts. Made at the Russell-Harrington factory, in Southbridge, the original Green River knife, Russell Dadley, and the Russell Buffalo skinner are still in current manufacture. Of course, some minor design adjustments have been made. Models with 5- and 6-inch blades are now available, as well as stain-free blade steel. However, the knives still have the same classic blade shapes and crosshatched wood handle slabs A top-grain, oiled leather sheath accompanies every knife.

As useful in the outdoors, as they were more than a century ago, the cutlery designs of John Russell ushered in an era that stands as a hallmark in American cutlery development. An era, that today continues to grow and develop far beyond anyone's wildest imaginings.

Russell-Harrington Cutlery, Inc.
44 Green River St., Dept. BT
Southbridge MA 01550
508/765-0201

D. Hollis

Faithful to their 19th century heritage, these three modern knives from the Russell-Harrington cutlery firm, (top to bottom) Buffalo Skinner, Hunter, and Dadley, incorporate in their individual designs features that have proven valuable to hunters in the field.

series—Large (Model 100), Standard (Model 101), Short Blade (Model 103), and Mini Skinner (Model 104), as well as the Deepwoods Hunter (Model 104)—each offering blade lengths from 5 inches, down to 2-1/2 inches, respectively. Available in either high-carbon stainless or carbon steel, with a choice of rosewood, resin-impregnated wood laminate, or horn handles (Deepwoods Hunter available in rosewood only), these knives are designed specifically for hide removal. Any model in this series has a host of features that a big-game hunter can well appreciate.

Imperial-Schrade Cutlery: In their Imperial Cutlery line, this cutlery producer lists a very affordable Skinner (Model AP13). The knife features a clip-pattern, stainless steel blade that has enough sweep to the cutting edge to effectively maneuver through skinning chores without a hitch. The glass-reinforce molded handle is designed to enhance blade control and reduce user fatigue. The belt sheath is made from nylon webbing with a hard plastic insert to protect the blade edge. This is an excellent choice in a skinning knife for those on a budget.

Ka-bar Cutlery: This well-respected cutlery firm recently brought out a line of small fixed-blade knives that are making a favorable impression on many big game hunters. Designed by knifemaker, Dan Harrison, this grouping of knives is without peer for innovative fixed-

D. Hollis

This Partner fixed-blade model from Columbia River Knife & Tool Company has the making of a fine edged skinning tool.

blade design. Two models within this Precision Hunter series are designed especially for skinning activities. Both knives are crafted from 440A stainless steel, with full-length blade tangs and thermoplastic handles. Not only are these knives functionally-designed, their abbreviated lengths make them easier to carry on a belt.

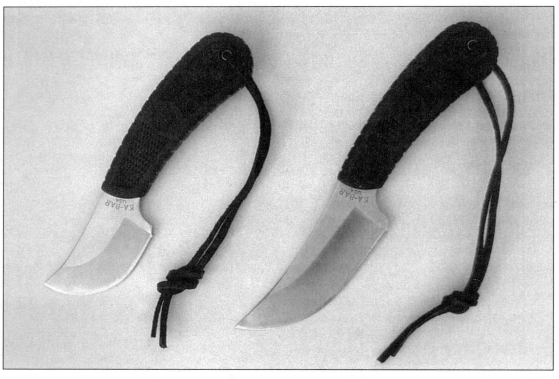

D. Hollis

This pair of Ka-bar Precision Hunters are both excellent choices for skinning big game.

136

Katz: The Katz Wild Cat is a hollow-ground skinner that features a 4-5/8-inch, satin-finished blade of XT-80 stainless steel (Rc 59). Blade spine serrations near the guard are designed as a thumb rest and allow amplified cutting edge management. The guard and buttcap are made from 400 series stainless steel for low maintenance. And there are several different (Kraton®, Sambar stag, and ivory Micarta®) handle material choices. A fitted Cordura® nylon belt sheath is included. With its full-tang construction and handle selection options, this is a quality skinner that can reflect its owner's own personal tastes.

Kellam: This Scandinavian cutlery importer carries knives made by a number of different makers. One of the best skinners in this assortment is the Gnome (Model F14) drop-point pattern folder with an abbreviated, 2-1/2-inch, 440A stainless steel blade. Interestingly, the blade has a somewhat rounded shape which tends to lengthen the edge radius. This exaggerated sweep of the cutting edge prevents accidental hide punctures and gives this knife a strong skinning appeal. The blade locks open for safety by means of an innerframe liner lock. And an opening stud on the blade spine allows the user to bring the blade into play with one hand. Handle scales are made from curly birch, which imparts a distinctive Nordic flare to this useful little knife. A nice little folder that is fully able to handle every skinning need, from deer to caribou.

Kershaw kai Cutlery: Markets a pair of very similar skinning knives. Both the Elk Skinner (Model 1014) and the Elk Skinner II (Model 2014) are crafted from AUS-6A stainless steel. Both have the same drop-point pattern blade with an integral guthook feature. The only differences between the two knives can be found in blade length and handle design. The Elk Skinner features a 4-3/8-inch blade and co-polymer handle with a molded-in guard. The Elk Skinner II offers a 4-1/2-inch blade with a stainless steel guard and the same "hand-print" molded handle. With either one of these two skinners, a big-game hunter can handle hide removal with confidence.

Russ Krommer: This Alaskan resident is both a knifemaker and a hunting guide in our most northern state. His experience in the field is reflected in his functional cutlery designs. Krommer's fixed-blade Guide knife is a fine skinning piece. The 3-inch blade is crafted from edge-holding ATS-34 in a drop-point pattern. The bolster and other fittings are all made from 416 stainless. The handle is stabilized Mammoth elephant ivory. The protective leather sheath is closely-stitched and provides nearly full-length covering. Russ Krommer knows his craft and it shows in the quality of his edged tools.

Normark: In their Rapala® knife line, Normark makes a Hunters Skinner™ that features a 4-1/4-inch, drop-point pattern, stainless steel blade. A chrome metallized ferrule provides a generous fin-

Kellam Knives

This Kellam lockblade folder may look a little on the squat side, but the blade design is just right for skinning activities.

Russ Kommer

Knifemaker, Russ Kommer edged designs reflect his experience in the field. Russ is pictured here with three bear hides that were taken near the Russell Glacier in southeastern Alaska.

ger guard and the rubberized composite handle offers a comfortable non-slip grip. An essential tool for the big game hunter, this Finnish manufactured skinner is as functional as it is good-looking.

Outdoor Edge: Earlier in this chapter, as well as in chapter nine, this firm's T-handle skinning knives were mentioned. The unique combination of a straight-wrist grip and a broad blade profile are a dramatic advantage in a skinning knife. Both the full-size Game Skinner (Model GS-100), and the smaller Whitetail Skinner (Model WT-10) have the T-handle design and are crafted from AUS-8A stainless steel. The blade is fully hollow-ground and the knives are available with a plain or combination (plain/serrated) edge grinds. The Kodi-Skinner Drop-Point (Model KS-10DP) is a more traditionally-styled fixed-blade knife. The blade is

4-1/4-inches long and made in a drop-point pattern. A similar model, the Kodi-Skinner (Model KS-10) adds a guthook feature to a slightly longer 4-3/4-inch blade. Both knives feature thermoplastic handles that are molded directly onto the full-length blade tangs. Each knife is supplied with a full-grain leather sheath. Innovative and well executed, any of these skinners is a welcome addition to a big-game hunter's field-care gear.

Puma: I've always appreciated the traditional designs and timeless beauty of Puma's edged offerings. This is certainly true when it comes to their Skinner (Model 11693). The 5-inch stainless steel blade is crafted in a trailing-point pattern, but manifests enough point to be useful in a broad range of field-dressing activities—much more than just skinning.

The Puma Skinner combines a 5-inch trailing-point stainless blade with genuine stage handle scales.

Coast Cutlery

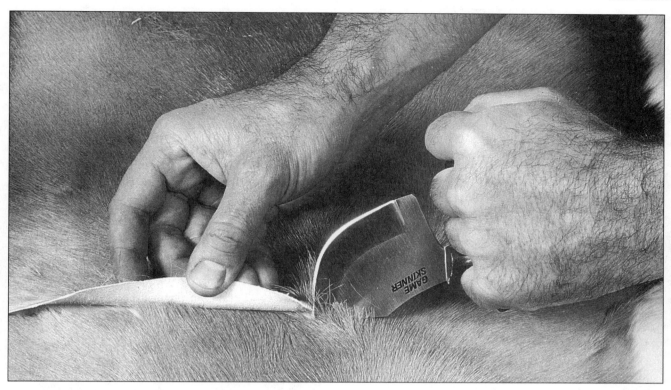

The T-handle design of the Outdoor Edge Game Skinner allows the user to work with a straight wrist.

Outdoor Edge

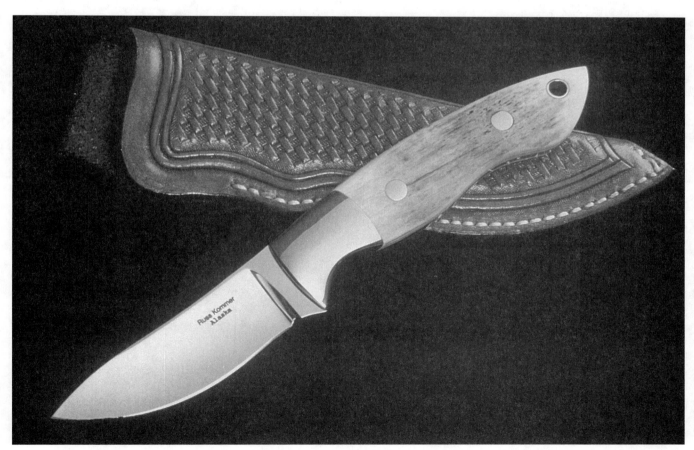

Russ Krommer

Obviously, Russ Krommer's skills as a knifemaker and big-game hunting guide are manifest in his Guide model fixed-blade, drop-point pattern skinning knife.

Skinning, One Step at a Time

Step One: When possible, position the animal where you can work on it easily. This may necessitate moving the carcass a short distance. Make all of the initial skinning cuts in the hide while the animal is on the ground. Removal of the hocks (lower legs) will facilitate the skinning process.

Step Two: Elevating the carcass off of the ground (deer size animals) makes it easier to skin without stooping over. Skin both lower legs to expose the opening between the large tendon and the leg bone. Insert a gambrel hook into this opening (both legs), attach a hoist to the central lifting point, and raise the carcass to a workable position. If the animal is too large to hoist, or there is no means to elevate the carcass, then all skinning will have to be conducted on the ground. To protect the exposed carcass, skin one side and lay the hide out flat, then roll the animal over onto the hide and skin the opposite side.

Step Three: Beginning at the rear, skin the hide free to the tail joint. Sever the tail, and continue skinning both hindquarters. Once you have the skin free from the hindquarters, you can pull the hide down with your hands just like taking off a sock. Skin the forequarters free and continue pulling on the hide (using your knife where necessary) until you reach the neck. Work the hide down the neck, then cut the head off at the joint nearest the skull. If you wish to save the hide and have it tanned, cut around the neck, lay the skin out flat (hair side down) and thoroughly salt. After skinning, cover the exposed carcass, or quarters, with a meat bag.

D. Hollis

Step One: Make all of the initial skinning cuts while the animal is on the ground.

D. Hollis

Step Two: Elevate the carcass off of the ground where it's easy to skin without stooping over.

D. Hollis

Step Three: Beginning at the rear, separate the hide from the underlying muscle tissue.

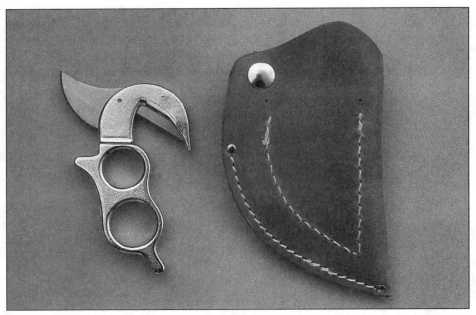

D. Hollis

While the design may be unusual, the Wyoming Knife offers a faster, easier and safer way to skin than a conventional knife design.

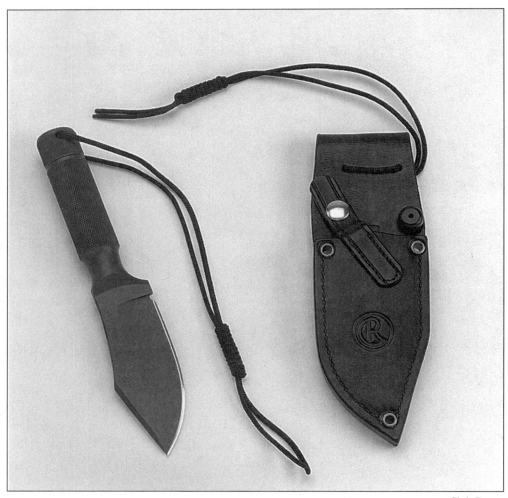

Chris Reeve

Knifemaker, Chris Reeve has designed a skinner to cover a wide range of tasks, including caping and breaking through cartilage and bone.

The full-length blade tang is mated to a pair of genuine stag handle scales. The natural irregularities of the stag offers a superior gripping surface under all conditions. The scales are triple-riveted and offset from the blade by a brass single guard. A bird's head stainless steel pommel completes the knife, and a fully protective leather sheath is also supplied as part of the package. Puma knives have been a favorite of mine for years and this skinning design is no exception.

Chris Reeve: While not a hunter himself, nonetheless, this knifemaker has designed a wonderful hollow-handle skinning knife. Made from a single billet of tough A2 tool steel, the broad, clip-point pattern blade can also be used for caping and cutting through cartilage and gristle. A non-reflective Kalgard® coating inhibits corrosion, even under the worst environmental invective. Hollow-handle knives are a Chris Reeve specialty and nobody does it any better. A knurled cap provides access to the handle cavity, which allows the user to store survival necessities. A well-made, oil-tanned leather sheath, with reinforcements at every point of strain, provides transport storage. Well worth every dollar spent in acquisition, Chris Reeve's edged tool's are simply the best, of the best.

Viking Knives: This firm is a lesser-known knife manufacturer, but the edged offerings are all top-drawer quality. The Large Game Skinner (Model 7) is a prime example of a fine skinning knife design. The clip-point, hollow-ground, stainless steel blade is extremely broad, with a nearly 90-degree sweep to the cutting edge. A serrated thumb rest on the spine, near the single guard, provides added blade control when skinning. And the stag handle is a handful of solid gripping surface. While this fixed-blade offering might be a tad too large for the average deer hunter, it is an elk hunter's dream come true.

Wyoming Knife: Probably the most unusual field knife design ever, the Wyoming Knife is all of that—and more! In addition to the die-cast, two-finger grip, chrome-plated, alloy handle, this little cutter has both replaceable gutting and skinning blades. Those who have used this knife claim that a faster, easier, cleaner and safer job of skinning can be accomplished than with conventional knife designs. By eliminating the hassle of resharpening and putting several game care features in a single, lightweight, easily carried tool, the designers of this unique knife have obviously had a lot of experience in the field.

Adding skinning to your big-game field-care skill set isn't difficult, especially if you have the right edged tool. Position the carcass where you can work on it easily, make all the right initial incisions in the hide, and use your knife blade sparingly. If the edge of your skinning knife is sharp enough, the weight of the blade can almost carry the assignment alone. When the carcass is warm, the hide will peel off as easily as a banana skin. If it has hung in the cold for several days, then you'll have your work cutout for you. Hands-on involvement in the skinning process is just one more component of responsible meat care.

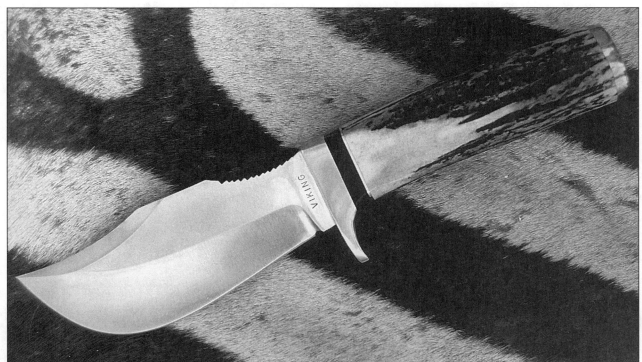

Viking Knives

Broad and sweeping, the cutting edge on this Large Game Skinner from Viking Knives almost cuts by itself.

Tan Your Hide

Unaffected by weather and wear, deerskin became the outdoor garment material of choice for American Indians, trappers, mountain men, and frontier folk. The natural suppleness and long wearing durability made it a natural for an outer body covering. Despite its value as a clothing material, after skinning, many deer hides are simply discarded. A few simple steps and that same buttery-soft skin can be transformed into wonderful garments and fine leather goods.

After skinning, salt, and lots of it, is the key to hide preservation. Lay the skin out on a flat surface (flesh side up) and liberally coat the exposed surface with salt. Some folks prefer rock salt, other use table salt, both will work equally as well. The important thing is to use enough so that a thick coating covers every inch of the skin. For most hides, three to five-pounds of salt should be enough.

After salting, check on the skin often and drain off any accumulated fluids that rise to the surface. If the salt gets damp, shake it off and re-salt the hide—repeating the procedure as many times as necessary. Salting will not only preserve the skin. It will also prevent insect contamination.

If you have immediate access to a freezer, you may eschew the immediate need to use salt as a preservative and simply roll the hide up, place it in an airtight plastic bag (to prevent freezer burns), and freeze. When it comes time to send the hide to a tannery, you can then thaw and salt it prior to that transport. If you live close to a tannery that handles deerskin, you can deliver the hide yourself, send it through the mail, United Parcel Service, or Federal Express, or let your taxidermist handle the matter.

Deerskin can be tanned at home. There are several different kits on the market. The only requirement is that you must have the commitment to follow the instructions to the letter, and the time to do the job right. Most of those who want to tan self-harvested deer skins use the services of a commercial tanning operation. The process will take anywhere from four to six months depending on the time of year when the tannery receives your hide(s). Finished deerskin leather color options are generally available. If you can't decide, then select the natural finish and have the skin(s) dyed at a later date.

If you send the hide directly to a tannery, make sure that no moisture remains on the skin surface. Shake off the crusted salt, roll the hide flesh side in (folding can leave permanent scars on the surface of the skin), and wrap it in several layers of newspaper. Do not use plastic, or airtight wrapping materials, since this will create a perfect environment for the growth of bacteria. The bacteria can rot your hide(s) during transit and all of your effort will be in vain. Place the skin in a cardboard box and ship it directly to the tannery. If you have any special instructions, make sure they are included with your hide, along with your return address. Pre-payment is generally not necessary. The tannery will bill you upon completion of the tanning process.

If you don't have enough hides to complete a particular project, additional tanned deerskin can usually be purchased from the tannery. It takes about four to five hides to make a jacket, two to three for a vest or handbag. And the average deerskin will make about two to three pairs of gloves or mittens. Many tanneries also offer sewing services, so you can order a garment made from your own hides.

Most tanning operations that handle game hides accept deer, elk, antelope, moose, buffalo, sheep and javelina skins. Tanned deer and antelope skin is the best material for gloves, shirts and jackets. Elk hide makes a much more durable leather and can be used for moccasins, heavy coats, and work gloves. All leather has two sides, the smooth outer face and the rough (suede) inner surface. Depending on your own preference, either side may be used as an outer surface.

Tanning and Garment Manufacturing Operations

Custom Coat
227 N. Washington St.
Berlin, WI 54923

Mid-Western Sport Togs
150 W. Franklin St.
Berlin, WI 54923

W. B. Place
P. O. Box 160
Hartford, WI 53027

Ubert Tanning Co.
Owatonna, MN 55060

Skinning is all part of game care, and the skinning knife is the mechanism by which hide removal is accomplished. The next time you find yourself engaged with that edge tool in a skinning activity, remember that you're dealing with a potentially valuable resource. When you turn that hide into a personal garment, the memories of the hunt become more than just a fleeting thought.

D. Hollis

Don't toss that hide in the trash. Tanned deer skin makes some very fine garments.

About 10 years ago, Camillus Cutlery was one of the first to combine three useful game-care blades into a single, triple-locking, folding knife configuration.

Chapter 14
All-in-one

When handling fish, fowl and game, you need all the edge you can get.

There is no such thing as an all-purpose knife. If you think so, then you'd better think again. When you push a knife beyond the limits of performance expectation, failure can and will result. That failure could be a botched job, broken blade, damaged knife, or a self-inflicted injury. Personally, I'd prefer not to enter that realm. This is the exact reason why multi-blade, exchange-blade and cutlery combination kits were developed. When it comes to field care of fish, fowl and game, all-in-one is better than one-for-all.

Okay, you're confused. Where is all this rhetoric going? The option to use an alternative blade, switch one blade shape for another, or even trade one style of a knife for something entirely different, is better than trying to use one knife for a wide range of cutting chores. Let's face it, field dressing, skinning, butchering, and trophy work are all different. And it's that difference that demands variation in blade shape, length, edge style and cutting implement category.

Multi-blade pocketknives are one approach to different cutting needs. The Swiss Army Knife (SAK) is the quintessential example of this theme. You name a sport, and it's possible to find a SAK for it. Since few SAK models are specifically designed for hunting, these handy pocket tool chests are not always what's needed. However, large two-blade folding hunting knives have been part of the product lines of many domestic cutlery manufacturers like Case (Models 189/192) and Ka-bar (Model 1184) for years.

Combining an elongated clip-pattern main blade, with what was referred to as a "skinning" blade (actually a straight blade with an edge curve that was somewhat rounded at the tip) in a single oversized folding knife frame, seemed to work for lots of big game hunters in the first half of the 20th century. The emergence of the single-blade locking folder in the early 1960s created a huge shift in hunter preference.

Cutlery manufacturers have begun to include more than one blade feature in many folding hunting knives. Some two-blade models offer a choice of a saw blade or a guthook blade as a secondary blade. As an alternative, the guthook and saw features may be combined into a single combination

blade and paired with a primary blade. These specialized game care features can also be individual companion blades in a three-blade folder.

Another approach to blade diversity can be seen in the pairing of two different edged tools in a common sheath. In Camillus' Western Cutlery line there are several such twin combinations. Also, United Cutlery is the distributor of a couple of fixed-blade twin sets. Most often, this approach joins two similar knives with disparate blade lengths. This allows the hunter to use the larger knife for field dressing and skinning, with the smaller knife held in reserve for detailed trophy work. Despite all of these attempts, however, the need for alternative blade shapes remained.

D. Hollis

Remington's Rattlesnake™ "One-Hander" places a drop-point main blade and a useful saw blade in the same folding knife frame.

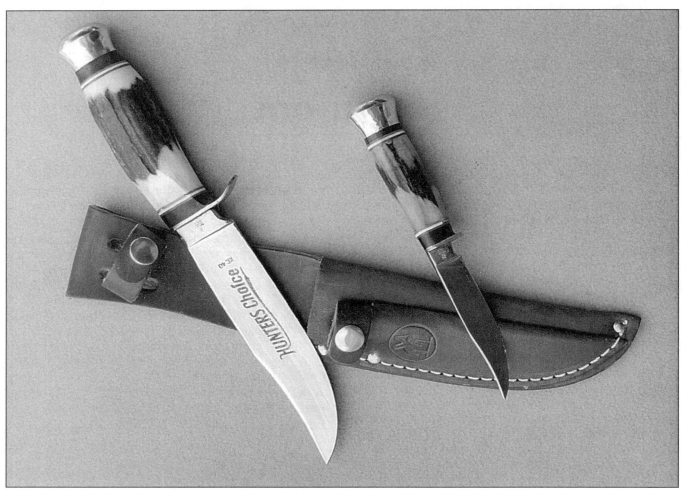

D. Hollis

United Cutlery's Hunters' Choice twin set pairs two similar clip-pattern fixed-blade knives, each with a different length blade, into a single sheath.

The advent of the exchange-blade knife concept in the early 1980s went a long way to solve the need for alternative blade types. The idea of exchanging one blade shape for another was a hot idea for a time. For whatever reason, however, this concept was not too popular with hunters. Quite possibly the choice of more than one blade shape was confusing, or maybe the quick-change mechanism was difficult to manipulate. I really can't pinpoint why hunters didn't flock to the idea. Today, only a couple of different manufacturers continue to produce exchange-blade knives.

Boker USA: This firm is one of the few cutlery manufacturers that has stayed in the exchange-blade game. The Boker *Optima* switch-blade folder has six different blade choice options (saw, clip-point, Damascus stainless steel clip-point, drop-point, drop-point with guthook, and ceramic drop-point), each of which are easily switched one-for-another in a single lockblade folding knife handle. The handle features nickel-silver bolsters and is available in either grey, bone or black Delrin® plastic. A leather or Cordura® nylon belt,

depending on knife model selected, is supplied with each knife.

Case: The Case *XX-Changer*®, available with either rosewood (Model 174), or stag (Model 186) handle scales is an exchange-blade folder. The knife comes with clip-point, drop-point, straight, and saw blades, and each can be swapped one-for-another in the same lockblade handle. Depending on the particular cutting application, this knife offers a specific blade design for that chore. For example, the clip-point blade can be used for general field dressing; the drop-point for skinning; the saw blade as an aid in opening the pelvic and chest cavities, and the straight blade to strip the meat away from the skeletal structure. The blades are easily exchanged by depressing the back spring lock and inserting whatever blade you desire into the handle frame. The knife, as well all three extra blades, is contained in a specially-designed leather sheath. While the popularity of exchange blade knives may have seen its nadir, nevertheless, this Case offering continues to be a well-conceived hunting knife design.

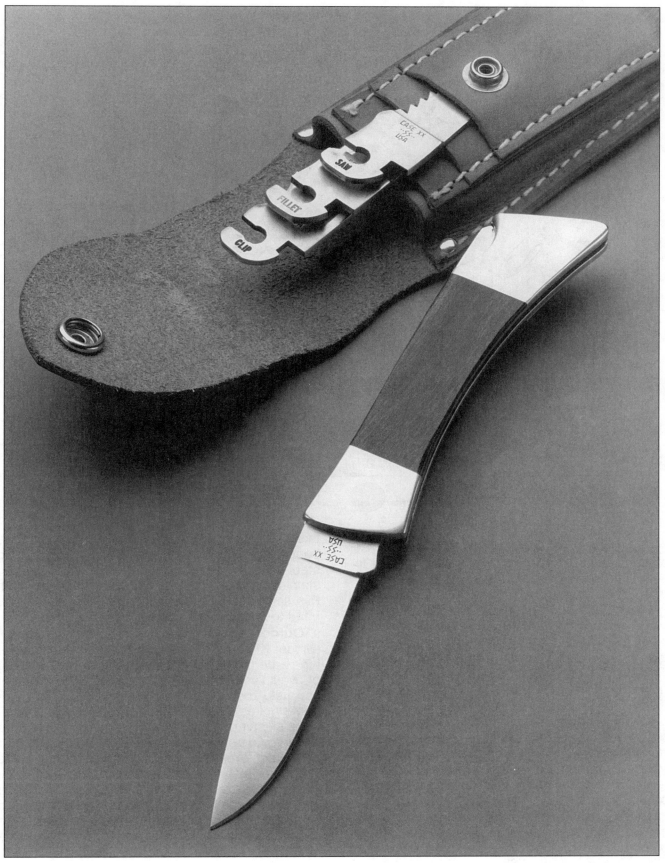

Case Cutlery

The Case XX-Changer® takes the exchange-blade theme to another level with its choice of clip-point, drop-point, guthook, and saw blades. Each blade can easily be swapped one-for-another in and out of the same lockblade handle.

D. Hollis

The Kershaw Alaskan Blade Trader allows the hunter to interchange a clip-point main blade with a large guthook skinning blade and a saw blade.

Kershaw: Blade exchange is the theme of Kershaw's Trader line of functional cutlery/kitchen tool sets. The *Alaskan Blade Trader* (Model 1098AK) is a three-blade set that features a 3-1/2-inch clip-point hollow-ground hunting blade, 4-1/4-inch skinning blade with a large guthook feature, and a 6-inch saw blade. All three blades interchange into a single handle by means of Kershaw's "Quik-Lock" mechanism. The entire set is contained in a leather sheath that holds the main knife and the other two blades.

Another approach to blade diversity is putting more than one knife in a kit. This way an entire group of specific-application (field dressing, butchering, etc.) cutlery can be assembled together in a single package. For the hunter, unitary containment allows for ready access and prevents loss.

L.E.M.: In this firm' s mail order catalog of meat processing equipment and sausage making supplies (L.E.M. Products, P. O. Box 244, Miamitown, OH 45041, 877/536-7763), they list a *Hunter's Kit* (Cat #099) that includes all of the knives you'll need for processing your own big game. Within this grouping of edged tools are a caping knife, a boning knife, a steaking knife and a sharpening steel. All knives are crafted from high-carbon stainless steel with thermoplastic handles. With this set of game-care cutlery, the only thing you need to supply is the meat and a cutting table.

Outdoor Edge: The Outdoor Edge *Kodi-Pak* (Model KP-1) is the most complete and effective big-game field-care set on the market. Consisting of two knives and a saw, with these tools a hunter can field dress, skin, quarter and cape any big-game animal. The main knife in this set is a drop-point skinning blade with a large guthook feature on the blade spine. Pointed enough to be useful in both field dressing and skinning activities, this knife features a 4-1/4-inch blade made from AUS-8A stainless steel. The checkered Kraton® handle is molded directly onto the full-tang and is shaped to fit the grip pocket of the hand. Likewise, the smaller caping knife is also crafted from the same easy maintenance steel. Its drop-point blade shape is extremely thin and pointed to facilitate the most delicate trophy work. A recessed choil provides for precision blade control when needed.

L.E.M

The L.E.M. Hunter's Kit has all of the knives, along with a sharpening steel, you need for field or home game butchering.

(*Traveling Kitchen Set*), and cookouts (*Picnic/Cookout Travel Set*). Each of these portable all-in-one sets comes in an impact-resistant molded carrying case. And the case is designed so all of the knives and other implements can snap into individual slots. The knives are crafted from 420-J2 stainless steel, with full-tang construction for strength and durability. Each thermoplastic handle is triple-riveted to the blade tang for permanent attachment.

Wildlife Enterprises: Designed by wildlife biologist, Rodney G. Marburger, the *Wildlife Processing* contains boning and skinning knives, a bone saw and a sharpening steel. Each of the implements fits snugly into individual pockets within a rugged Cordura® nylon carrying case and the case has a fold-over flap cover, hook and loop fasteners and is compact enough to slip into a pack or saddle bags. The stainless steel knives in this kit are the same type that professional butchers use. The boning knife blade is slender with a slightly upswept tip for enhanced control when working close to the skeletal structure. The skinning blade is based on a trailing-point design, with the broad, rounded tip that works best in hide removal activities. Both knives have ergonomically-designed, thermoplastic handles that are heavily texturized for complete cutting control. The sharpening steel is basic to blade edge main-

The same molded thermoplastic handle makes even the most tedious caping assignment manageable. The saw features an aggressive tooth design that can handle quartering game or brush work with equal aplomb. And the unique T-handle allows for straight wrist cutting. Best of all, all three edged tools are contained in a compact, full-grain leather belt sheath. This is an awesome game-care set that can effectively deal with all game-care assignments.

United Cutlery: These folks are into cutlery kits in a big way. The *Big Game Field Dress Travel Set* (Model UC1117) contains a large butcher knife, boning knife, skinning knife, bone saw with two replaceable blades, sharpening steel and one-dozen disposable field-dressing gloves. Best of all, these individual items are all contained in a molded plastic case. Equipped with one of these kits, a hunter could easily skin, quarter and butcher a carcass in the field, camp or at home. From carcass to chops, this kit contains all the tools and equipment you'll need. United also makes cutlery kits for anglers (*Fisherman's Travel Set* and *Fisherman's Travel Set*), camp kitchens

United Cutlery

United Cutlery's Big Game Kit contains everything you'll need to skin, quarter and butcher a big-game carcass.

151

tenance. Just a few strokes on the steel and the user can smooth over and straighten rough spots on the blade edge. The bone saw is nothing more than a simple hacksaw frame fitted with a bone-cutting blade. This kit has everything you need, when you need it and in a handy kit form.

In the Field

There are a number of widely different game-care chores in the field. Of course, basic field dressing (evisceration) is the most fundamental of these assignments. There are some hunters who never go beyond this primary task. They prefer to leave skinning and butchering to professional meat cutters. Others may decide to skin, quarter, bone and even butcher a carcass in the field. In the first instance, nothing more than a single blade knife will suffice. In the latter situation, several different blade shapes and tools may be necessary. This is where the option of selecting multiple-edged tools offers a clear advantage. This specifically falls into the theme of this chapter. With either an exchange-blade knife, or a cutlery field kit, one can switch from one type of tool to another as the need arises. Furthermore, this allows for the use of application-specific cutlery.

United Cutlery

The Kitchen Kit from United Cutlery is another edged tool set that's right on target.

Photo Credit: Weyer of Toledo

This Sebenza knife by Chris Reeve is a magnificent one-hand opening folder with a Damascus blade.

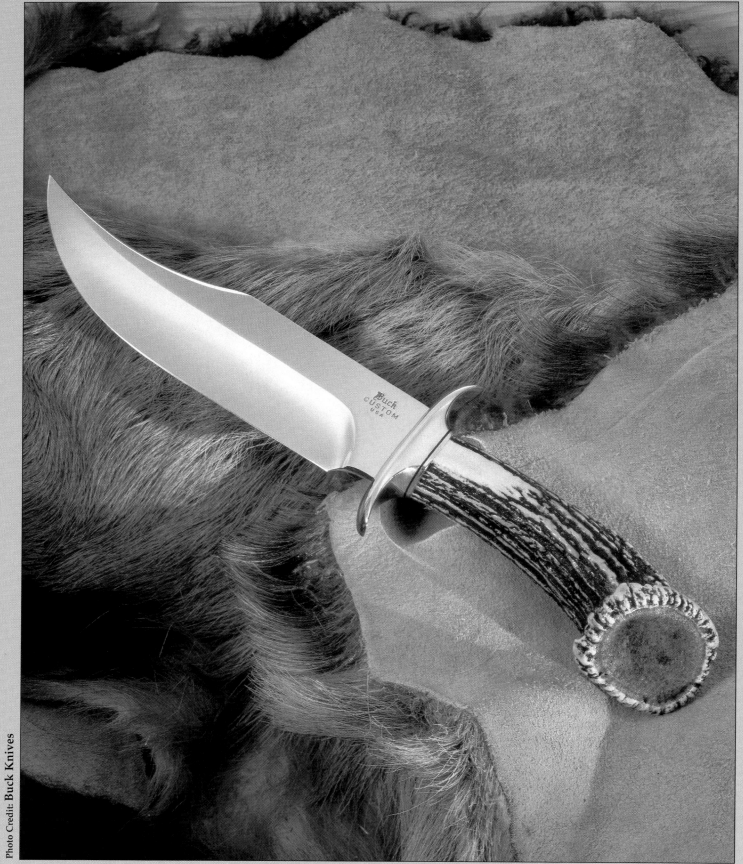

This fixed-blade Bowie knife from the Buck Custom Shop
is just the ticket for black powder hunters.

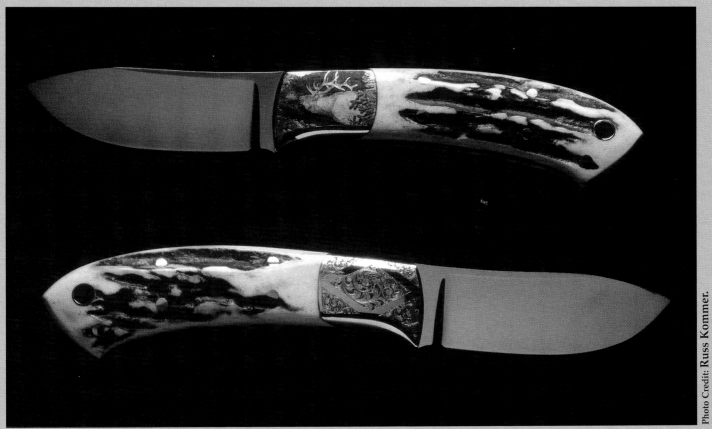

Russ Kommer made these fine drop-point skinners.

These Paragon and Junglee (Gutmann Cutlery) pieces exemplify
the wide-range of hunting knives today.

This all-integral constructed, drop-point skinner, is by Edmund Davidson.
The engraving on the guard and pommel was done by Jere Davidson.

Photo Credit: Images Group

Schrade Cutlery offers this fixed-blade collaboration with knifemaker D'Alton Holder.

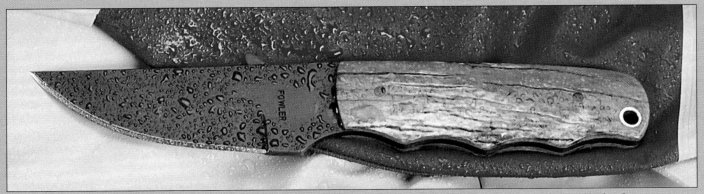

A Ricky Fowler skinner with O-1 blade coated with Precision Brand Tool Black.

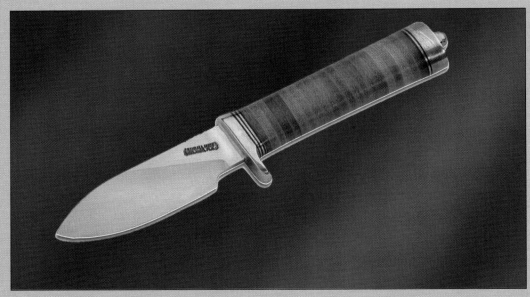

The A.G. Russel-Randall skinner is ground for perform-ance.

Marbles drop-point hunter based on a Bob Loveless design.

This lightweight fixed-blade hunter is a Spyderco collaboration with Bill Moran.

Knifemaker Joe Szilaski cold forged the D-2 blade of this drop-point hunter.

An assortment of field steel ranging from shears to camp knives, from top to bottom:
Spyderco, A.G. Russel, Remington, Knives of Alaska(2), and Kershaw.

At Home

Outside of a small town, it's getting more and more difficult to find a butcher shop or meat cutting operation that handles game. Federal and state regulations forbid the mixing of domestic and wild meat storage and cutting areas, tools, cutting blocks, boards, and wrapping stations. A small meat cutting operation, with limited demand for wild game butchering, just can't afford to provide both kinds of services. This means that the hunter must have his meat butchered near the hunting area where this specialized service can be located. To accomplish this, an extra day or two has to be tacked onto the time you allotted for your hunting excursion. In some situations, adding additional unplanned time isn't practical.

Out of necessity, many hunters have become home wild game butchers themselves. Even without formal training, some guys get really good at this chore. This is where sets, like those available from L.E.M, United Cutlery, and Wilderness Enterprises become the solution to this problem. Any one of these cutlery kits has all you need to transform a game carcass into roasts, chops and steaks. Add a couple of large plastic tubs (like those restaurants use to collect dirty dishes) for meat containment, a meat grinder, wrapping materials, as well as inked marking stamps and you have your own butcher shop. The basic tools of this activity, however, will be found in a game care cutlery set.

In my experience, if you have to look all over camp or the kitchen for the right tools, then a simple job becomes complicated. When I first began cutting up my own game, my knives and other meat cutting paraphernalia disappeared in between jobs. Some were "borrowed" by hunting buddies that forgot to return them. Others were appropriated by my wife for her own culinary needs. Even if I managed to gather everything up, there wasn't a sharp edge in the lot!

After several seasons of frustration, I now use a game care cutlery set. When the meat cutting chores are concluded, all the knife edges receive appropriate attention. Each knife is then returned to the kit. All of the other butcher gear receives thorough cleaning, sharpening and adjusting. For safe keeping in between jobs, everything is kept under lock and key. This way, when next year's hunting season comes around, I am ready to go. Even then if my hunting friends want to use my meat cutting gear, the answer is—no!

When I first became a big game hunter, I never realized just how involved things would become. At first glance, hunting seemed to be nothing more than a accurate rifle, a handful of shells and a sharp knife. I don't where it all began, but I now find myself the master of several related skills. It seems that somewhere in all of this, the acquisition of more than one edged tool became a necessity. All I can say is that experience has taught me that it's better to have all-in-one, than one-in-all.

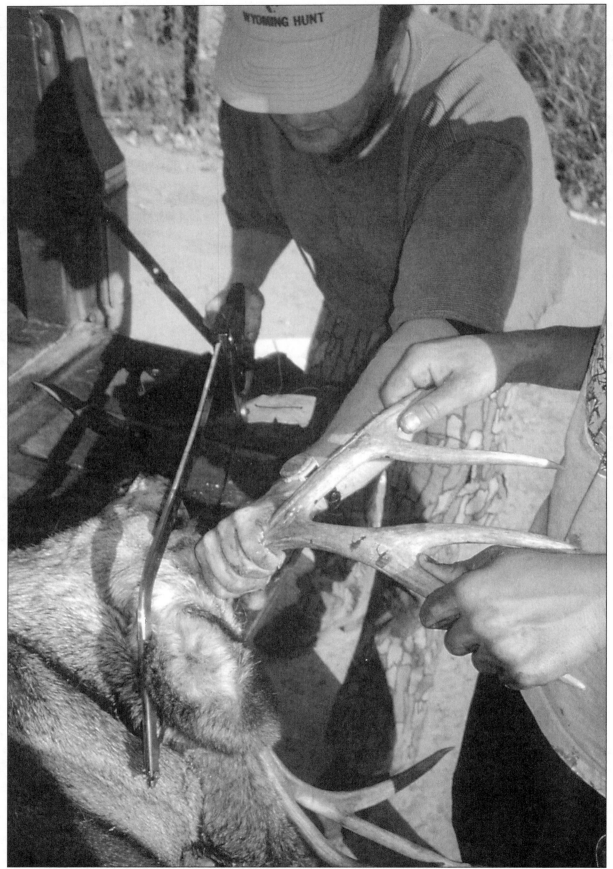

D. Hollis

When it comes to rough cutting assignments, a saw or an axe is the hunter's tool of choice.

Chapter 15
Rough Cutters

Why push the cutlery performance envelope? When things get tough, you need to get rough!

A flash of color, in the otherwise verdant landscape, caught my eye. Sweeping the slope with my binoculars, it didn't take long to pick up the form of a blaze-orange-clad deer hunter. I could see a rifle and a daypack leaning up against a tree. I could also see there was a forked-horn mule deer laying in the grass not far away. Obviously, the hunter's efforts had paid off.

I watched the hunter pull a knife out of its sheath, and then bend over to start field dressing the buck. In a minute or so he jumped up and started bellowing like a bull caught in a barbed wire fence. I couldn't make out what he was saying, but obviously he had some kind of problem. Seeking to provide assistance to a fellow hunter in distress, I headed down the slope in his direction.

In a minute or two, the yelling subsided. By the time I was within speaking distance, the only sound that came from his lips seemed to be some unintelligible mumbling. Not wanting to startle him, I made sure he could see me.

"Hi, what's going on?" I asked in a calm voice.

"My knife gave out on me," he replied

He held up what looked like a really nice handmade fixed-blade knife, with about two inches of the tip missing. Then, a complete description of the preceding events was provided. Apparently, my newfound friend had tried to split the deer's pelvic bone with his knife. Placing the tip of the blade at what he assumed was a bone suture. He gave the knife a *whack* with a stout piece of branch. The pelvic bone

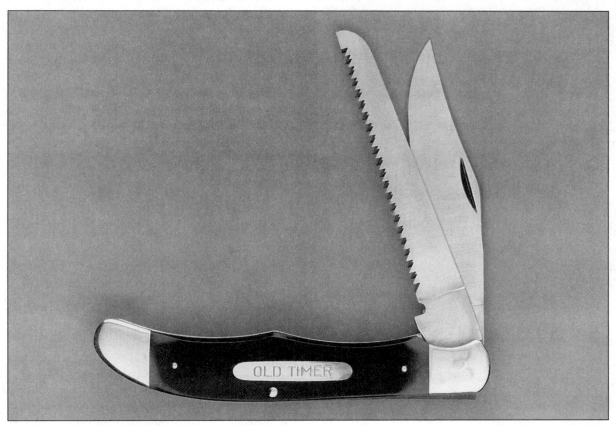

Images Group/Schrade

With an oversized locking saw blade in the same knife frame as the clip-pattern main blade, this Schrade Old Timer Son-of-a-Gun (Model 225OT) folding hunter is a handful of cutting power.

didn't give way, but his knife blade did. All of the hollering, including the mumbling I heard when we first met, was nothing more than his way of venting frustration.

"Could I use your knife?" he inquired.

I didn't even have to think about my reply. After all, one busted knife could have been an accident; two would surely be an act of pure stupidity. No, my knife wasn't about to leave its sheath.

"I think there's something in my pack that can solve this problem," I answered.

It didn't take but a second or two to lay my hands on a game saw. I handed the little saw to the guy and stood back to watch. At first he struggled a minute, but then cutting mastery kicked in. It took him about a minute to saw through the deer's pelvic bone.

"That was easy," the hunter stated.

"Of course, you had the right tool for the job," I replied.

A knife is designed to cut materials that present very little resistance. A sharpened blade can easily handle animal hide, muscle tissue, and to a lim-

D. Hollis

Butchering big game in the field isn't easy. Outfitter and guide, John Winter, selected a Dandy Saw to quarter this bull elk.

ited extent—gristle and bone cartilage. While it is possible to force a blade through a deer's pelvic suture, I wouldn't recommend it. When you need something more than a knife, but less than a chain saw, it's time to bring in the rough cutters.

An ax, or a saw, is the best field tool for tough cutting assignments. Both tools are made in a variety of styles and sizes for every need, from lumbering to game care. Axes can cut faster than saws, but you'll need plenty of room to use them. Plus there are safety issues surrounding ax use that don't apply to a saw. The average outdoors person will probably find a saw easier to use in most situations, but that doesn't lessen the importance of the ax as a cutting tool. The choice of either tool is purely personal.

There are several manufacturers that produce hand axes and saws that can handle both camp and game-care needs. A review of what's available will assist readers in selecting their own "right tool for the job."

Bay Knife Company: A unique outdoor tool, the *Cobra* knife from this firm can chop and hack with wicked efficiency. The 10-3/4-inch blade is 1075 high-carbon steel of .125" thick stock. Protected with a zinc phosphate, fluorocarbon resin and graphite coating, the blade has a high degree of rust resistance. A unique "S" curve in the blade configuration is the directing force of all of the cutting power. The apex of the edge belly and the tip hook become the focus of this inertia. The tough polypropylene handle scales are attached to the full-length blade tang by two stainless steel screws. A padded nylon sheath affords either pack or belt transport. Shorter than a machete and lighter than an ax, this handy tool is great for brushwork.

Bear MCG: This firm's *Sportsman's Saw* combines a tough Zytel® handle with a 5-1/2-inch, folding, locking saw blade. The tooth edge cuts on the upstroke and can handle green and dry limbs. A useful tool at camp or deep in the backcountry, this lightweight saw is capable of handling most tough cutting chores with ease. Clearing an archery shooting lane, making a blind, or quartering game, this edged tool is a great asset.

Browning: The Browning *Folding Game and Camp Saw* (Model 900/901) weighs just 7-ounces, but can tear through wood and bone with surprising efficiency. The blade features self-cleaning, offset teeth that aggressively bite into the cutting medium. During transport, the ergonomically-designed handle contains the folding saw blade. A great tool for camp work and game butchering, it's as functional as it is compact. This company also makes a *Take-Down Saw* (Models 903/907) that can be instantly put together to form

D. Hollis

The Buck Camper's Axe is a heavy duty cutting tool that can handle big-game field dressing and campfire kindling cutting chores with equal aplomb.

D. Hollis

Muzzleloaders can appreciate the historical significance the Cold Steel Frontier Hawk brings to hunting camp.

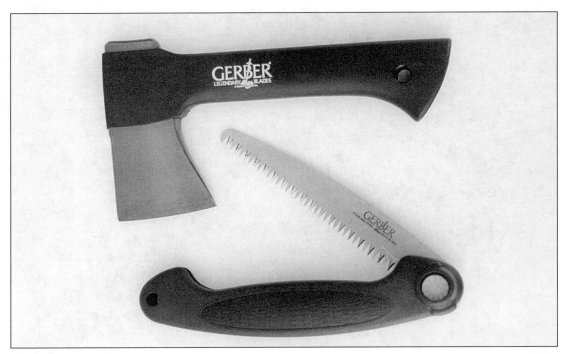

D. Hollis

The Gerber Back Paxe and Exchange-a-Blade Sport Saw are tools specifically designed to handle tough cutting chores.

a full-size outdoor saw with a 16-inch cutting blade. Available with blades for both wood and bone cutting. The square tubing construction provides complete stability when the saw is in use. A rugged tool for tough jobs, this compact saw is a serious performer.

Buck Knives: While Buck doesn't currently list a saw in their product line, they do offer the *Buck Camper's Ax*. The one-piece design is crafted from a 1/4-inch thick billet of 400 series stainless steel. The 3-1/4-inch cutting face is tapered well back from the actual striking edge for use in tight places. A pair of black thermoplastic handle scales have been contoured to fit comfortably into the hand. A protective leather sheath allows the user to carry the tool directly on the belt. Measuring 12-1/4-inches overall and weighing 1 pound 10 ounces, this Buck tool is a lot of power in a small package.

Cold Steel: Many hunters have taken up muzzleloaders as their weapon of choice. This provides the opportunity for many to take a step back in time when it comes to edge tools. On the mark with this theme, Cold Steel markets a couple of tomahawks that can fit into any frontstuffer's plans. Both the *Rifleman's Hawk* and the *Frontier Hawk* are modern recreations of early American outdoor tools. Both tomahawks have forged steel heads and straight-grain hickory handles. Welcome steel companions in hunting camp, or at a rendezvous, either tool will remind you that the past is still alive.

Gerber Legendary Blades: This cutlery firm lists three ax models and a fine sport saw. All the ax models feature a virtually indestructible, hollow, fiberglass handle. To prevent the separation of ax head and handle, the handle is injection molded round the forged steel ax head. The largest model, the *Sport Axe*, is almost big enough to be a two-hander. The mid-size *Camp Axe* is great for the campsite and yard work. The tiny *Back Paxe* is just the right size for backcountry game-care chores and camp chores. Rounding out Gerber's line of heavy hitters, the *Exchange-A-Blade Sport Saw* features lots of cutting versatility. This lightweight, folding, lockblade saw is supplied with both coarse and fine tooth blades for wood or bone work. Either blade can be swapped one-for-the-other in seconds. The thermoplastic handle features a button-lock mechanism so the blade can be locked open and closed. A nylon carrying pouch holds both the saw and the extra blade.

Kellam: This importer of Nordic cutlery offers a rugged billhook that's one of the best brush whackers I've ever used. The blade and handle design allows the user to wade in and clear the worst brush with speed. The carbon steel blade edge holds up well to even dry limbs and resharpens easily with a file. The handle design provides for a one- or two-hand grip and the smooth finish won't raise blisters. If you want to remove unwanted brush, tree limbs and other vegetation without wasting time, then this is the tool for you. In fact, this rugged cutter is so efficient that it warrants inclusion in every outdoor enthusiast's gear.

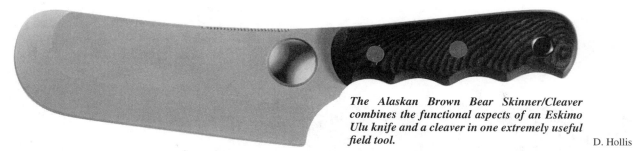

The Alaskan Brown Bear Skinner/Cleaver combines the functional aspects of an Eskimo Ulu knife and a cleaver in one extremely useful field tool.

D. Hollis

Knives of Alaska: The *Alaska Brown Bear Skinner/Cleaver* was developed with the big-game hunter in mind. Made from D-2 tool steel, this unique cleaver was the winner of the "Most Innovative American Design" at the 1994 International Blade Show. The design utilizes the rounded Eskimo Ulu knife point, which increases the edge radius and facilitates hide-removal activities. Furthermore, the blade has an integral index-finger hole that provides a positive three-point locking support for enhanced control when skinning. The blade is a full 1/4-inch thick, providing the necessary weight for chopping through bone and campfire kindling. Handle materials include a black rubberized "Suregrip" with a deeply-impressed diamond pattern, linen Micarta®, or genuine stag. This handy cleaver is a fine heavy-duty chopper and skinner all-in-one highly functional tool.

L. E. M. Products: This mail-order catalog firm carries a neat little saw that cuts fast and breaks down to fit into your backpack. Measuring 15-3/4-inches long, the saw uses a long-lasting stainless steel blade (replacement blades are available). An extra blade can be stored in the saw's body. Easy-to-clean and affordable, this saw is a fine tool for hunting camp or backcountry work.

McGowan Manufacturing Company: The newly introduced *Firestone Belt Axe* is one of this company's premier products. Described as "the perfect hunting tool," this little gem features a radical edge curve that allows a secondary use as a skinning tool. The ax head is investment cast from 440C stainless steel, appropriately heat-treated and annealed to provide superior edge retention. The laminated birch handles feature a user-friendly curve that enhances the power of each cutting stroke. A stainless setscrew and a spring steel pin firmly connect the handle and ax head. With this type of coupling, there is no way the head and handle can ever come apart. A leather carrying sheath with a double-snap closure provides safety and security during transport. A well-made tool that is able to stand up to the worst kind of treatment, this is one whacker that deserves consideration.

McGowan Manufacturing

The Firestone Belt Axe can be used for camp chores, as well as quartering and skinning big game.

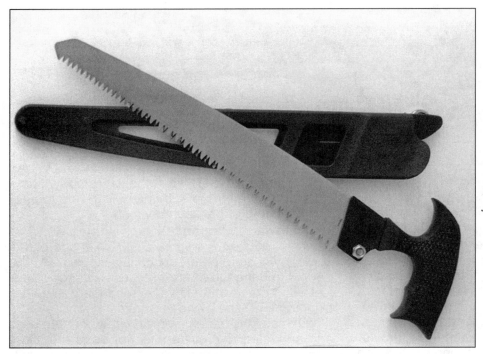

The Outdoor Edge Grizz Saw sports a T-handle for enhanced user comfort and a molded thermoplastic sheath for safe carrying.

D. Hollis

Muela Cutlery: Obviously, the folks at this Spanish cutlery firm have a strong hunting background. This is certainly reflected in their fine hunting ax. Featuring a stainless steel head permanently attached to a rugged thermoplastic handle, this game ax can handle big-game field dressing and quartering activities with ease. Furthermore, the user can grip the ax right behind the head and use it as a skinning tool. Dual capability and rugged construction make this a fine choice for camp chores or in-the-field game care.

Outdoor Edge: Among the many innovative designs that this firm markets are two fine game saws. The *Kodi-Saw* is included with a caper and a skinner in a combination game-care cutlery set. This efficient little rough cutter features a 6-inch long replaceable blade with triple-ground diamond-cut teeth. Best of all, the deeply checkered molded Kraton® handle is T-shaped to allow cutting with a straight wrist. Equally as effective on bone and brush, this is one tough little cutter. A slightly larger saw, the *Griz-Saw* (Model GW-2) features a replaceable 8-inch blade with the same triple-ground diamond-cut tooth pattern. The T-shaped handle grip provides secure hand-to-saw contact, even when wet. A quick-release, molded Delrin® sheath with a swivel-clip attachment allows the user to carry the saw on the belt or in the pack. Either saw is a serious outdoor tool that cuts through nearly anything with unbelievable ease.

Normark: The Normark *Hunter's Skinning Axe* (Model HSA-1) is designed for use not only as a field-dressing tool, but also as a skinning aid. Not unlike the Eskimo Ulu knife, the stainless steel ax head has a pronounced edge curve.

Specifically honed and precisely angled for use on bone, cartilage and gristle, this ax is not intended for chopping seasoned hardwoods or other dense materials. The thermoplastic handle is permanently fused to the ax head so there's no worry about separation. An ideal tool for any big game hunter, this ax can speed field-dressing and skinning chores.

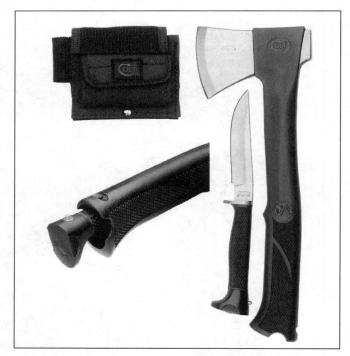

United Cutlery

The Colt® Trailblazer Axe (Model CT2) combines an efficient hunting and camping axe with a companion knife that is carried inside of the axe handle. A built-in spring mechanism holds the knife securely until released with a simple push of a button.

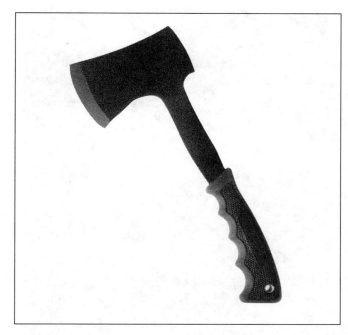

The Remington Camp Axe features a resilient, finger-grooved Kraton® handle grip for safe and untroubled use.

United Cutlery: Leave it to this innovative cutlery distributor to come up with something unusual. The Colt *Trailblazer* hatchet is all that, and more! Starting with the stainless steel ax head, this product breaks new ground by secreting a slender clip-point fixed-blade knife within the hollow thermoplastic handle. A pin positively locks the knife in place until it is needed. The handle itself has a molded-in, deeply checkered grip for a superior two-handed gripping surface. A solid combination of edged tools for the big-game hunter—this is definitely a do-it-all-duo.

Remington: Rounding out their cutlery line, Remington markets a *Camp Axe* that can handle fire kindling, tent stake driving or field-dressing chores. With a one-piece steel head and handle, there is never any danger of accidental separation. The molded thermoplastic grip is finger-grooved for added control, as well as resilient enough to protect the hand from jarring impact. A snap-closed Cordura® nylon belt case provides protection from the cutting edge when carried. Thin, light, and tough enough for most chopping chores, this little ax is a right at home on the belt or in a pack.

Robertson Enterprises: Especially-designed for hunters, campers, backpackers, and outdoor folk of every persuasion, the *Dandy Saw* is a quick-cutting, lightweight and easily-carried outdoor tool. The blade is made from Swedish bandsaw steel and the teeth are about as aggressive as it gets. The 12-inch blade *Mini Dandy* model (other blade lengths are also available) can handle both wood and bone with ease. The laminated hardwood handle provides all the cutting comfort you need. The handle can be removed and the blade resharpened at any saw shop. My own experience with this tiny cutting terror is that when it's time to get serious about cutting, then this little saw is nothing less than a "Dandy."

Available in several blade lengths, the Dandy Saw is a "get serious" rough cutter.

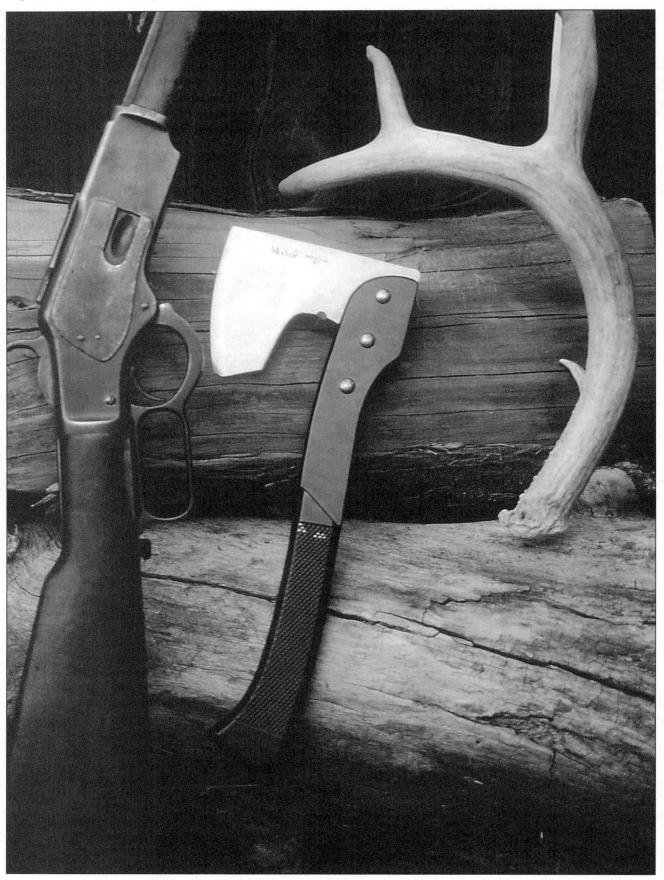

The Muela ax features a stainless steel head triple-riveted to a thermoplastic handle.

D. Hollis

Turner Knife Manufacturing: Paul Turner is the maker of an ingenious tool called the *Uluchet®*. Basically, this rough cutter is a folding hatchet based on the Alaskan Eskimo Ulu knife. The sleek, curved blade is made from cryogenically treated D-2 carbon steel. The shape is specifically designed for chopping, cutting and skinning. The folding handle is glass-reinforced thermoplastic that can hold up to the worst abuse. In the closed position, the handle is folded up against the cutting head. This configuration allows the tool to be used for cutting and skinning chores in the same manner as an Ulu knife. When the handle is folded open and locked, the *Uluchet®* can be used for chopping, clearing limbs and quartering game. The tool weighs 10-1/2 ounces and measures just 6-1/2-inches in length when closed. Easily carried on the belt, this rugged little cutter is hard to equal. While it may not have the raw chopping power of an ax, as an edged tool it is far more versatile.

Western (Camillus) Cutlery: Similar in design to the Remington ax, the Western *Mighty Hunter's Axe* provides many of the same features. The one-piece, carbon steel ax head and handle are powder painted for protection from the elements. Available singly, or in an ax/knife combination sheath, this hand ax is just the right size for most big-game butchering chores. As well, it can be used to chop fire kindling or clear brush.

Muscle Machines: In some situations, you need more than hand tools to get the job done. After one particularly hard snow storm, the dirt track we'd used to get to camp was completely blocked by fallen timber. With a saw or an ax, it would have taken two, or maybe even three days of hard labor to cut my way through what looked like a timber maze. However, with a small chain saw it only took about six hours to make my way out to the main road. If it's legal to use power tools in the areas where you hunt, you might consider acquiring a small chain saw and a carrying case. Make sure

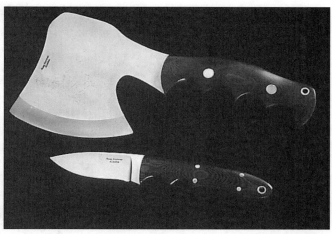

Russ Kommer

Knifemaker Russ Kommer, makes a great Hunter Pak with a compact hatchet from D-2 tool steel and a companion knife with a drop-point pattern blade of ATS-34. Both hatchet and knife feature linen Micarta® handle scales.

you include eye and ear protection, whatever other tools are necessary for chain adjustment, and some means of resharpening the cutting chain.

The Last Cut

There are times that it takes something other than a knife to accomplish a particular cutting assignment. Attempts at splitting or cutting through bone with anything less than the right tool can be an invitation to danger. While it is possible to split an animal's pelvic bone and cut through ribcage cartilage with a knife blade, in most cases a saw or an ax is a better choice. Likewise, trimming off small branches, cutting wood and splitting kindling all place heavy demands on any cutting implement. A serrated knife blade might be able to handle the small stuff, but more often than not, the right tool for the job is a hand ax or a small saw. There are enough choices in either product category that one, or the other, should be part of everyone's game-care and camp gear.

What's the Difference?

Webster's New World Dictionary defines an axe (or ax) as "a tool for chopping trees and splitting wood: it has a long wooden handle and a metal head with a blade usually on only one side." On the other hand, a hand-axe (or hand-ax) is defined as "a stone tool of the Paleolithic period rounded at one end for grasping, and flaked to make sharp edges and a point at the other end." Furthermore, this same word authority defines a hatchet as "a small axe with a short handle, for use with one hand." This means that the tomahawk (or the more concise "hawk") is nothing more than a type of hatchet. The term, "hunter's axe," is one of cutting application, rather than a definition of tool type and a "belt-axe" is an ax small enough to be worn on the belt.

The terms, axe (or ax), hand-axe, hunter's axe, belt-axe, hatchet, and tomahawk (or "hawk') are often used haphazardly by cutlery manufacturers. What is often referred to as a hand-axe is usually a hatchet. Likewise, most belt-axes and hunter's axes are also hatchets. The tomahawk alone seems to have the most precise definition. Unfortunately, the entire nomenclature issue has been clouded over enough to make it confusing to even the informed observer. However, you may call these tools whatever you will—just make sure you have one with you when the need arises.

Big-game trophies are dramatic remembrances of the hunt.

Chapter 16
Trophy Work

Knowledgeable knife work is the first step in preserving trophies and capturing memories.

The stop at Dan Herring's taxidermy shop in Thermopolis, Wyoming, was an annual event. Over the years, Dan has become an occasional companion in the field, as well as a regular consultant on matters dealing with game trophies. When I walked into his shop, this energetic artist was busy removing the head skin from a magnificent whitetail buck.

"Give me minute and I'll be finished," Dan said, never taking his eyes off of the work at hand.

Watching Dan toil, I was amazed at just how quickly he could remove a cape from an animal. From start to finish, I'll wager he didn't take more than four or fives minutes. Of course, he has decades of experience. Even so, watching him deftly wield nothing more than what looked like a slender paring knife was impressive.

After Dan finished with the cape, he wiped the little knife blade on his apron (*de rigueur* attire in the taxidermy business), settled back on his stool and commenced to fill me in on his latest hunting accomplishments. I can't recall at this moment whether it was an African adventure, another trip to Canada for caribou, or just the fact that he'd finally drawn the deer license of his dreams. You see, Dan Herring is not only a skilled taxidermist, he is also an experienced hunter. When it comes to trophy work in the field, as well as in his shop, Dan is definitely "the man."

"What kind of caping knife does a guy need to carry with him?" I asked.

Reaching across his work bench, Dan pulled out a box of inexpensive German-made paring knives. Each knife had the same tiny stainless steel blade and thermoplastic grip. Since they were paring knives, the blade was only about one-third as long as the handle. He picked out a new knife and held it up for my scrutiny. Dan went on to say:

"Some guys use those replaceable blade knives that you can find where model airplanes are sold. Replaceable blades are as thin as a razor blade. A razor-thin edge just doesn't hold up well when you work it hard. This is especially true when you're cutting the cape away from a horn or antler butt. Since you're working close to bone, there's a tendency to muscle the blade a

bit too much. If it breaks during this procedure, you're likely to impale yourself on a broken piece. Believe me—those replaceable blades just don't hold up. What I like best about these little paring knives is that in normal use, they won't break."

Okay, a caping knife blade needs to be tough. It was something I hadn't really thought much about. After Dan mentioned that fact, it became readily apparent. When you remove a head skin cape, there is a significant level of blade edge-to-bone contact. Even in the usual field dressing process this can happen. When you're caping, it happens all the time. When the edge hits the bone, it impacts the integrity of the blade's ability to negotiate the cutting medium. When portions of the edge are repeatedly compromised, this extremity can turn, chip, or even fracture. If this blade failure occurs unexpectedly, there's always the possibility of damaging the cape, or inflicting an accidental injury. Obviously, caping is far more destructive to a blade edge than I really imagined.

"And another thing about knives for trophy work, is that they don't have to be fancy. I go through a lot of knives, so I buy them by the box. In a lifetime, most hunters don't use their knives as much as I do in a single year. If I had a bunch of showy knives around, they would either disappear, or get torn up real fast. Of course, the average guy doesn't cape the number of animals this shop handles. Most hunters will cape, if they have confidence in their ability to do so, no more than one or two animals a season. At that rate, most caping knives will last forever. If you don't use your knife all that much, then you can afford to spend a few bucks to acquire what you want. Personally, I use the heck out of my knives, so it doesn't pay for me to spend a lot on them," Dan said.

My taxidermist friend had hit on another knife feature that is important to many of us—cost. According to him, a knife for trophy work doesn't have to cost the better part of a week's salary. The fact that Dan used simple paring knives made that point very clear. Over the years, I met a lot of guys who owned some real upscale caping knives. The

D. Hollis

When doing trophy work, you will need to use your knife like a scalpel.

fact that they had invested a lot of money in a specialized tool certainly didn't guarantee that they knew how to use it. Even worse, the knife they thought was designed for trophy work often wasn't the right size or shape for the job. It takes more than just calling a knife a "caper" to make it useful in that assignment.

"I use a caping knife like a scalpel. My index finger and thumb are often right on the blade controlling the cutting force. What I like in a caper is a thin, short, almost straight blade, with a sharp point and not a lot of blade belly. Since the blade is small, the handle needs to be long enough to balance like a quill writing pen. I could care less about the artistic design balance between knife blade and grip. What I want in a caper is total functional control of the blade at all times. The length and design of the handle are what makes this possible," Herring went on to say.

In the matter of a few sentences, Dan Herring had encapsulated the essence of a caping knife. Blade shape, length and the relationship of those elements to the handle are all critical to adequate performance. In the case of a caper, the blade should have the characteristics of a medical scalpel, and the length of the knife handle must not necessarily be influenced by aesthetics.

According to Dan, "The final consideration is that you must keep your knife sharp. If you begin to sense that the work isn't going well, then it's time to hit the sharpening stone. Don't put this needful chore off for later. The little time you spend on knife sharpening can save you lots of grief in the long run. A dull knife can make a mess out of a good cape. I have an aversion to hospital emergency rooms and sutures. Having a physician sew me up because of a dull knife isn't my idea of a good time."

Let's look at a representative sampling of caping knives and see how well they stand up to Dan Herring's criteria.

Columbia River Knife & Tool Company (CRKT): The *NECK P.E.C.K.* (Model 2410) is one of CRKT's Precision Engineered Compact Knife models. This slender cutter is made from AUS6M stainless steel and features a Wharncliffe pattern blade just 2.31-inches long. Weighing in at a mere 0.9 ounces, the skeletonized handle has a finger notch along with top and bottom grooves for complete blade command. Available with either plain edge, or a combination edge (50% plain/50% triple-point® serration), this is a serious-edged tool. A molded Zytel® sheath features a locking detent that assures complete carrying security. Molded-in clothing/belt clip fittings at either end of the sheath (clip and attachment screws provided) provide for alternative wearing choices. The ultimate sportsman's scalpel, this little number can handle caping assignments like no other.

Gerber Legendary Blades: The smallest fixed-blade in the Gerber *Pro Guide*™ series is the *Caper* (Model 04268). As the name implies, this knife is specifically designed for caping big-game animals. The 400 series stainless steel, drop-point pattern blade is just 2-3/4-inches long. The full-tang extends completely through the handle and is nearly three times the length of the blade. Handle scales are molded, glass-filled nylon and have a lanyard hole at the end. The knife is contained in a Cordura® nylon belt sheath for a safe belt carry. A rugged knife that can handle the blade stress of working around horn and antler butts, this is a great choice for trophy work.

Ka-bar: In the Ka-bar *Precision Hunter*™ line, the smallest drop-point (Model 1440), would be my choice as a caping knife. This tiny fixed-blade features a 2-1/8-inch, hollow-ground blade crafted from 440A stainless steel and tempered to a final Rockwell hardness of Rc55-56. The Kraton G® thermoplastic elastomer handle is molded directly onto the blade tang. This material is slightly resilient for a non-slip grip and maximum blade control. A top-grain leather sheath with snap closure completes the package. This Ka-bar offering is a great little knife that's big on performance.

174

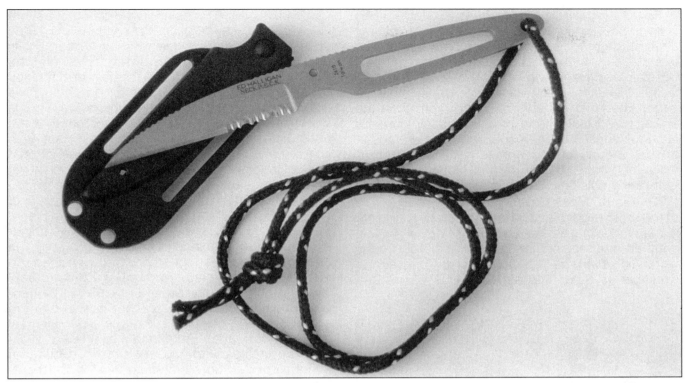

D. Hollis

The NECK P.E.C.K. knife from Columbia River Knife & Tool Company is the ultimate sportsman's scalpel.

Head Skin Removal

This assignment calls for the use of a caping knife. If you're new to the game, then plan on spending a lot of time and some real calories doing the job right. Old hands at caping will peel off a deer cape in about 15-20 minutes.

Step one: Starting at the bottom of the skull, make a "Y" incision that runs up the back of the head and branches to the back of each ear.

Step two: Slide your knife blade under the skin and sever each ear butt flush with the skull.

Step three: Using careful knife work, continue freeing the skin from the head until you reach the eyes.

Step four: Carefully free the skin from around each eye socket, including the tear duct directly in front of the eye. If the animal is a mule deer, you'll have to dig the tear duct out with the tip of your knife.

Step five: Continue peeling skin off until you reach the base of the nose. Sever the nose cartilage at the skull and cut the lips free where they attach inside of the mouth.

Step six: Turn the cape completely inside-out. Use your knife to split the top and bottom lip about halfway through. This will allow the salt to penetrate the lip tissue and prevent spoilage.

Step seven: Turn both ears inside-out, leaving the ear cartilage attached to the front of the ear. This will take a lot of patience, very little knife work, and a flat, slender, blunt-pointed object to separate the back of the ear skin from the cartilage. Some folks use a spoon, a flat stick, or very careful knife work.

Step eight: Once the head skin has been removed from the skin, the lips are partially split and ears turned, then filet off any pieces of meat that remain on the cape. When this has been complete, salt (every nook and cranny), roll and keep cool. As soon as practical, transport the cape to the taxidermist.

There's a lot more to trophy work than just caping. Of course, you'll need a saw to cut the antlers or horns out of the skull. In some instances, you'll have to use both a skinning knife and a caper. This is particularly true when removing the entire skin, including the head cape in a single piece. Laboring with an animal as large as a grizzly bear can be real work. The paws alone are almost as much work as head skin removal. Mountain lion, bobcat, and wolverine are no different, and the same goes for trophy work on African lion and leopard.

Transforming a game animal into a trophy that captures the essence of the hunt isn't easy. The process takes special skill sets, some of which go well beyond the hunter. In this realm, the taxidermist is the person most knowledgeable of the how, what and why of that craft. However, the hunter is the first person on the scene and his or her choice of edged tools is often the deciding factor.

Katz Knives: The *Kitty Caper®* (Model C-5 BB) knife, with its lean profile, 2-1/2-inch, almost straight, drop-point pattern blade, is a fine choice in a blade for trophy assignments. Made from XT-80 stainless steel, with a Rockwell hardness of Rc59, this little sleek slicer can really hold its edge. The knife handle is nothing more than the skeletonized blade tang, precisely sculptured for superior edge management. The knife weighs in at just 2-ounces and comes with a Cordura® nylon belt case. Easily carried along with a primary knife, this tiny marvel is all about hard work.

Knives of Alaska: Designed and tested in one of the most rugged and inhospitable environments in the world, the Alaska *Cub Bear Caping Knife* is another near-scalpel-like edged tool for trophy work. The blade is just 2-3/4-inches long and is available in either 440 series stainless, or high-

carbon D2 steel. The elongated drop-point pattern is available with a plain or combination (50% plain/50% serrated) edge. Double finger choils provide a gripping surface for the thumb and the forefinger. Standard handle scales are molded "Suregrip," with the option of choosing stag. This is an ideal knife design for all of the delicate blade work needed to work effectively around eyes, nose, lips and ears. Newly introduced, the *Alaskan Super Cub* was, according to Company President, Charles Allen, "designed specifically to provide the hunter with a folding caping knife." Measuring just 4-1/4-inches overall when closed, with a 2-1/2-inch long VG-10 stainless steel blade, this is my kind of caper. The knife employs a liner lock to secure the blade in the open position. The blade-mounted opening stud can be switched to either side of the blade for right or left-hand use. Since trophy work can leave the knife with a generous coating of blood and other nasty stuff, the space between the frame liners is wide open for easy cleaning after use. Handle scales are available in the easy-to-grip rubberized "Suregrip" material, or the more high-tech looking G-10 carbon fiber. Need I say more?

Outdoor Edge Cutlery: This innovative cutlery firm makes two knives specifically designed for trophy work. The *Kodi-Caper* (Model KC-1) is a slender, full-tang, fixed-blade caping knife, with a

D. Hollis

The Katz Kitty Caper® weighs just 2-ounces, but it's a heavyweight caping knife with "all the right stuff."

D. Hollis

The Cub Bear Caping Knife from Knives of Alaska is an ideal choice for all of the delicate blade work needed to free the cape skin from around the eyes, nose, lips and ears.

D. Hollis

You'll need considerable patience to skin a full bear hide. The right knife, however, is a real asset.

Caping Basics

No matter the species of the animal, head-skin cape removal is the same. The most important thing to remember is to leave plenty of cape attached to the head. This can be accomplished by cutting completely around the body of the animal, directly behind the shoulders.

Step one: I usually begin the incision at the bottom of the ribcage (this is the point where the initial field dressing incision stopped). Working in a straight line, the cut should run up one side, over the back, down the opposite side, and meet itself at the point of origin.

Step two: Run a cut down the rear margin of both front legs, across the chest at an angle and extending all the way to the bottom of the ribcage.

Step three: Beginning at the top of the back, use your knife to cut forward following the spine, between the shoulders, and along the top of the neck to the bottom of the skull.

Step four: Use your knife to skin the hide free from both side of the carcass, including the front legs, chest, shoulders and neck.

Step five: Remove the head, leaving the cape attached, by cutting around the exposed neck musculature and then severing the spine at the bottom of the skull.

Step six: Roll the cape and head up into a ball and cover it with a cloth bag. If the weather is cold, you can keep the cape and head intact for awhile. If the ambient temperature rises much above 45-degrees, you'll need to skin the cape off of the head and salt it down, or immediately transport the head and cape to a taxidermist.

2-1/2-inch blade crafted from AUS-8A stainless steel. The knife itself measures 7-3/8-inches overall, with over two-thirds of that length consisting of a thermoplastic covered full-tang handle. Finger recesses are located at the blade choil and the leading end of the handle. These provisions for alternative grip locations allow for full hand control or the use of just the thumb and forefinger. Outdoor Edge also produces the T-handle *Game-Caper* (Model GC-20). This knife features a drop-point pattern blade that is just 3-inches in length. A short section of the blade, just behind the leading edge, is serrated to handle tough cutting chores. The handle is encapsulated with a resilient thermoplastic that offers a comfortable gripping surface. Measuring just 5-inches overall, this little caper takes a straight wrist cutting approach to trophy work.

United Cutlery: The United Hunter's Choice *Twin Set* (Model KC40) is made by the famous Kissing Crane cutlery folks, in Solingen, Germany. The trophy-work feature that I like about this fixed-blade paring is that in addition to the main knife, a smaller similarly-designed caper rides along in the same sheath. Both knives are made from high-carbon steel and feature stag handles, brass guards and polished steel pommels. The knives have clip-pattern blades that are 5-inches and 2-7/8-inches long respectively. These traditionally-styled hunting knives are a solid choice for those who prefer carbon steel blades.

Wyoming Knife Corporation: Touted as "the world's most versatile utility knife," the *Wyoming Camp Knife* is just that! While it works well as a small-game, bird, kitchen and steak knife, the cutting forte will be found in trophy work. Made with a slender, hollow-ground, stainless steel blade, along with a pair of equally as slim laminated wood handle scales, this is one of the most scalpel-like capers available anywhere. Supplied with a pouch-type leather sheath that covers both the blade and most of the handle, this handy little knife can be carried on the belt or in the pack. I've caped a whole pile deer, antelope, and several elk with this tiny terror. From that experience came the realization that this is almost the ultimate in caping knife design.

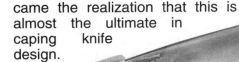

Ed Fowler

This tough little carbon steel caper came from the forge of knifemaker Ed Fowler.

Handmade Caper: Caping knives are not a design in big demand. However, Lynn Griffith is one knifemaker that really understands trophy-work cutlery needs. Lynn makes a full-tang caper from ATS-34 stainless steel, with a drop-point blade just 2-inches in length. The knife handle is nearly three times the length of the blade, and

Russ Krommer

You haven't caped anything until you've had to deal with a caribou. Knifemaker Russ Krommer (pictured here) makes edged tools that can handle every game-care need, from basic field dressing to trophy caping.

features Micarta™ scales with a forefinger cutout for added edge management. The extended handle length of this knife design not only allows optimum cutting control, but also permits the user to impart added edge force when necessary. It's nice to know that at least one knifemaker hasn't forgotten those who perform their own trophy work.

Wyoming rancher and knifemaker, Ed Fowler, forges his fine knives from carbon steel ball bearings. One need only to imagine Ed at work with his hammer and anvil to realize all of the effort that goes into his premium edged products. His *Fawn* fixed-blade model may be small, but that doesn't mean it can't handle rugged caping chores. Featuring a blade of either 2 or 3-inches in length (cus-

tomer choice), brass single guard and sheep horn handle, this little caper is one tough cutter.

Trophy work takes a certain level of knife skill, lots of time and infinite patience. If you don't know what to do, then practice ahead of time. I worked on several non-trophy animals just for experience. When the time came for me to work my first record-book mule deer, I already had the skill sets necessary to accomplish that assignment. If you have a taxidermist in your area, spend some time making a friend out of him. The effort you put into learning how to cape an animal, along with selecting the proper knife for that chore, will insure that you play a knowledgeable part in preserving your own memories of the hunt.

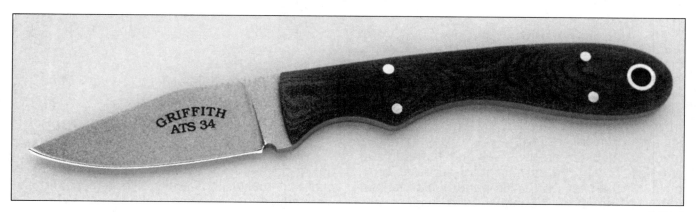

C. Ward

Here is a simply "perfect" caping knife by Lynn Griffith. The ATS-34 stainless steel blade is just 2-inches in length and the Micarta™ handle offers plenty of gripping surface for precise blade control.

Game Bird Trophies

How well I remember my old friend Don Pine spending evenings at home mounting quail, pheasants, and various species of ducks. Wood ducks were his specialty and he really could make those colorful little waterfowl princes come alive. Don was a wildlife biologist for the California Department of Fish and Game and nobody knew game birds any better than he did. His familiarity with birds and their natural habitat was evident in his taxidermy. Since Don was also one of the most serious deer hunters I'd ever known, I once asked him why he didn't focus his taxidermy on big game. "Too much trouble," he replied. Indeed, in many ways primary game-bird trophy care is a lot easier than dealing with big game.

If you decide to mount a game bird, then select one that has the least amount of shot damage. Smooth the feathers out, fold the wings closed next to the body, place the bird in a paper bag (a plastic bag will contain body heat and accelerate decomposition), and close the bag so dirt, debris and insects are excluded. If you can reach your taxidermist in a reasonable amount of time, just keep the bird cool. All the rest can be left to a professional taxidermist. If the weather turns unseasonably warm, then refrigerate the bird carcass. If all else fails, then follow the steps outlined below.

Step one: Make a shallow horizontal incision through the skin, just below the point of the breast. Try to cut between the feathers, rather than through them. Make no effort to remove the visceral material at this time.

Step two: Set your knife aside, and use your fingers to separate the skin from the breast, legs, and back of the carcass.

Step three: Push each leg up and out of the initial opening in the skin until you reach the lowest joint (the beginning of the scaled portion of the leg). Sever the leg at this joint, leaving the scaled portion and the foot attached to the skin. Repeat this procedure on both legs.

Step four: Carefully cut through the fatty tissue that connects the tail feathers to the body. Leave most of this fatty tissue, along with the base of the tail feathers, attached to the skin.

Step five: Carefully turn the skin inside-out, working forward to the wing butts.

Step six: Sever the wings at the joint closest to the body. Leave the wings attached to the skin.

Step seven: Continue peeling the skin off of the body until you reach the neck.

Step eight: Push the head down into the neck and sever the spine at the bottom of the skull. Leave the head attached to the skin.

Step nine: Separate the skin from the carcass (you can now remove the viscera and prepare the carcass as usual).

Step ten: Turn the entire skin, with the head, wings, and feet attached, right-side-out. Smooth all of the feathers out, place in a paper bag and refrigerate until you can transport it to the taxidermist.

On the wall, or under glass (my choice), game bird mounts are dramatic remembrances of those special moments afield. While work, parenting, or some other important responsibility may have kept me out of the field on occasion, the game bird mounts in my home always provided a sense of the hunt. I just remember that it all began with a sharp knife (maybe even a pair of shears) and a little patience.

Looks real, doesn't it? That's what trophy work is all about.

D. Hollis

In addition to a clip-point main blade and a serrated sheepsfoot secondary blade, the Remington Waterfowl folder also carries a choke tube tool and a drift pin punch.

Chapter 17
Bird and Small-Game Blades

Waterfowlers, uplanders and small game hunters are just as much in need of a sharp edge as any big-game hunter.

The weather was about as rough as it gets. The constant downpour all through the night, by first light, had settled down to a fine mist. Most folks would have kept to the confines of home and hearth. To a duck hunter, however, the inclement weather was heaven sent. You see, on those mild days when the sky is as clear as gin, the waterfowl will raft-up and seldom flutter a wing. Without birds in the air there would be no ducks in the bag. This day, however, birds were everywhere. In less than an hour, my hunting companion and I had our limits.

I'll be the first to agree that plucking and gutting ducks is not my first love. But if you're going to hunt waterfowl then it's just part of the game. When my friend pulled his pocketknife out and began to go to work on his limit of birds, I was fascinated. First, the main clip-point blade was used to open the visceral cavity. Holding the duck by the neck, he gave the bird a yank and the guts fell out. Next, an aggressively serrated sheepsfoot blade was used to remove the wings and the feet. It only took a couple of discreet slices with the main knife blade to free the visceral mass from the fowl. Finally, he used a combination of blade and hand manipulation to separate the skin from the bird. The whole process only took a few minutes. In fact, he had his whole limit ready for the ice chest in the time it took me to work my way through two birds.

Afterwards, I received a little cutlery education. My friend had experienced all of the same problems with field dressing wild fowl that I had. Sensing that there had to be a better way, he spent some real calories looking into the problem. His solution came when he noticed a Remington "Waterfowl" knife for sale in the local cutlery shop. All it took was one use to convince him that some ingenious designer had finally put every field-care tool necessary for birds and small game in a single folding knife configuration.

The importance of the knife to the waterfowl, upland bird, and small-game hunter cannot be emphasized enough. Prompt and adequate field care of birds, rabbits and squirrels is as important as it is with big game. Once the internal balance in a living creature is altered through death, tissue deterioration ensues. Ruptures caused by penetrating wounds of the stomach and intestines will spill acid juices into the abdominal cavity. Accelerated by warm weather, or the contained heat of a game bag, or trunk of a vehicle, the growth of bacteria will be unrestrained. If not forestalled by the removal of the compromised viscera, the ultimate result is premature spoilage.

To counter this process, both birds and small game must be gutted as soon as possible. The first and foremost defensive tool to prevent tainted meat is a knife. With the exception of turkeys, geese and swans, most winged game is fairly small. Likewise, only the largest mountain hare will weigh much more than a couple of pounds, and squirrels less than that. This means that there's no need for an overly-large edged tool. A blade no greater in length than the index finger is more than enough to open birds and small game. Additional blades, such as a gut hook, serrated sheepsfoot blade, choke tube wrench, screwdriver, and pin punch are handy tools for the shotgunner to carry, but not necessarily essential.

The choice between fixed-blade and folding configuration for a bird or small game hunter is fairly easy. Since most shotgunning and small caliber rifle hunting takes place on foot, the lightest and easiest carried edged tool possible is the knife of choice. Moreover, the game pursued is small enough to be carried in the back of a hunting vest. One of the reasons why my dad never got very enthusiastic about big-game hunting was he couldn't carry a deer back to camp in his vest! For all of these reasons, pocket folders predominate in the bird and small game hunting venue.

There was a happy occasion when my selection of a small fixed-blade knife was the right choice. It was spring turkey season and I'd tried all morning to convince a reluctant gobbler that my box call was a legitimate love proposal. Like so many of his kind, he steadfastly refused to budge an inch. In all likelihood, the old boy probably had a hen or two of his own. Not wanting to stray from the conquests he'd already made, the gobbler was disinclined to come to the call. With

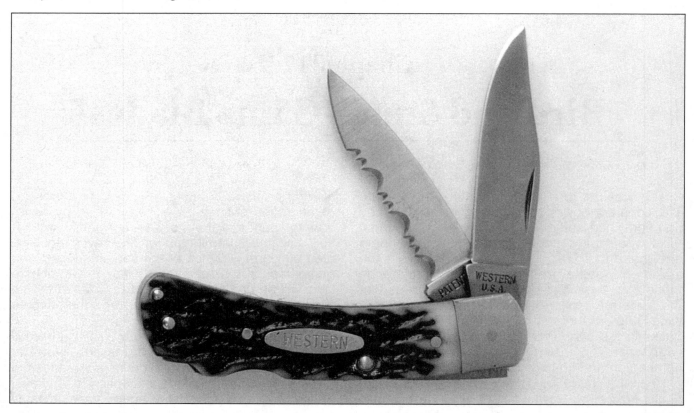

D. Hollis

This handy little Western pocket folder, with its clip-point main blade and serrated drop-point companion, is just the right size for game and wild fowl. Best of all, both blades lock open for safety.

no other prospects available, I persisted with my forlorn love calls on the cedar box.

About the time I started to get edgy about the entire affair, I heard some movement on the other side of a line of brush. Thinking it was the cagey old turkey gobbler, I hunkered-down and prepared for action. To my surprise, a sounder of wild hogs emerged. I always carry a couple of rifle slugs for just such an occurrence, so what happened next was a logical extension of that preparation. Cracking open my double barrel, I traded some magnum #6 shot shells for a couple of solid lead projectiles. About the time a fat young boar crossed in front of me at less than 20 yards, I sent a slug his way.

To abbreviate a much longer chronicle, the ultimate result of this encounter was one bar-b-que pig with all four feet in the air. Fortunately, that day I carried a Grohman, D. H. Russell *Bird & Trout Knife* on my belt. The added size of the blade provided much needed assistance when dealing with field dressing, skinning, and boning out the freshly harvested wild pork. Sure, I could have handled the job with nearly any kind of knife, including the smallest bird knife. It was just more convenient to have a blade with a greater level of versatility.

In some jurisdictions, deer season often runs at the same time as bird season. It's not all that

Jim Matthews

Cottontails can spoil quickly if not field dressed immediately. Always remember to slip a knife in your pocket.

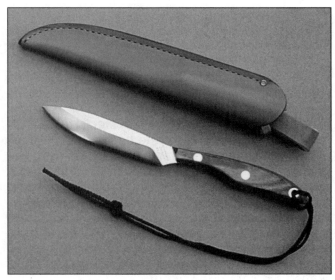

D. Hollis

The Grohmann D. H. Russell Bird & Trout Knife is large enough to do double duty on deer, antelope, and wild boar.

uncommon for a shotgunner to stumble upon a buck at near range. I know, because it's happened to me.

During a quail hunt, I once jumped a nice little buck that stood rock-still not 20 feet away. In reality, I think he was as startled as I was. Fortunately, along with my hunting license, a deer tag was nestled away in my wallet. While the deer had taken me by surprise (or was it the other way around?), I had the presence of mind to see venison chops in the freezer. All it took was a trigger squeeze to put one quail hunter elbow-deep into field-dressing activities. The whole affair proved once and for all that a load of low brass #8 shot can be devastating up close. It's a sure bet that I am not the only one who has taken a buck with a load of bird shot. In that instance, I was certainly thankful that my knife wasn't somewhere back home, or in the glove compartment of the truck. One things for sure, no matter how hard you try, a field-dressed buck deer just won't fit into a quail vest.

In Europe where both wild fowl, small game, and big game can be hunted in the same venue, the drilling evolved. A drilling is just a double-barrel (occasionally other multiple barrel configurations can be seen) shotgun with the addition of a rifle barrel as part of the package. No matter what kind of game they are confronted with, European hunters can handle feathers or fur with equal aplomb. And you'll never find one without a knife—most often a fixed-blade model—on their belts.

While the Remington folder mentioned at the beginning of this chapter is a solid choice for shotgunners, it isn't the only cutlery choice for wild fowl and small game. A glance at the edged product lines of several cutlery firms suggests that

there are other selections to consider in the bird and small game cutlery venue.

A. G. Russell™: This mail order firm carries an excellent fixed-blade *Bird & Trout knife*. Available in ATS-34 stainless (Model AGBT-34), or AUS-8A (Model AGBT-8A) stainless steel, the 3-inch, drop-point blade is just .080" thick—so thin that it slices like a razor! The handle is an injection-molded fiberglass composite that is textured for positive hand contact. The sheath uses a unique Thumbbolt® containment design created by Black Collins. The lock securely holds the knife in place until it is freed by gripping the handle and pressing on the release button. A metal swivel holds the knife to the belt, or pack. Perfect for wild fowl and small game, this tiny wonder weighs less than 2 ounces.

The small, fixed-blade *A. G. Russsell Woodswalker* (Model AGPRS with hip pocket sheath) is designed specifically for bird and small game hunters. The knife weighs 1.2 ounces and measures just 6-inches overall. The high-carbon, stainless steel, drop-point pattern blade is just the right shape and length for a variety of game-care chores. The triple-riveted, dark, laminated wood handle scales are seemingly impervious to environmental invectives. The knife fits snugly into a patented hip pocket sheath that's easily carried out-of-the-way. Both simple in design and well-made, this non-folding pocket knife is a great all-around field tool for waterfowlers and upland hunters.

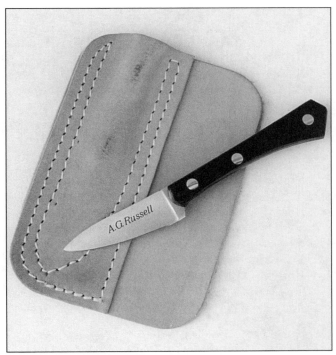

D. Hollis

The A. G. Russell™ Woodswalker is my idea of a handy little knife. The blade is just the right size for rabbits, squirrel, and wild fowl of every kind. The knife fits neatly into a heavyweight leather sheath that fits into the back pocket of your jeans.

Case: The tiny Case *Finn SS* (stainless steel) is a great little bird and small game knife. The slender, 3-inch, straight blade can deal with all the basic field-dressing chores, including cutting through bone joints, sinew, and cartilage. Satin-finished and concave-ground for maximum edge retention when worked hard, the size and design of the blade are just right for rabbit, squirrel, and all manner of wild fowl. A set of stacked-leather-washers forms the handle, and despite the miniature size it offers adequate blade control. Weighing in at a mere 2-ounces, this diminutive fixed-blade is hardly noticeable on the belt.

Cold Steel: This firm makes their own version of a century old cutlery concept. Possessing an incredibly lean outline, this diminutive knife is lighter than most in this category. Made from Carbon V® steel, the blade has a black epoxy powder coat to protect it from the vicissitudes of nature. The blade is just 2-1/4-inches in length and could be characterized as a spear-point pattern. Cold steel has made some subtle improvement in the blade design, providing slightly greater width with a narrower tip than the other versions of this pattern. Likewise, the finger ring at the end of the skeletonized handle has been enlarged. The knife comes with a Concealex™ molded sheath that can be worn in several different ways. Simply

straightforward and easy-to-use, this slick slicer can deal with wild fowl and small game as easily as a limit of trout.

Columbia River Knife & Tool Company (CRKT): This Pacific Northwest firm makes the unique *Stiff K.I.S.S.* that's a fixed-blade adaptation of their highly-successful folding version. Made from AUS-6M stainless steel, the 3-1/2-inch, drop-point pattern blade has friction grooves on the spine's rear that serve as a thumb rest. The knife is available in either a plain or combination (plain/serrated) edge models. Weighing a mere 1.5 ounces, the full-length, skeletonized tang functions as the knife handle. A form-fitting Zytel® sheath completes the package. With the handle wrapped with nylon cord (supplied with the knife), this slick little knife is capable of any bird or small game field-care assignment.

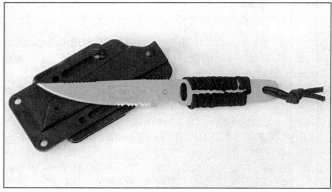

D. Hollis

Light and thin, the Stiff K.I.S.S. from Columbia River Knife and Tool weighs just 1.5-ounces and comes with a molded Zytel® belt sheath.

Grohmann: In this manufacturer's line of D. H. Russell Belt Knives, my choice would be the *Trout & Bird Knife* (Model R2S). Available with either a carbon, or high-carbon stainless steel, the 4-inch, elliptical-shaped blade, this knife is suitable for any angling, upland, or waterfowl game care need. The hand-burnished rosewood handle scales fit naturally into the hand. There's a brass-lined lanyard hole complete with a braided nylon wrist thong. An oil-tanned leather belt sheath provides complete carrying containment. Lean and tough, this is a knife that has earned the respect of outdoor folks on both sides of the Canadian/U.S. border.

Kabar: It's hard to beat a diminutive fixed-blade for bird and small game work. **The Kabar Little Finn** is all that and then some. Featuring a slender, hollow-ground, stainless steel blade, this little knife is hard worker. A brass single guard, aluminum pommel, and traditional stacked leather washer handle finish the design. Supplied with a leather sheath for belt carry, it doesn't get any better than this!

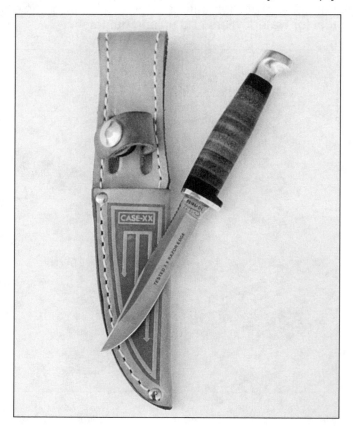

D. Hollis

Hardly noticeable on the belt, this diminutive fixed-blade from Case Cutlery weighs a mere 2-ounces.

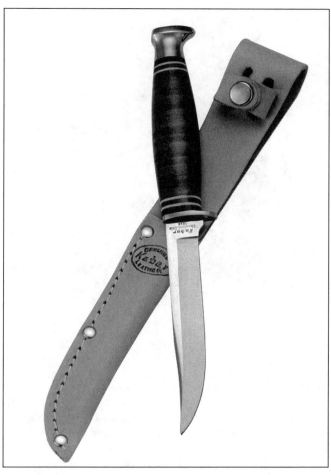

D. Hollis

This Ka-bar Little Finn features a slender AUS-6 stainless steel blade and contoured leather washer handle. Great for both birds and small game, this is a high-performance field tool.

Kershaw kai USA: Realizing that most scatter-gunners occasionally need more cutting power than just a knife, this firm combines their fixed-blade *Bird Knife* in a tandem sheath that holds both the knife and a pair of shears. The knife features a 3-1/2-inch, drop-point pattern blade that is made from AUS-6A stainlesss steel. A thermoplastic handle is molded directly onto the full-length blade tang. Simple and straight-forward in design, this knife is a rugged performer.

Outdoor Edge: I can't say enough good things about this firm's little *Wedge* (Model W6-1) knife. This minuscule fixed-blade offering has a 2-3/8-inch blade that is incredibly functional. Made from 6M stainless steel, the blade is crafted in a broad drop-point pattern. For superior cutting control, the full-length tang has a tear-drop shaped Delrin® handle that easily fits into the hand. The knife snaps into a rugged thermoplastic sheath that is supplied with both a swivel-clip and a length of nylon cord for a variety of carrying options. Lightweight, versatile, and a real serious-edged outdoor tool, this is a knife that any bird or small-game hunter can well appreciate.

Queen Cutlery: Another Lilliputian-sized fixed-blade, the Queen *Game Bird Knife* (Model 85/85A) offers a 3-inch, somewhat elongated, clip-point pattern blade crafted of 440A stainless steel. The simulated stag handle (Model 85), or the yellow Delrin® handle (Model 85A), single guard and bird's head pommel all combine to offer secure control when the knife is in use. At just 6-1/4-inches overall, this slender little wonder has been the choice of many shotgunners over the years.

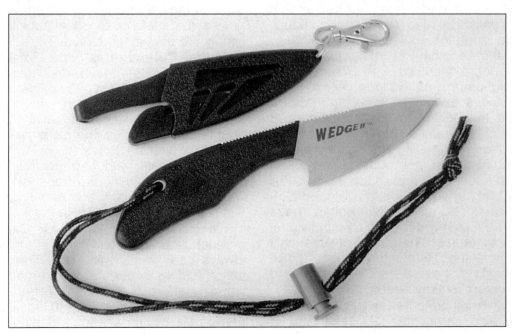

D. Hollis

The Wedge by Outdoor Edge features a drop-point pattern blade that is just 2-3/8-inches long. The teardrop-shaped handle offers non-slip blade edge control.

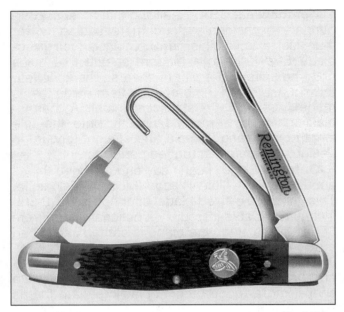

Remington

Designed specifically for upland hunting, this pocket folder by Remington features a choke tool with a screwdriver that handles most 12- and 20-gauge choke tubes. The knife also has a Turkish clip-point main blade and an entrails hook.

D. Hollis

This slender and delicately balanced folder by G. Sakai has the makings of an outstanding small-game and bird knife.

Remington: This manufacturer has jumped into the bird knife arena in a big way. The fixed-blade *Bird and Trout Knife* is an excellent example of this theme. It features a narrow, 3-9/16-inch, hollow-ground, clip-point 440A stainless steel blade. A molded Kraton® handle encapsulates the full-length blade tang, and the non-slip checkered finish is the ultimate in a gripping surface. A lanyard hole at the handle's end allows for the attachment of a wrist leash. A leather belt sheath completes the package. Also, Remington makes a pair of multiple blade folders—*Upland* and *Waterfowl* knives—that combine a main blade with some shotgun tool essentials. The *Upland* folder combines a clip-pattern main blade with a 12/20 gauge choke tool/screwdriver blade, and adds a fowl gut hook. In addition to this assortment of blades, the *Waterfowl* knife also has a serrated sheepsfoot pattern for cutting through bone and cartilage, and a useful pin punch. Two great knives, with blades that are made from 440A stainless steel, along with the same rugged Delrin® handle scales and nickel-silver bolters, have what it takes to effectively deal with their individual game-care assignments. The maker of America's favorite shotgun, the Remington Model 870™ pump-gun, seems to have a handle on bird and small-game hunters' cutlery needs.

Spyderco: In addition to its line of CLIPIT folders, this firm also carries the G. Sakai line of knives. My favorite is the *Road Runner*, a narrow, clip-pattern, lockblade folder. The 2-7/8-inch blade is made from AUS-6A stainless steel, which has

been hollow-ground for ease of blade edge maintenance. The lustrous appearance of the knife is enhanced by the contoured Micarta® handle scales and satin-finished stainless bolsters. A flat Cordura® nylon carrying case keeps the knife close to the belt. Founded in the tradition of Japanese sword making, G. Sakai cutlery products are simply the best of the best.

United Cutlery: This firm's *Small Game Skinner* features a 2-1/2-inch, drop-point pattern cutting blade, crafted from 420 stainless steel. Based on a decades-old design, the skeleton tang serves as the knife handle. A useful little finger-ring is positioned at the tang extension which enhances user control of the knife. A black nylon webbing sheath with a protective plastic insert contains the knife during transport and storage. Extremely light, highly adaptable, and affordable, this slender cutter is never in the way.

Western Cutlery: Part of the Camillus Cutlery product line, Western's edge products have always been well engineered. The Western two-blade, folding *Bird Knife*, pairs an elongated Turkish clip-pattern blade with a European-style fowl gut hook. Both blades are 440 stainless steel, and the handle scales are tough Delrin® plastic in a simulated pick-bone pattern. Closed, this pocket wonder is just a tad under 4-inches in length. The right size, with a blade combination that's suitable

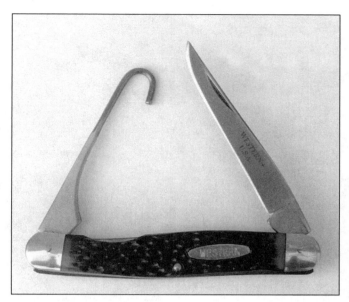

D. Hollis

A typical "bird knife" pattern, this Western folder pairs a Turkish clip-pattern blade with a fowl gut hook.

for both small game and fowl, this little folder is a shotgunners dream.

Handmade Bird Knives

Many handmade knifemakers have developed their own bird knife versions. Some of these edged tools have unique features that make them real "stand outs." Those who want something just a little out of the ordinary might consider one of the following offerings.

John Barlow makes a fine fixed-blade bird knife in 440C stainless steel, ATS-34 stainless steel, or Damascus steel. The 3-inch, drop-point pattern blade is hollow-ground for a fine edge. Interestingly, there's a sharpened slot in the choil area for holding and severing bird wings and legs. The bolsters are 416 stainless steel and offer a shallow finger-grip recess. Handle scales are available in a wide range of materials, but desert ironwood, Micarta® and stag are favorites.

Jarrell Lambert makes a bird knife that is quite popular and capable of handling small or big chores equally as well. Available in either carbon steel or hand-forged Damascus, this knife features a slender, 4-inch, drop-point blade configuration. Dark ebony wood is used for the handle, the guard is 303 stainless steel, and no cap or pins detract from the smooth lines.

Brett Laplante makes a fixed-blade bird knife with a thumb-activated, retractable gut hook that easily slides in and out of a scrimshawed ivory handle. The 4-1/4-inch, 440C, drop-point blade has a modified elliptical shape with thumb-rest file work on the spine. An exquisite piece, this lean knife combines innovative design and functional

operation into a handy game-care tool.

William S. Letcher employs a user-friendly curve on the handle of his bird knife. Crafted from 440C stainless steel, the narrow blade features functional file work on the spine. The nickel-silver bolsters are engraved for an artistic touch, and the laminated wood handle is epoxy impregnated for a durable self-contained finish.

Joe Malloy makes a custom bird knife that comes in a sheath with a laminated "feathered-lizard" facing. This slender, full-tang, fixed-blade knife features a 3-inch blade crafted from ATS-34 stainless steel. The knife has a recessed choil and thumb rest serrations on the blade spine for superior blade control. The Sambar stag handle adds a measure of elegance to an already dramatic-looking knife. Interestingly, the "feathered-lizard" sheath facing is actually tanned chicken-foot skin. After all, scientists are now telling us that the dinosaurs of the past may have had feathers! The common barnyard fowl might just be a descendant of one of those horrible lizards.

Loyd Thomsen makes a magnificent bird knife from Damascus steel. The 2-1/2-inch, drop-point pattern blade is mated with an impala horn handle for a dramatic appearance. The knife itself is only 6 inches in overall length, but in this game-care arena, size isn't all that important. The knife comes in an embossed leather sheath that just reeks of quality. For those who like the look of layered steel, then it doesn't get any better than this.

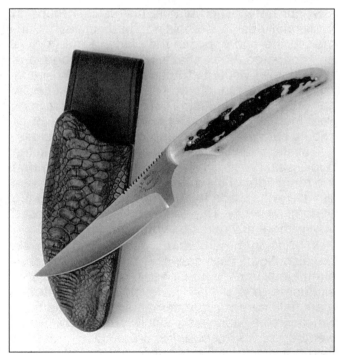

D. Hollis

This custom bird knife by knifemaker Joe Malloy, features a ATS-34 stainless steel blade, stag handle scales and a "feathered lizard" sheath facing.

Even custom knifemakers are into bird knives. The delicate Damascus piece by Loyd Thomsen features an impala horn handle.

In the Field

My best advice is to clean game birds as soon as practical. Furthermore, don't forget to clean out the crop (located at the base of the neck). This is particularly true when field dressing wild turkeys. Left intact, the crop will spoil and taint the breast meat. The same thing is true with all birds, from quail to ducks, woodcock to geese.

Some hunters are bewildered by the use of a fowl gut hook. Such blades are usually found in traditionally-designed folding "bird knives." Situated at the end opposite the blade, a gut hook is an elongated hook that's used to engage and remove fowl viscera. To use the gut hook, simply make a horizontal cut across the skin, just below the point of the breast. Then, insert the gut hook into the abdominal cavity and twist. The hook should catch onto some part of the internal digestive system. Once the viscera are entangled in the hook, simply extract the intestines, stomach and the remainder of the internal organs. You can then use the knife blade to sever any connection to the abdominal cavity. The end result is a field-dressed fowl without any mess on your fingers.

In addition to game birds, rabbits and squirrels are also big hunting draws. There is nothing more sumptuous than either one in a hardy stew, or simmered in a skillet. However, dealing with primary field care is more demanding than wild fowl. Small game can also spoil quickly in warm weather, so it's important to promptly take care of field-dressing activities as soon as possible. If you do nothing more than just immediately open the abdominal cavity and remove the viscera, you'll prevent decomposition from setting in early.

Carry a pair of plastic gloves, along with a few paper towels to assist with clean up. The gloves are essential to not only keep the mess off of your hands, but they also will help protect you from Tularemia, plague, and Rocky Mountain spotted fever. Tularemia is carried primarily by rabbits and is a bacterial disease. The blood and tissue of infect animals can transmit the disease to humans through the skin, mucous membranes and the eyes. Likewise, gloves provide some protection from bubonic plague

Field dressing upland birds and waterfowl is easy. Just make an incision into the abdominal cavity at the point of the breast, then remove the entrails.

D. Hollis

Pheasant are best prepared by skinning and cutting them up into individual wing, leg, and breast pieces.

that is associated with the fleas that can be found on squirrels. Rocky Mountain spotted fever is a tick-borne disease and these arthropods can also be found on both rabbits and squirrels. Aside from helping keep the mess off of your hands, using disposable gloves just makes good health sense.

On the Table

Traditionally, wild fowl are plucked (feather removal). As an alternative, use your knife blade to filet the breast meat off of the skeletal structure. You'll end up with two plump boneless breast meat filets that can be cooked in a variety of ways (cut into strips, rolled and stuffed, or bar-b-qued). It's a lot easier to deal with filets than the entire hassle associated with feather plucking. Some of the older birds, especially sage grouse, can be as tough as old boot leather. Try running the breast meat through a meat grinder, combining it with pork sausage and using it in a meatloaf. In the same vein, sausage made from wild fowl is a real gourmet treat.

The Final Word

My freezer, it seems, has become the repository for a number of unwanted game birds. The usual scenario includes a hasty telephone call from one of my hunt-

ing friends, whose wife refuses to cook the game birds he has brought home. After the fowl are dropped off at my house, it doesn't take too long to figure out why the spouse refused to deal with them. The limit of pheasants that I recently had to handle hadn't been cleaned and were on the verge of spoiling. I don't blame anyone for refusing to handle game in that condition.

Many waterfowl, upland bird and small game hunters don't consider the matter of primary field care very seriously. The same guys who are fanatic about field-dressing big game promptly, somehow fail to manifest the same urgency when it comes feathered and furred game. Most are probably more interested in bagging their limit, rather than taking the time to pursue game-care chores. Even at the conclusion of the hunt, some just toss hunting vest contained game in the back of their vehicle and drive home. Sometimes, the family cat gets to the game before they do. Never forget, the quality of what reaches the table is directly related to the care it receives in the field.

You certainly don't need a specialized knife to deal with wild fowl, rabbits and squirrels. Quite frankly, almost any pocket knife or small fixed-blade can do the job. The advantages inherent in many of the so called, "bird knives," are all of the other blades that can be included in a folding knife configuration. In this age of specialization, it makes sense to carry the right tool for the job at hand. They may not be essential, but additional blades—even tool blades—can deliver distinct advantages. I don't know about you, but when it comes to shotgunning, I need all the *edge* possible!

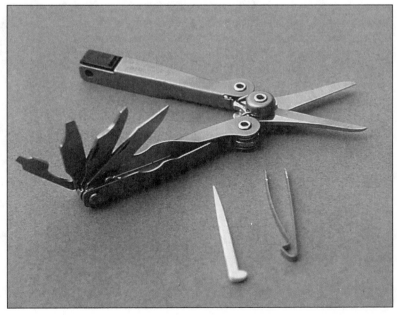

Images Group/Schrade

A compact multi-tool, like this Schrade Tough Chip™ should be on every bird and small-game hunter's belt.

Cleaning a limit of ducks is hard work. The use of a pair of game shears can speed the job.

Chapter 18
Shear Magic

If you want to learn a new trick, then discover the magic in a pair of field shears!

Long before marriage, children and the responsibilities that come with connubial bliss, I was a carefree young man. In those days, hunting was my life. I'd hunt before work, after work, and any other time. Most of the time, I had the right gear. On other occasions, however, I had to "make do." It was during one of these "make do" adventures that I learned about the magic in a pair of shears.

Rabbit season was in full swing. Even better, the cottontail population seemed to be at an all-time high. Not one to forego filling the freezer with a mess of tasty rabbit meat, I hunted bunnies nearly every day. The limit of five rabbits a day necessitated immediate field dressing and skinning. With a sharp knife, the chore took me about 20 minutes to accomplish. And all of the skin, viscera and other body parts not intended for consumption were discarded in the field (after all, the coyotes have to eat every once in awhile).

The scheme of hunting and field care worked well, until the inevitable happened. I absent-mindedly left my knife at home. Even worse, my hunting buddy also didn't have a knife. The ambient temperature was pushing triple-digits, and the prospect of spoiled rabbit meat loomed on the horizon. Scrambling for a solution, we looked in every corner of the truck for a knife. The only edged tool we came up with was a pair of tin snips.

Amazingly, the tin snips handled the rabbits better than any knife. It had always proven difficult to cut through heavy vertebrae and leg joints, but nothing seemed to slow the cutting action of the snips. It was easy to understand, once you realized that the compound leverage provided by the added length of the handles increased the cutting force. The tin snips worked so well, that we had both of our limits of rabbits skinned, cleaned, and cut up in less than fifteen minutes. That was a big improvement over what we had experienced in the past with a knife.

Upon my return home, I searched and searched for something a little more compact than a pair of tin snips. My first selection was a pair of bandage scissors. Those little cutters also worked well, but they didn't stay sharp too long. With no provision to resharpen them, I realized that there had to be a better way. Rummaging around in my mother's kitchen junk drawer (every kitchen has a junk drawer), I came across a pair of Case kitchen shears. Interestingly, the shears had a bone notch in one of the blades. The notch provided a distinct advantage when cutting through joints and vertebrae, and the sharp blades did all the rest. Eventually, I graduated to a pair poultry shears, and then to an actual set of game shears. There must have been a lot of other shotgunners with the same idea, because over time a pair of game shears became a welcome addition to many cutlery lines.

After my initial experience with the rabbits, I began to try the shears out on other game. Inter-

D. Hollis

It's certainly a lot easier to cut through tough wing and leg joints with a pair of game shears.

191

D. Hollis

Jack rabbit or cottontail, field dressing, skinning and cutting the meat into meal-size portions are best handled with a pair of game shears.

estingly, there wasn't anything with fur or feather that a pair of game shears couldn't handle quicker and easier than a knife. And I wasn't the only one who realized this. I preached game shears to all of my hunting buddies, and after one use they too became converts. Always one to experiment, I even used the shears on a limit of trout. Well, I can testify to the fact that game shears clean trout as easily as any knife. Especially because the shears put a little distance between the user and the game being cleaned. This alone prevents the resultant mess from getting on your hands, clothing and gear. Simply put, game shears were, and are, a better way to go.

There are several different types of game shears on the market, each with its own individual strength. Let's review a selection of these useful tools and see if there's one that might catch your interest.

Buck Knives: This firm makes a pair of *Utility Shears* (Model 815) that are as useful in the field as they are in the kitchen. Measuring 7-1/2-inches overall, these shears feature stainless steel construction, a take-apart design, and molded thermoplastic handles. A multiple-featured tool, these

shears have screwdriver blades at the end of each handle, as well as a bottle opener and jar lid pry feature. Easy-to-clean and rugged enough to cut through bone, cartilage and gristle, these shears are indispensable field tools.

Case Cutlery: The Case *Multi-Purpose Shears* are chrome-plated for rust resistance. The take-apart design allows the user to easily clean up the shears after use. The additional features, like cap lifter, jar lid pry opener, and a narrow hammer face, all combine to make this one handy tool. Just 8-1/4-inches overall, these shears come with or without a leather carrying sheath. In camp, or in the home, these shears can handle a mess of quail, or a limit of rabbits with equal assurance of successful job completion.

Columbia River Knife & Tool Company (CRKT): I hate it when a good product is no longer in production. Unfortunately, this is just what happened to the CRKT shears. I have a friend who has a pair and he won't part with them at any price. The take-apart design, stainless steel construction, and molded handles are hard to beat for functional application. A solid product, but one that has apparently been withdrawn from the market.

EdgeCraft Corporation: The Chef's Choice® *Kitchen Shears* and *Poultry Shears* are both top-quality, forged shears. Designed to handle rugged cutting chores, the cutting edges are long-lasting and easily resharpened when needed. The all-stainless steel construction provides easy cleaning and superior rust resistance. You can find both of these products in my home, and my camp kitchen. Need I say anymore?

CRKT

Not only does Columbia River Knife & Tool Company make fine knives, at one time they also made an excellent pair of stainless steel game shears.

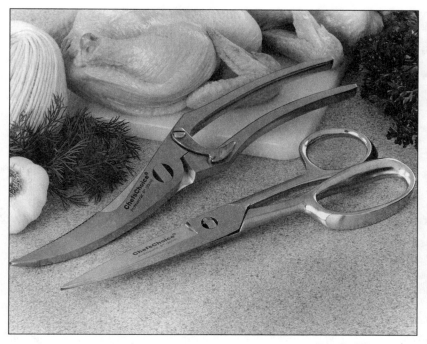

The all-stainless steel construction of the Chef's Choice® Poultry (top), or Kitchen (bottom) shears, combined with their take-apart design, provides for simple maintenance of these rugged shears.

The Kershaw Sportsman Shears can handle small game, fowl, and when taken apart—the drop-point guthook blade is a functional big-game field-dressing tool.

Gerber Legendary Blades: The Gerber *Shear and Sheath Set* (Model 46001) features stainless steel construction and serrated cutting blades with an integral bone notch. Measuring 9-1/4-inches in length, these shears fit nicely into their Ballistic Cloth® carrying sheath. At home, or in the field, these handy shears can make quick work of small game and birds, as well as a whole host of other heavy cutting chores.

Kershaw: This cutlery firm makes a pair of AUS-6A stainless steel *Sportsman Shears* (Model 1130) that features resilient thermoplastic handles for added comfort in use. Measuring 7-1/2-inches overall, this is a serious-edged tool that can maneuver its way through any tough cutting assignment. Interestingly, the shears unhinge and one half quickly becomes a drop-point knife with a guthook feature.

Recently, a friend of mine came across a deer that had a run-in with a truck. Laying beside the road, the animal had just expired. He telephoned the game warden on his cell phone and requested permission to salvage the carcass. The warden met him at the scene, certified that the deer had been accidentally killed by a vehicle (there was a serious paint scrape on the antlers), and released the animal to my friend. The only thing resembling a knife that my buddy had with him was a pair of these Kershaw *Sportsman Shears*. He then promptly unhinged the shears and used the knife half as a field-dressing tool. Every salvageable scrap of venison went into the freezer and the Kershaw shears made it all possible.

Kershaw also makes a pair of *TaskMaster Shears* (Model 1120S) that are crafted from AUS-6A stainless steel. These shears have a

Small-Game Cooking Hints

Even the toughest jack rabbit or stringy squirrel can be tenderized in a pressure cooker. Rinse the meat thoroughly and place in the pressure cooker. Follow directions for cooking whatever quantity of meat is being prepared. Serve with gravy, over a bed of brown rice, add a helping of summer squash, and you will discover a taste treat that is a delight to the taste buds.

As an alternative, filet the meat off of the bone, grind and mix with a quantity (25%) of pork sau-sage, add spices, stuffing mix, egg and form into a loaf. Place the loaf in an appropriate size pan and bake for 60 minutes. The resulting meat loaf will be delicate and light, without the loud flavor of beef.

Young cottontail rabbits and squirrels can also be battered (beer batter works great), seasoned, and pan fried. Use care not to overcook the meat. Serve with rice, home fries and a salad. Get prepared for a real gourmet treat.

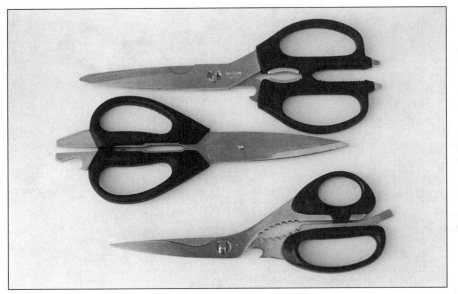

D. Hollis

Here's a trio of shears from Kershaw (top), Schrade (middle), and Buck Knives (bottom). Any one of these handy cutters is able to effectively deal with a host of home, camp and field chores.

useful bone notch in one cutting edge that makes bird and small game work a delight. Other features, like a bottle opener and screwdriver tips at the end of each handle, add functional utility to an already great tool. Even better, the rubbery thermoplastic handles are easy on the hand. For carrying in the field, the shears come with a leather sheath.

Normark: Combining power leverage with super-sharp blades, the Normark *Game/Fish & Fowl Shears* can make short work of anything with feathers or fur. The precision-serrated blades are crafted from stainless steel and can hold the cutting medium firmly in place. The blades quickly detach for cleaning in the sink or dishwasher. The thermoplastic handles are comfort-designed for cutting ease. A snap-closed leather sheath, with an extra wide belt loop, is supplied with the shears. A fine cutting tool for the bird and small game hunter, the Normark shears are hard to beat.

Remington: Until very recently, Remington listed a pair of traditionally-styled kitchen shears in their catalog. Chrome-plated steel with all the usual features (a bottle opener, hammer face and jar lid pry opener), these shears are great for the home, or the camp kitchen. And the shears are easily taken-apart for quick cleaning. It seems as if this product might have also been taken off of the market, but you probably can still find a pair somewhere. If you do, don't hesitate to get your hands on them.

Schrade: In their Imperial Apex® line this cutlery manufacturer lists a pair of *Wilderness Utility Shears* (Model AP8). Made in Schrade's manufac-

turing facility in Ireland, this pair of shears is on the mark for serious performance. Featuring a stainless steel blade that can handle a wide range of tough cutting mediums, these shears are just right for game care chores. The molded thermoplastic handles enable the user to apply added force without discomfort. Furthermore, the shears have other integral functions (screwdriver, cap lifter, bottle/jar opener) built into their design. Well made and affordably priced, these shears are backed by a solid 10-year warranty.

The Angler's Friend

Game shears are just as useful for anglers as they are small game and bird hunters. I've used shears on trout, catfish, largemouth bass, and several different species of saltwater fish. For example, catfish have some very nasty spines in their dorsal and pectoral fins. If you've ever put one of these barbs into your hand, you'll know what I am talking about. It seems no matter how I handle whiskerfish, I end up with at least one puncture wound that seems to take forever to heal. Now, I just cut the spiney fins off flush with a pair of game shears, and then continue on with my usual field-dressing activities. In addition to a fillet knife, a pair of shears ought to be in every angler's tackle box.

Other Uses

More times than I can remember, a pair of shears has come in handy with vehicular repair. It never seems to fail that something untoward happens to the truck or motorhome on the way to and from hunting camp. Some of these breakdowns involve engine cooling system failure. It can be difficult to find the right size hose in a one-horse town. You can cut the right size in any junkyard, however, if you have a pair of shears. Shears can also cut aluminum trailer siding, duct tape, wire, and you name it.

In many instances—small game, wild fowl, some fish, and other heavy duty cutting assignments—a pair of shears can be the best choice. I have found shears to be an invaluable outdoor cutting asset. My only problem is keeping them out of the kitchen and in my hunting gear where they belong. You try explaining it to my wife, but then that's another story entirely.

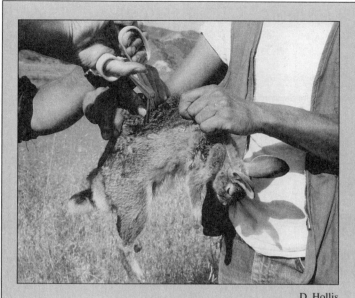

D. Hollis

Make a small incision at the mid-point of the animal's back.

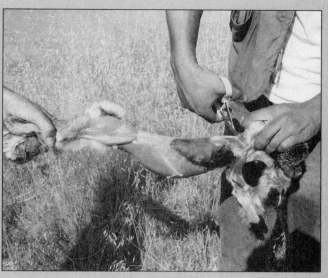

D. Hollis

Cut the head, tail, and all four paws free and discard along with the skin.

D. Hollis

Insert your fingers into the skin and pull in opposite directions.

D. Hollis

Use the tip of the shears to cut into the abdominal cavity and then up through the rib cage. The internal viscera can then be easily removed.

Ten Steps to Easy Small-Game Care

Step One: Make a small incision into the skin on the animal's back.

Step Two: Insert a couple of fingers into the incision and pull in opposite directions.

Step Three: Continue to pull the skin down to the tail, and up to the skull's base. Peel the skin down to the last joint on each of the four legs. Sever the tail, head, and each of the four paws free from the carcass. Discard the skin.

Step Four: Snip a small opening into the abdominal cavity. Make a lengthwise slit in the abdominal wall, extending this cut all the way up through the middle of the ribcage. Scrape out all of the internal organs, using the shears to snip any adhesions.

Recommendations: Cut the forequarters, hindquarters, and lower back (loin area) into individual pieces and place them in a plastic bag. Discard the ribcage. When you return home, remove the rabbit or squirrel pieces from the plastic bag. Use running water to clean the meat. Place the pieces in a bowl or other receptacle. Cover the meat with a combination of cold water and cooking wine (this will help tenderize the meat) and refrigerate. If the meat isn't used within a reasonable amount of time (3-4 days), remove from this solution, rinse, place in a plastic freezer bag and freeze. The frozen meat should be used within a four to six-month time period.

The most important prerequisite of big-game field-care is a sharp knife.

Chapter 19

On Edge

A sharp knife is accident prevention in action.

It never ceases to amaze me just how quickly a dull knife can inflict a serious injury. One would think that dull connotes an inability to perform in the prescribed manner. Given this fact, a dull knife should, therefore, be incapable of cutting. Unfortunately, in the real world, things don't work like that. Impart enough force to a dull knife blade and it will carry out its intended assignment. With a sharp blade a measure of cutting control is possible. The sharper the edge, the greater the level of performance management. Conversely, a dull blade becomes increasingly more unmanageable as usage continues. The issue of manageability becomes a factor when the edge deteriorates beyond the containment envelope of acceptable performance. It is here, in an unmanageable arena, that the knife user enters a potentially dangerous performance zone.

A few deer seasons ago I stepped right smack in the middle of the dangerous knife performance zone. I knew that it was possible that an untoward event, causing serious physical injury, had the potential to occur. However, possibility and potential are entirely different phenomenons. Possibilities deal with such issues as averages, odds, and mean points of occurrence, while potential centers solely on capability. Any knife has the capability of inflicting injury. The possibility of such an event is directly proportionate to blade edge integrity and safe handling practices. If the edge becomes increasingly compromised, and safety practices are overlooked, then the likelihood of an unplanned incident increases proportionately to the usage time line. Fundamentally, if something can happen it will—and when it does, expect the worst. In my case, the worst was a serious laceration, lots of blood, more pain than expected, and lots of sutures. However, let's back up to the beginning.

It was opening day of California's central coast deer season. Not long after daybreak, I took the opportunity to validate my deer tag with a fat forked-horn buck. It's hot during this early season, with midday temperatures often reaching triple-digit figures. To ensure that the venison remained in top shape, I quickly field dressed the animal. Since it was a couple miles back to the main ranch house, I decided to skin the carcass, bone-out the meat and haul it out in my pack.

Everything went as planned. My knife sailed through one cutting chore after another without the slightest hesitation. It was a beautiful day, I had punched my deer with little effort, and now the meat was under refrigeration. Things couldn't have been better—right! After lunch, a dip in the nearby river, and a snooze, it was time to finish the job. Assembling a cutting board, some meat wrapping paper, and my knife, I began to further cut up and wrap the venison into kitchen-ready packages.

The project was going so well, that I didn't think about blade edge maintenance. Nearing completion, the blade began to drag a bit. Overconfidence can be a deceptive demon. I had confidence, too much so, in my own ability to push the blade right on through to project completion. Nothing could have been farther from reality. Working too fast, I didn't watch where my left thumb was positioned. When the edge stalled in the meat, I muscled the blade a bit too much. Since edge integrity had already been compromised, the knife uncontrollably lunged right through the venison. Unfortunately, the blade edge also made direct contact with my left thumb.

Right off, I knew the cut would take more than a Band-Aid to close. If there was a question, what seemed an unstoppable upwelling of blood removed any doubt. I wrapped the wounded appendage up in a towel and headed off for the nearest hospital, nearly 50 miles away.

Upon my arrival in the hospital emergency room, the nurse whisked me into a treatment area. You can imagine my embarrassment when the physician walked in wearing his hunting boots, a pair of jeans and a blaze orange shirt. The doctor was a deer hunter—just my luck!

"Don't tell me. Let me guess. You cut yourself with a dull knife?" the doctor inquired.

I went on and told my sad story. The doctor just smiled. As it turned out, my case would be one of many similar lacerations that he would be suturing during the six-week deer season. Apparently, there were more deer hunters with dull knives

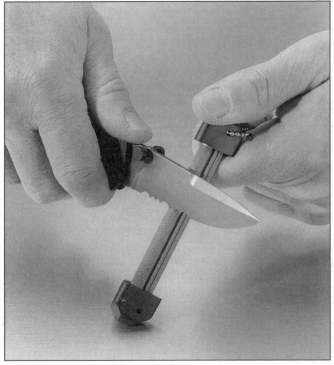

Jim Bush/GATCO

The GATCO Tri-Steps knife sharpener can handle both plain and serrated blade edges. Made from alumina ceramic, this tiny sharpener is a must-have for any outdoors person.

than you'd imagine. After it was all over, I didn't know which was worse—my damaged pride or my wounded body. One thing was for sure, the thumb looked like it came out second best in a fight with a Singer sewing machine!

I'll agree. Knife sharpening is a nuisance. However, until someone discovers a material that never needs sharpening, the need for edge maintenance isn't going to go away. If you use a knife for very long, at some point in time you'll find yourself involved in edge restoration activities. The success of that effort will be directly related to what you use and how you use it.

There is a virtual plethora of knife-sharpening tools on the market. For the sake of clarity, most of these implements can be divided into the following categories: sharpening steels, sharpening rods, whetstones (natural and manmade), clamp-on edge guides, edge-angle tools, edge-angle fixture tools, and electrically-powered sharpeners. Depending on the particular product, some sharpeners are simple. Others are more complex demanding assembly before use. And with some, the need for a power source is inevitable.

I've used every one of the aforementioned types of sharpeners, and have been satisfied with the results achieved. In some venues, however, certain types of sharpeners work better than others. For example, it's hard to find a place to plug-in an electric sharpener in the backcountry. In the

woods it's also easy to lose things. If a particular type of knife sharpener has several component parts, even if contained in kit form, it's possible to lose something. Without a critical sharpener element, you may be out of business!

Sharpening Steels: If you watch the butcher in your local supermarket, you'll see him repeatedly work his knife blade across a round sharpening steel. Most butchers have their knives sharpened regularly by a commercial sharpening service. A sharpening steel performs very little abrasive sharpening. Its forte is edge alignment. When a knife is initially sharpened, the resultant edge is generally very thin. Over time, the thin edge becomes rounded by contact abrasion, chipping, or being bent or turned away from the center. The act of "steeling" actually helps keep the edge straight. To be effective, the sharpening steel must be used at regular intervals, or at the first sign of edge deterioration. I view the sharpening steel as an interim edge-maintenance tool, rather than an actual edge-restoration device.

There is one kind of steel that really does sharpen. This is a rod coated with tiny diamond particles, set into a hand-held tool. These rods are

D. Hollis

Working on a wild boar in the field will quickly erode the best blade edge. A pocket sharpener is an absolute necessity.

198

A pointed diamond-coated sharpening rod can handle every kind of knife edge, plain or serrated.

made in a variety of sizes, from full-size models an inch or more in diameter for professional butcher use to shorter lengths in smaller diameters for field use. With the widespread acceptance of serrated and combination edge knives, most of the smaller diamond rods feature a tapered tip for sharpening scalloped serrations. Likewise, these little wonders work well on guthooks. To restore an edge, hold your knife securely and engage the edge at a slight angle (20-22 degrees) with the rod. Maintaining the angle, work the sharpener along the length of the edge in tiny circles, alternating from one side of the blade to the other. At first, you'll feel the diamond particles dig into the edge, but after a couple of passes with the rod, things will smooth right out. The longer you work on the edge, the smoother it will be. Lightweight, with a low profile, and extremely efficient, a diamond-coated sharpening steel is often my own personal choice for field use.

Stone Abrasion: The oldest sharpening methodology is stone abrasion. There are two kinds of whetstone material—manmade and natural. Manmade whetstones are nothing more than abrasive granules bonded together into a functional configuration. Natural whetstone material is basically silica quartz crystal. Known as novaculite (from the Latin *novacula*, meaning "razor"), this material was originally marine sediment deposited during the Devonian and Mississippian geological periods (405-345 million years ago). The tiny crystal nodules are similar to diamonds in hardness, but less abrasive with enhanced polishing qualities. Encompassed in a 20-mile radius of the town of Hot Springs, Arkansas is the largest known deposit of novaculite. The firms of Smith's Abrasive, Washita Mountain Whetstone, and others have been mining novaculite for decades in this area.

Whether manmade or natural, whetstones come in several different sizes (pocket to bench), shapes (rectangular, round, and triangular) and abrasive quality (coarse to soft). The abrasive quality or grit can range from extremely granular (soft) to exceptionally minute (hard). Depending on sharpening needs, one or more different grits may be needed for edge restoration. Whetstones are produced with an absolutely flat surface, or sharpening bed. Over time, this surface wil! erode and become "dished-out." Since the sharpening bed is no longer flat, it can exacerbate the problem of maintaining a consistent sharpening angle.

Whetstone sharpening is traditionally performed by repeatedly stroking the blade edge back and forth across the abrasive sharpening bed, alternating sides on each pass. The most important element in this process is the consistency of the edge-to-stone presentation angle. Freehand sharpening depends entirely on eye-hand-coordination to replicate this angle across the entire length of the sharpening bed. If this angle is not replicated accurately during the sharpening process—a significant challenge in

A natural whetstone, like this Tri-Hone by Smith's Abrasives, is one of the oldest and most reliable methods of edge restoration.

and of itself—then the edge is both gained and lost during each abrasive stroke across the stone.

Stone sharpening is popular because the process is simple, relatively safe and effective. Furthermore, whetstones are affordable and last for many, many years. I still use the same bench-size whetstone that my father purchased more than 75 years ago. Sure, it's a little "dished-out" in the middle, but if you use the right technique, that old piece of Devonian deposit can still do the job. A small pocket stone is a handy field sharpener. Rather than attempting to stroke the blade edge across the stone, try an alternative approach. Lay your knife down flat and stroke the stone across the edge. If you have a hard time maintaining the same angle while sharpening, move the blade edge across the stone (or vice versa) in tiny circles, switching sides on every pass. I've found it easier to maintain consistent edge-to-blade angle contact using this approach.

The natural whetstone is Mother Nature's answer to knife sharpening needs. A manmade product isn't a lot different. If you prefer tradition to technology, then a whetstone may be your "cup of tea." Full-size whetstones are too big and heavy for field use, but a slender pocket stone is a welcome companion. Priced affordably and widely available, the whetstone is often the preferred edge-restoration tool.

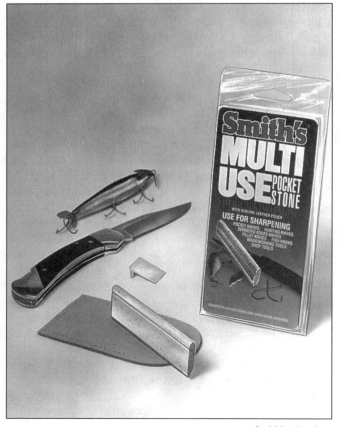

A portable pocket stone, like this 4-inch model from Smith's Abrasives, is just the ticket for field use.

Edge Guides: An excellent adjunct to whetstone sharpening is a clamp-on edge guide. When attached to a blade, the guide positions the edge at a predetermined edge-to-stone sharpening angle (most edge guides are adjustable to different presentation angles). This takes all of the freehand guesswork out of stone sharpening. Simply clamp the edge guide to the knife blade and sharpen away. I don't care how much experience you've had whetstone sharpening. It's not humanly possible to maintain a precise edge angle throughout the entire sharpening process. You may only vary the angle slightly, but any deviation will detract from edge precision. The use of an edge guide eliminates any possible angle variance and works every time, on any abrasive surface. Whether you're a novice knife sharpener, or an old pro at the game, an edge guide can obviate both experience and skill level. Believe me. It's a better way to go.

Edge-Angle Sharpeners: Affectionately referred to in the cutlery industry as "drag-and-scrape" tools, this edge restoration tool is the ultimate in speed sharpening. The sharpening task is accomplished by means of a pair of tungsten-carbide tips set in a hand-held tool, at a previously established sharpening angle. To restore a dull knife, you actually scrape a new edge with the sharpening tips. The end result may be somewhat ragged, but the new edge will be sharp. Even though sharpeners of this ilk are extremely efficient, they are also profoundly erosive. If you opt to use one, over time, you will see a marked difference in

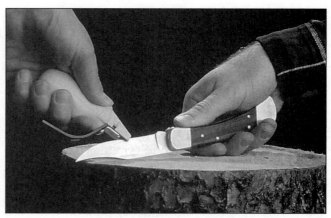

Creative Sales

The carbide tips in the "drag and scrape" type of hand-held sharpener actually scrape a new edge on the blade.

blade geometry (the sharpener will actually strip metal off of the blade edge). I might be reluctant to use this kind of sharpener on an expensive handmade knife. Nevertheless, when daylight is fading and I need an edge fast, then this is the tool for the job. The hand-held *Super Sharpener*, by the folks at Creative Sales & Manufacturing, as well as the *Accusharp* sharpener by Fortune Products, and Smith's *Jiff-V-Sharp*, are representative samples of this technology.

Edge-Angle Fixture Sharpeners: Several manufacturers produce knife-sharpening tools that feature fixture-mounted edge-restoration material. The fixture pre-establishes the edge-to-abrasive contact angle, and the user only has to pass the blade edge across the abrasive, or the abrasive

Spyderco

The Spyderco Triangle Sharpmaker uses triangle-shaped alumina ceramic abrasive stones, set into keyed holes and slots molded into the polymer base. No lubrication is required for mess-free sharpening.

over the blade, to produce the desired effect. The so-called "V" hone is an excellent example of this category of knife sharpener. This category of edge restoration tool mounts lengths of abrasive material (stone, ceramic, diamond-coated, etc.) into angled holes in a freestanding base. To use this sharpener, the knife blade is drawn vertically down and across the abrasive medium, alternating sides on each pass. If the sharpener is used properly, the pre-established angles into which the abrasive material is mounted create a consistent sharpening angle on either side of the edge. The only variable is that the blade must be held absolutely vertical when the edge is passed over the abrasive medium.

An alternative approach, which is manifest in knifesharpeners marketed by Lansky, Great American Tool Company (GATCO), Diamond Machine Technology (DMT), and others, clamps the knife blade into a fixture. The abrasive is mounted on a base with an extension that can be inserted into an angled slot in the fixture. To effect sharpening, the user holds the fixture-attached knife in one hand and passes the abrasive over the blade edge with the other hand. Usually, the sharpening fixture, various abrasives, and lubri-

cant are all contained in a carrying kit. For fear of losing one of the sharpener pieces, I probably wouldn't use this type of tool in the field. At base camp, in a trailer, motor home, or similar location there is far less chance of misplacing one of the individual kit components. Regardless of how the knife is held, or the abrasive presented, this type of sharpener is without peer for superior edge production.

Other Choices: Another method of edge sharpening employs a set of fixture-mounted, roller-stone and abrasive wheels. The fixture is held in one hand, while the knife blade is drawn through the wheels. The blade's movement across the abrasive causes the wheel to rotate in opposite directions. This combination of movements reestablishes the proper edge angle. Some of this class of sharpeners features two-stage edge restoration. The first step straightens the old edge and establishes a new angle on both sides concurrently (not unlike the "drag and scrape" approach). The next step establishes a secondary bevel and polishes the edge. The fixture is made from a rugged thermoplastic that is almost indestructible, and the abrasive roller-stone wheels last forever. (Okay, how about, you'll never wear them out?) The Edgecraft *Manual Diamond Hone* (Model 450), and the McGowan Manufacturing *Firestone Two-Step Knife Sharpener* (Model 11302), are both representative samples of this sharpening approach.

The folks at Diamond Machine Technology (DMT) have for several years marketed sharpeners that feature a perforated nickel plate with monocrystalline diamond particles fused directly on the flat surface. Available in all traditional whet-

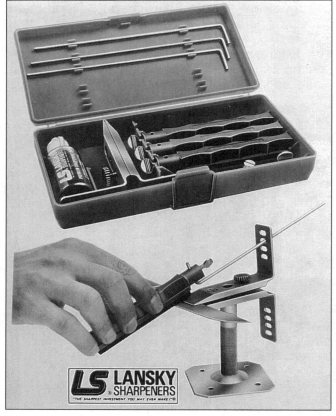

Lansky

The Lansky Three Stone Sharpening System features a multi-angle, flip-over knife clamp, a selection of different abrasive hones, lubricant, and a molded case that holds all of the components.

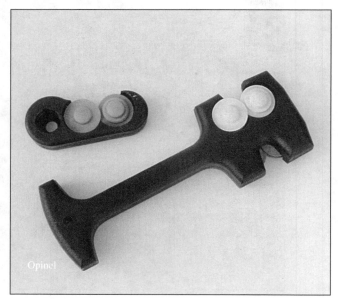

D. Hollis

The Firestone roller-stone sharpeners from McGowan Manufacturing quickly establish a new blade edge at the proper angle.

DMT Technology

The DMT Diamond Whetstone™ is available in full-size and pocket models, several different abrasive grits, and works with just a few drops of water as a lubricant.

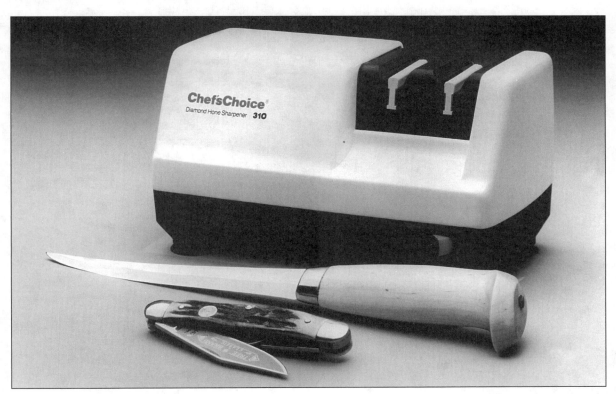

Edgecraft Corp.

When you really want to get serious about knife sharpening, then "Power Up." The Chef's Choice® Multistage Electric Sharpener (Model 310) uses patented "orbiting diamond" sharpening plates, magnetic blade guides, in a two-stage process that produces an incredibly sharp, long-lasting edge.

stone sizes and in fixture sharpeners, this type of abrasive surface provides rapid edge restoration. The other feature I like is that the perforations in the sharpening surface catch and hold the ground-away material (fines). This prevents the sharpener from clogging-up as edge maintenance proceeds. This firm's *Diafold* model features an attached handle that folds to contain the sharpener when not in use.

Power-Up: Electric knife sharpeners have been around for a long time. The problem with most is the fact that the sharpening wheel revolves so fast that the abrasive effect produces considerable heat. Enough heat, in fact, that the sharpener compromises blade hardness along the length of the edge. I guess these kitchen marvels worked all right on inexpensive kitchen cutlery (there's not much harm that can be done there!). Anyone that treasures their knives, however, should avoid these blade eaters like the plague.

Today there is a new generation of electric knife sharpeners, which don't affect blade integrity. This is a blessing for those of us (and that should be everybody) who demand sharp knives. Edgecraft makes the popular *Chef's Choice* electric sharpener that's the best I've ever used. The secret to this device is the paired diamond-coated plates that pass over the blade edge in a figure-eight pattern at slow speed. No matter how long you spend working on your knife (it takes only a few minutes to achieve a razor-edge), no heat will be produced. Furthermore, a strong magnet holds the blade at a precise edge-to-abrasive angle throughout the entire sharpening procedure. You don't have to muscle your blade through the sharpening procedure. In fact, a light touch works best. One use and you'll be amazed at how easy knife sharpening can be with this plug-in edge restoration miracle worker.

The Final Cut

There are several reasons why some knives cut better than others after they're sharpened, even if all are subjected to the same edge restoration methodology. The characteristics inherent in the

Edgecraft Corp.

The Chef's Choice® 2-Stage Manual Diamond Hone™ (Model 450), assures razor-sharp edges by using two different pre-angled sharpening slots, each with its own special diamond abrasive.

blade material, the degree to which these properties are enhanced by heat treatment and edge geometry are all factors that influence the ability of a sharpener to perform its assigned task.

Freehand knife sharpening is a skill that must be repeatedly practiced to be learned. Unfortunately, few have the time and patience to acquire this skill. I have a friend Don, who has experienced so much failure at the task, he has given up knife sharpening entirely. Rather than trying to hone a dull edge to an acceptable cutting level, he just buys a new knife! At last count, he had more than two dozen dull knives. I guess there's more than one way, albeit an expensive method, of avoiding knife sharpening.

Because freehand knife sharpening is such a challenging task for most, methods to overcome the edge-to-abrasive angle problem have devel-

oped. In this chapter we've discussed several tools that go a long way toward improving anyone's competency. None of us have the same level of eye-hand-coordination. For this reason alone, what works for one may not provide suitable satisfaction for someone else. Moreover, edge restoration needs may be manifest at home, in camp, or at a backcountry locale. No single sharpener is best in all situations.

If a knife is sharp, the cutting energy is focused at the apex of the paired edge angles. The edge of a dull knife, having been eroded by contact abrasion, is several times wider than a sharp edge. Because energy is focused over a wider area, it takes greater force to overcome resistance. Furthermore, the movement of a dull edge is less predictable. This is why a dull knife is an accident waiting to happen!

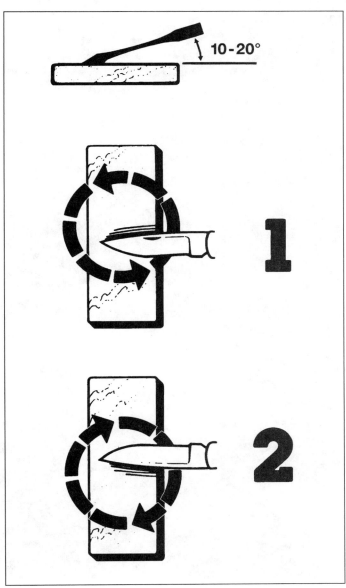

Knife sharpening is easy and quick if you use the right method. Step One: Establish a sharpening angle between 10- to 20-degrees. Step Two: Work the entire length of the blade edge along the whetstone in small, counter-clockwise circles. Step Three: Flip the blade over and repeat the procedure, this time in small clockwise circles.

Buck Knives

Bob Robb

The delicate taste of fresh-caught trout is best preserved by prompt field care. A pocket folder is all you need to do the job right.

Chapter 20
The Angler's Edge

Everyone who hunts finned quarry needs an edge!

The presence of a chapter on edged tools for anglers may seem somewhat out of place in a book on hunting knives. It is not uncommon, however, to find that many hunters also have an interest in angling. On most of my hunts, a fishing rod has always been close at hand. Some of my most memorable hunts have also produced some equally unforgettable fishing. For all of these reasons, I have chosen to include some thoughts on the subject.

My father started me fishing at the tender age of five years old. It all began one April at Lake Henshaw, in San Diego County, California. This location was a favorite of my father because the lake held a burgeoning population of magnum-size crappie. Dad was a fly fisherman, so tempting the slabsided "paper mouths" was his idea of a great time.

I was too little to manage a fly rod. However, there was an old steel bait-casting pole and reel that could handle the adversity of being in the hands of a little boy. All day long, I'd toss a night-crawler out into the deep and keep my fingers crossed for a bite. Of course, being yet a child an occasional nap was an absolute necessity. It was during one of these slumber periods that my dad waded out into the lake and attached a freshly-caught bluegill to my hook. When I awoke, the old man suggested that I check my bait. Amazingly, I had a hookup. Over the next few minutes, I fought it out with that little bluegill. Even though I found myself thigh-deep in the lake before it was all over, in the end I landed my first fish.

I would have been none the wiser to my father's skullduggery. However, when I was fully grown, married and had my own children my mother told me the truth about that long-ago experience. Of course, I pulled the same trick on my own five-year-old little boy and it worked just as well. Who knows, maybe someday I'll tell him. For now, however, maybe it's just as well if it remains a secret between the fish and me!

From year to year, my angling prowess improved. By the time I was eight or nine years old, it was no trick to actually catch as many fish as anyone else in the family. After awhile, the old man got tired of cleaning all of the fish his youngest son brought back to camp. One afternoon, he found me on the lake and suggested that it was about time that I learned how to dress my own fish. Hauling the stringer out of the water, he grabbed the first finned candidate and proceeded to demonstrate primary field care.

Dad always carried a slender-bladed pocket folder when he was fishing. Removing the knife from his jeans, he carefully opened the blade and reminded me that the edge would cut me as well as the fish. Then with the accomplished ability of someone who was well acquainted with the chore, he commenced to gut the fish on the spot. Then, it was my turn. Handing me the knife, he coached me through each one of the remaining fish on the stringer. When it was all over, I had fish guts on my shirt, slime on my pants, and a smile on my face. From that moment on, dad never had to clean another fish for me.

Dad, mother, and my brother are all gone now, but the lessons learned in the outdoors have remained. The first lesson in knife work occurred when I was about nine years old, and that little boy (now a father and grandfather himself), has been learning about angling knives and field care ever since.

Remington

A traditional folding fishing knife, the clip-pattern blade of this Remington Fisherman (1987 replica "Bullet" knife) is just right for field dressing most game fish.

One thing for sure, it's hard to beat a Turkish clip blade pattern (the same slender blade on dad's pocket folder) for gutting fish. The fine point and slender blade are just right for opening trout, bass, panfish, and a whole host of salt water species. Such a blade is traditionally found in folders marketed as "fishing knives," as a solo blade, or in tandem with a scaler/hook remover blade. Sometimes, there's even a hook sharpener on one side of the handle scales.

Cutlery design has moved into a high tech mode of late, so it's hard to find a traditionally-styled fishing knife. No matter, the new patterns have just as much, if not more, to offer an angler. Let's look at a sampling of folding fishing knives and see what the cutlery designers have put together for the hook and sinker crowd.

Browning: Once again, this firm has put together what may be the ultimate fishing folder. The *Angler* (Model 620) incorporates three useful blades into a single folding knife frame. Made from AUS-8A stainless steel, each 3-inch blade is designed for a specific application. The chisel-point main blade is perfect for gutting fish, and its serrated edge can cut through bones without hesitation. The pliers/nipper blade can be opened from the handle with one hand and works great at straightening hooks and adjusting lures. Finally, the scaler/hook remover blade has both of those assignments well in hand. All of the blades lock open in place and the tough Zytel® knife

handle has a checkered rubber insert, which provides a comfortable, non-slip grip.

Buck: While most fillet knives are fixed-blades, Buck makes the *FishLocker®* that takes a 5-1/4-inch fillet blade and places it into a folding knife frame. Slender and flexible, the stainless steel blade locks open for safety. The black thermoplastic handle is texturized for a secure grip, even when wet. In place of a sheath, a 6-inch nylon lanyard is attached to the knife handle. When the knife is closed, the lanyard can be looped over the belt for safe transport. This is an excellent design, which makes it easy to carry a fillet knife in your pocket, or pack.

Case: Within this cutlery manufacturer's extensive line of pocketknives, the *Single Blade Utility Knife* is my idea of a fine fishing knife. The Tru-Sharp® stainless steel blade is a slender, elongated clip-point nearly 4-inches long. The bolsters are nickel-silver and the handle choices are yellow Delrin® (Model 031), or jigged brown plastic (Model 135). Lightweight and easily carried, this single blade is a sure fit for pocket or tackle box.

Schrade: In their Imperial cutlery line, this manufacturer produces a folding *Fish Knife* (Model 943) that combines a clip-point main blade with a scaler/hook degorger companion blade in the same serpentine knife frame. Both blades are crafted from low maintenance stainless steel and require little more than an occasional rinsing to

Buck Knives

The FishLocker® folding fillet knife by Buck combines a 5-1/4-inch, high-carbon, rust-resistant, modified stainless steel blade with a black thermoplastic handle. Lightweight and rugged, this folder fits easily inside of any tackle box.

keep them clean. The bright yellow Delrin® handle scales are a standout advantage when this edged tool gets mixed in with tackle box clutter. A proven design, this practical folder should be on every angler's "must have" list.

Spyderco: Designed as a folding fillet knife, the abbreviated blade length (4-3/4 inch) of the *Catcherman* (Model C17) makes it an equally efficient field-dressing tool. Interestingly, the AUS-8 stainless steel blade is a trailing-point design. Of course, the characteristic blade spine hump and opening hole provide easy access to the cutting edge. The knife utilizes a front lock mechanism, which allows the user to close the blade with one hand. The curved thermoplastic handle features a texturized surface ("Volcano Grip") for positive contact, even when fish slime and moisture are present. A molded clothing clip, which affords attachment to the edge of almost anything, is present on one side of the handle. An extremely versatile folder, this angler's tool is definitely more than a fillet knife.

Wenger: Nobody does multi-blade folders any better than the producers of Swiss Army Knives. This is certainly true of the folks at Wenger. In their product line, this cutlery producer has four different knives that are designed expressly for anglers. Ranging in size from the *Bass*™ folder (Model 16990) that features eight implements with 13 functions, to the *Catch & Release*™ version (Model 16956) with 12 implements and 19 differ-

Spyderco

Spyderco's handy Catcherman folder (Model C17) features a MBS-26 stainless steel blade with a combination edge (75% plain/25% serrated), and a fiberglass reinforced nylon resin handle.

ent functions, each knife model provides a host of blades that serve in many capacities. My pick of this lot would be the *Master Fisherman*™ (Model 16934), which places eight blades (large spear-point main blade, scaler/hook disgorger/line guide, springless scissors, three screwdriver blades, cap lifter/wire stripper, can opener,

D. Hollis

Here's a selection of handy edged tackle box tools. With this trio an angler is prepared for any fishing chore, from field care to tackle repair.

reamer/awl, and a nail file) in the traditional red handle Swiss Army Knife folding frame. Quite frankly, there's everything an angler could ever need (except a sandwich and a cold drink) contained within this folding knife configuration. The chain and key ring make it easy to attach this handful of edged tools to any fishing vest.

While a folder might be convenient for carrying, many popular fishing knives are fixed-blades. This is particularly true of fillet knives. Filleting, or the act of separating meat from bone, is often the best field-care option. Thin, flat-sided fish, like panfish, are best filleted. Likewise, larger trout, salmon, bass, and most ocean fish (even a halibut) are easier to deal with when filleted. While almost any long, slender blade will work, the best fillet knife features a thin, flat-ground, flexible blade. If the blade doesn't have enough flex, it will cut through, rather than sliding over the bone structure. Almost every cutlery manufacturer makes one or more fillet knife models. Most share common features (slender blades and molded handles), so selection has more to do with brand name allegiance than particular knife features. Even so, let's take a look at a representative sample of what the market has to offer.

Browning: In their cutlery line, this firm offers two different size *Featherweight™ Composite Fillet* knife models. Both knives are made from premium AUS-8A stainless steel and feature a short serrated section of the edge near the handle. Available with either a 6-1/2-inch (Model 906), or a 9-inch (Model 909) blade, both knives have the same Zytel® molded handle with a great-looking wood insert. Supplied with a top-grain leather sheath, either one of these fillet wonders can make quick work out of a mess of fish.

Case: Known for their pocketknives, this firm also makes some fine fixed-blade models. This is particularly true of their thermoplastic-handled fillet knife. The Tru-Sharp® stainless steel blade is a handy 6-inches in length. The molded grip is ergonomically designed and fits well into even the largest hand. Supplied with a full-length leather sheath with a puncture-proof plastic liner, this is a fillet knife with few peers.

Cold Steel: Made in three different blade lengths (6-, 7-1/2-, and 9-inch), these beauties feature Carbon V® blade steel, which seems to hold its edge longer than most stainless formulations. The blades are 20% wider than most traditional fillet designs. The added width allows the blade to lie flat and slide almost effortlessly between the bone and the meat. The handle is made from deeply checkered Kraton®, which offers a slightly "tacky" feel. Individual finger grooves and a thumb rest have been molded into the comfortable grip. Outfitted with a self-drain-ing, hard-sided, polycarbonate molded sheath, the knives can easily be carried on the belt. From saucer-size panfish to Alaskan halibut, these knives offer outstanding performance at an economical price.

Columbia River Knife & Tool Company: This firm has a wide range of cutlery, including a couple of very fine fixed-blade fillet knives. Made from AUS 6M stainless steel, the *Big Eddy Fillet* knife is an exceptional value. Two different blade lengths are available, with the choice of a taper-ground plain edge or partial edge serration near the handle. The thermoplastic handle is molded directly onto the full-length blade tang. The checkered pattern on the handle provides excellent hand-to-knife contact—even when wet. There's also a convenient lanyard hole at the end of the handle. The plastic sheath has been molded to precisely fit the knife and encloses both the blade and a significant part of the handle. Slots are placed in the sheath so moisture can quickly dissipate. A well-designed fillet tool, these CRKT offerings can be a valuable addition to any angler's tackle box.

Grohman: Responding to the needs of Canada's fishing industry, as well as the individual requirements of sport anglers, this firm makes a lovely fillet knife in four different blade lengths. The high-carbon stainless steel blades have enough flex to slide over major bones, yet are able to slice with efficiency. The warm rosewood handles are triple-riveted to the full-length blade tang for strength. Supplied with a leather sheath, which protects both the blade and a significant portion of the handle, this is a solid choice in a fillet knife.

CRKT

Columbia River Knife & Tool Company's Big Eddy fillet knives are an exceptional value. The razor-sharp AUS 6M stainless steel blades are taper-ground for mid-point flex and the serrated portion of the blade near the handle is just the ticket for handling bones. The soft, comfortable textured grip takes all the strain out of fish handling.

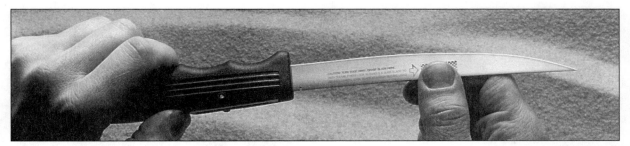

Kershaw kai Cutlery

The blade length of the Kershaw Seven-Step Adjustable Filet Knife can be changed to accommodate fish of different widths.

Kershaw: Realizing that different size fish need varying fillet knife blade lengths, the Kershaw *Seven-Step Adjustable Fillet Knife* (Model 1240) is the functional solution to this quintessential problem. The high-carbon 420J2 stainless steel blade adjusts from 5-1/2 to 9-inches in length. The adjusting mechanism is contained within the molded TaskMaster handle and engages positive stops engineered into the blade spine. A molded ABS plastic sheath completes the fillet knife package. Covering a wide range of finned species, this knife is a tackle box essential.

Knives of Alaska: This firm makes some of the most functional-edged field tools I've ever used. The *Grayling Fillet and Boning Knife* features a 440 series stainless steel blade that has a bit more spine than most fillet knives. While still flexible enough for fish work, it also makes a great hunter's boning knife (I told you that this chapter isn't out of place in a book on hunting knives). The 6-inch blade incorporates a serrated point to facilitate entry into tough fish skin. Double finger choils at the blade base allow for alternative handgrip positions. Both stag and a deeply checkered "Suregrip" material are available as handle choices. Built to last a lifetime, if you can only afford one fillet knife—then this is the one!

Schrade: In their Old Timer® knife series, this cutlery manufacturer lists one of the best designed fillet knives I've ever used. The *Minimum Flex Fillet* (Model 146OT) features a full-tang Schrade+ stainless steel blade. Best of all, the blade is thin and flexible enough to handle even small trout and panfish. The ergonomically correct handle is molded from TPR (thermoplastic rubber), which provides superior hand-to-knife contact in any situation. The protective knife sheath is made from quick-drying nylon webbing for low maintenance in a damp environment. Featuring a limited lifetime warranty, this is one fillet knife that you can count on.

For Globetrotters: Made for the folks at Stanley® Tools by United Cutlery, the Deluxe Traveling Fisherman's Set is the perfect accessory for anglers on the move. This complete set features MaxEdge™ stainless steel blades with a black rubber handle and yellow ABS inserts.

Images Group/Schrade

Schrade recently introduced the Old Timer® Maximum (Model 246OT) and Minimum (Model 146OT) Flex fillet knives that feature slender 6-inch blades and ergonomically designed grips. Joining this pair is the new Safe-T-Grip Pro Fisherman (Model 147OT) with a slight longer 7-inch blade. All three knives feature Schrade® stainless blade steel.

United Cutlery

About the only things that are missing from this Deluxe Traveling Fisherman's Kit are a rod, reel, terminal tackle and someplace wet!

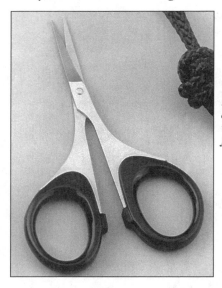

The Kershaw Skeeter™ Fly-Tying Scissors are as handy in your fishing vest as they are at the fly-tying table.

Kershaw kai Cutlery

D. Hollis

While the author's daughter Kristin isn't about to let her older brother catch all the fish, she will let him handle the field dressing.

The assortment of edged tools includes large (8-inch blade) and small (6-inch blade) fillet knives, and a serrated fish knife with scaler feature. The kit also holds a pair of utility scissors, a sharpening steel, cutting board, cut-resistant Kevlar® gloves, scale and tape measure. All any angler needs to do is add a rod, reel, terminal tackle and someplace wet.

What Else?

There is a whole assortment of cutters, crimpers, and snippers that can find their way into an angler's gear. In my experience, you can throw everything away except a good pair of scissors. The innovative folks at Kershaw catalog a pair of *Skeeter* ™ *Fly-Tying Scissors* that can "do it all." Made from

Basic Fish Cleaning

The very best way to insure that the delicate flavor of fresh-caught fish remains intact is to immediately remove the viscera. This chore isn't at all difficult and it takes only a few minutes to perform. The entire process can be accomplished in four simple steps.

Step One: Position the fish so the belly side is turned-up. Use your knife blade to cut completely through the attachment of the gills to the gill plate.

Step Two: Holding the fish firmly, insert the tip of your knife blade into the anal vent and slit open the midline of the belly upward to a point just below the gills.

Step Three: Set your knife safely aside. Holding the fish firmly with one hand, grasp the gill structure and pull it down and away from the fish (when gutting larger fish, you may have to cut the gill structure attachment to the spinal column first). Should you meet any resistance, use the tip of your knife blade to sever adhesions. Discard the visceral material appropriately.

Step Four: With the gills and the visceral mass removed, a dark line of congealed blood can be seen along the spine of the fish. Using the back edge of your thumbnail (small fish), or a suitable rounded object (the tip of a teaspoon works great for this chore), scrape the blood up and away from the body cavity.

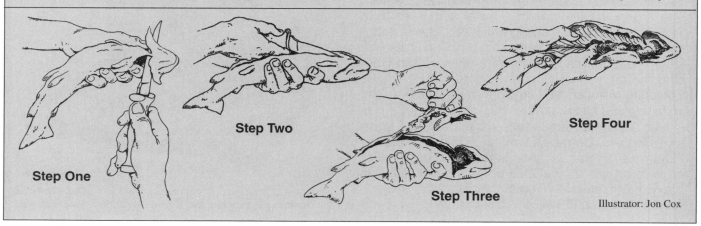

Step One

Step Two

Step Three

Step Four

Illustrator: Jon Cox

high-carbon stainless steel with thermoplastic handle inserts, these little beauties can snip line, cut monofilament, or a trim fly hackle with ease. And the pointed blades are useful in opening clogged hook eyes, or lifting a splinter from beneath your hide. Available with plain (Model 1210), or serrated (Model 1215) blades, this is one pair of scissors you won't leave on the fly-tying bench.

Another useful tool for anglers is the Gerber *Multi-Lite*™ (Models 07200 and 072005). This multi-purpose tool combines seven locking tool blades (scissors, can opener, awl, screwdriver/bottle opener, serrated blade and a drop-point blade) and a bright amber emergency light in a frame just 3-1/2-inches long. The compact design also includes a storage compartment that can accept matches, extra batteries, or even a couple lures. The tool also accepts an accessory tool kit for added functional applications. At high noon or darkest midnight, this tool can be the answer to fishing tackle adjustment and repair needs.

Finally, every angler should have a Schrade *Tough Chip*™ tool (Model ST2) in their fishing vest. Made entirely from maintenance-free stainless steel, this miniature multi-tool offers a pair of folding scissors, four locking implements (including a knife blade), a tooth pick and a pair of tweezers in a package that's just 2-1/2-inches long when closed. Quite frankly, it just doesn't get any better than this practical little tool.

I've hauled a fishing outfit to hunting camps all over the globe. Along with that setup, edged angling tools have also been part of my gear. Whether it's cutthroat trout on a Rocky Mountain elk adventure, or a mess of bluegills during a southern whitetail deer hunt, it seems that the hunt always includes some time on the water. For my part, I like to be prepared!

Fish Filleting

The act of filleting is simply the removal of the meat from the skeletal structure. This chore calls for a long, thin, and flexible knife blade. While it may take more practice than simple fish cleaning, filleting isn't difficult to master. The basic steps are outlined below:

Step One: Lay the fish on a flat surface. Use the tip of your knife blade to make an incision through the side of the fish, just behind the gill cover. The incision should run from the dorsal midline (top) of the fish, down to the rib cage. Avoid cutting into the visceral cavity.

Step Two: Holding the fish firmly, insert the tip of your knife blade at a right angle (90-degrees) to your initial incision. Then, work the knife blade down along the backbone to the top of the rib cage. Working carefully, slice the meat away from the backbone to the end of the visceral cavity. At the visceral cavity's end, slide the tip of the knife blade over the spinal column and out the ventral (bottom) end of the fish. Then, continue cutting the fillet free, all the way to the base of the tail.

Step Three: Grab hold of the upper end of the fillet and pull it down and away from the rib cage. Use the tip of your knife blade to cut through any adhesions. Turn the fish over and repeat steps one through three on the opposite side.

Step Four: Lay each fillet out, skin-side-down. Using your fingertips, hold the fillet at the tail end with one hand. Take your knife and cut into the fillet just forward of the fingertips of your opposite hand, all the way down to the skin (don't cut through the skin). The wedge of meat that is made at the tail end of the fillet will serve as a gripping point while you cut the meat free from the skin. Turn the knife blade against the skin. Using a sweeping motion cut the fillet free from the inner side of the skin. Repeat this procedure on the remaining fillet

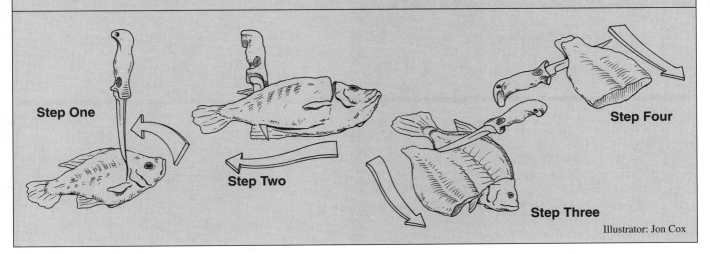

Step One

Step Two

Step Three

Step Four

Illustrator: Jon Cox

Darden Hollis

Home away from home is what camping in the woods is all about.

Chapter 21

Camp Cutlery

At one point, or another, every hunter is a camper and every camper needs all "the right stuff."

Watching my dad prepare for a road trip to hunting camp was an education in itself. In those days, long before interstate highways and roadside emergency telephones, it was a long distance between service stations. And professional roadway assistance was almost unheard of. If trouble happened along way, most vehicular operators were left to their own devices. Furthermore, when you finally reached your destination, most campsites were "unimproved."

Before anything was packed into the trunk of our family sedan (dad was a Ford man), the old man placed a tarp in the driveway and began laying out his emergency supplies on it. In rapid succession, he laid out a set of tire chains, a tow strap, an ax, a saw, a shovel, a machete, road flares, first aid kit, and assortment of hand tools. He rolled the whole mess into the tarp and put it into the trunk. Of course, this didn't leave much room for our camping gear. Somehow, dad managed to stuff in a tent, cots, sleeping bags, Coleman lantern and stove, and an entire camp kitchen into the trunk. When he was reasonably assured that we could survive an on-the-road emergency, or spend a week in the woods, then the old man felt adequately prepared.

Once we made it to camp (at times its own ordeal), there was brush to clear, firewood to gather, kindling to chop, and grub to cook. Of course, when the meat pole was filled, there would be deer to cut up. Brushwork belonged to the shovel and ax brigade (my brother and myself). The gathering of firewood, chopping kindling, and cooking was dad's assignment. And cutting up deer meat was a chore that concerned every successful hunter in camp.

It always seemed to me that my brother and I got the worst part of deer camp drudgery. Clearing brush and digging up tree roots—that always seemed to grow where dad wanted the tent pitched—took all day. This was especially odious because we would have rather been scouting for game. Even when we were done, dad had a way of involving us in firewood duties and cooking clean up. I do remember, however, his complaining that boys were poor substitutes for the right tools.

When it came to edged tools, the ax did a yeoman's choice of chopping all of the big stuff. However, the head occasionally came loose, and more than one handle broke. It was hard to improve on the shovel, but the kitchen cutlery needed thorough revamping. Most of the knives were homemade numbers that couldn't cut butter on a summer afternoon. They were either too big or not big enough, and there wasn't a sharp edge in the group. This meant that dad had to spend a disproportional amount of time on edge-restoration duties.

Today, the old man is gone. However, the same preparation for the annual trek to hunting camp still follows a traditional path. Instead of overly-large tools and unsuitable knives, a manageable-size tool kit and cutlery specifically designed for camp work has been selected. These choices didn't happen overnight. It has taken several years and careful culling to find just the right equipment for hunting camp. In the paragraphs which follow, let me share with you some of those choices. Hopefully, this commentary will help you develop your own selection of tools and cutlery for hunting camp.

On the Road

Instead of a collection of hard-to-pack, cumbersome tools, I now carry the Gerber *Sport Utility Pack* (Model 05638). This handy grouping of tools includes a folding shovel, the handy *BackPaxe*, a versatile *Exchange-a-Blade* saw, first aid kit, and instead of several hand tools—a Gerber multitool. The one thing I like about this kit is that everything is packed into a zippered Cordura® nylon case. There are times when a professional mechanic and a whole garage full of tools can't put your vehicle in good running order, but for all of the other times this kit can be heaven sent.

At the Campsite

Throughout many parts of this country there are wide spots along most backcountry jeep trails that are loosely designed "camp areas." These locations give a whole new meaning to the words "unimproved camp site." Whatever improvement is enjoyed, those who use these spots must put

D. Hollis

The Gerber Sport Utility Pack has all the primary tools and accessories to get you out of a tight spot off the road.

into it themselves. This usually means moving rocks and cutting brush, or whatever else gets into your way. The two indispensable edged tools for these assignments are an ax and some kind of brush whacker.

Through the *A. G. Russell, Catalog of Knives*, it's possible to acquire one of the best serious field axes I've ever used. The *Marbles #9 Belt Axe* was always one of the most popular tools this manufacturer ever made. The current version is a re-

creation of an earlier model (pre-1911), but made with 1085 carbon steel and high-tech production methods. The 24-ounce head and the 14 inch hardwood handle with a goat's foot style butt impart a maximum chopping attack on green or dry wood. This ax is a fine choice for clearing campsites and one that will last for generations.

For brushwork, no other tool does it any better than an old fashioned bill hook. Designed for cutting brush, small trees, and splitting logs, such a tool is standard fare in nearly every Scandinavian home. Hunters, anglers and outdoors enthusiasts of every persuasion carry one of these nifty whackers in their vehicles. Kellam Cutlery markets a billhook that is forged out of impact-resistant carbon steel. This tool has a long cutting edge, with a hook to protect the blade should one hit the ground accidentally. The hook is also handy for snatching brush and pulling limbs out of a tangle of vegetation. The hardwood handle is shock absorbent, making the tool comfortable to use. A true woodsman's implement, the Kellam billhook comes with a leather sheath for carrying safety. In my experience, there are occasions when this tool is better than an ax or a chainsaw for many camp cutting tasks.

In their Becker Knife & Tool line, Camillus cutlery makes several ultra-rugged edged tools that any camper will appreciate. The *TacTool* (Model BK3) is one of the most versatile chopping tools you'll ever handle. The 7-inch blade has a square point, combination edge, and a hook cutter on the spine. The ergonomic handle scales are bolted to the full-length blade tang for permanent attachment. Chopping, cutting, or even prying, it doesn't get any tougher than this incredibly sharp and useful tool design. Likewise, the *Machax* (BK4) is a combination machete-ax-Bowie knife all rolled into one extremely powerful cutting implement.

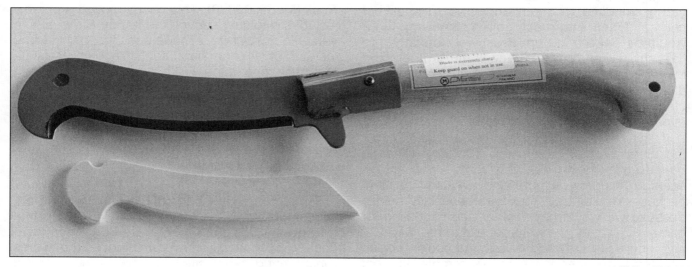

Kellam Knives

When it comes to serious brushwork, the Kellam billhook is the right tool for the job.

The 9-1/2-inch blade has a dramatic curve that works together with the angled handle to increase cutting force. Like all the tools in this series, each full-tang blade is crafted from carbon steel, flat ground and epoxy coated, a Kydex® sheath, with a unique multi-carry system, comes with each of these hardworking tools.

The Camp Kitchen

It wouldn't be hunting camp if there weren't camp stove meals. Despite all improvements in freeze-dry food (nasty), nothing quite beats a pre-dawn breakfast of bacon and eggs. In my book, slab bacon is the only way to go. However, it takes a decent slicer to cut this kind of bacon into thin pieces. Furthermore, there is a broad assortment of other camp cooking that calls for knifework. Let's look at a few of my own personal selections.

Typically, kitchen knives get rough treatment in hunting camp. They're usually thrown in along with all the rest of the cook gear, resulting in edge damage. Even worse, most camp kitchen knives never see a whetstone—a sad state of edged affairs. Fortunately, the folks at Cold Steel have come to the rescue. Their *Kitchen Series* knives come with their own protective polypropylene blade sheath. This alone makes these keen kitchen cutters the only pick for the grub box. Available in two useful drop-point pattern blade lengths (5" or 7"), these knives feature serrated blade edges and Kraton® handles. Flat-ground to an extra thin edge, these knives can slice vegetables into thin wafers, yet cut through meat and vegetables with complete ease. Full-tang construction for added strength and years of hunting camp use, a set of these knives is a "must-have" for any hunting camp kitchen.

A mail order catalog exclusive, the A. G. Russell™ *Hocho* folding cook's knife is a camp kitchen necessity. Made entirely of stainless steel, this slicing marvel has double liners with a detent in each to make sure that the blade doesn't fly open at an untoward moment. The blade locks with a back spring mid-lock that positively assures safety when cutting in any medium. The 4-1/4" blade is crafted from edge-holding ATS-34 stainless steel that will hold up to an entire week of chopping salad vegetables or stew meat. Not only does the blade fold up into the handle for storage, the knife has a clothing clip for attachment to the edge of anything. This is a well-made tool for the kitchen that deserves to be in every hunter's camping gear.

The folks at Kershaw kai Cutlery have made what appears to be the ultimate camp utensil kit.

Kershaw kai Cutlery

In the camp kitchen, the interchangeable blade assortment in Kershaw's Blade Trader set is heaven sent.

The *Camp Tool Trader* (Model 1091CT) features two interchangeable handles, two knife blades (6-inch fillet, and 6-inch drop-point cook's blade), spatula, large spoon and a serving fork. All of the blades and utensils are made from 420-J2 stainless steel to resist the formation of rust that can result from meat and fruit juices. All of these handy kitchen tools are contained in a zippered, Cordura® nylon storage/carrying case. Likewise, the Kershaw *Blade Trader* is another excellent cutlery set for camp use. This set combines six different blades (French chef's blade, slicing blade, bread blade, a frozen food blade, a fillet blade, and a serrated utility blade) with an interchangeable handle. Like all other Kershaw exchangeable blade sets, the blades are made from 420-J2 stainless steel. The patented exchange mechanism assures quick and easy blade switch with solid lock-up. No more box full of knives and kitchen utensils rattling around in the camping gear. These Kershaw exclusives are my idea of a good thing!

In the Pocket or On the Belt

Known as a traveler's pocket tableware, an all-in-one folding set of eating utensils is a design that has been known for more than 200 years. W. R. Case & Sons Cutlery has been a prominent maker of this style of pocket cutlery. The *Case Hobo* is one of the best, and certainly most collectable, of this category of knives. Measuring 4-1/8" overall, the knife frame contains a clip-point cutting blade and a fork/cap lifter blade. The blades and liners are made from stainless steel and the bolsters are nickel-silver. Interestingly, the knife frame slides apart when the fork is opened halfway. This effectively disconnects the knife from the fork and allows the use of separate utensils. Place the two halves together, close the fork blade and the two halves are joined together again. This functionally designed knife is available with rosewood, jigged chestnut, bone, or India stag handle scales. I carry one of these folders in my pocket and find it useful no matter whether it's mealtime on the mountain, or back at camp.

Every hunting camp has an assortment of ropes, straps and cordage. All of this fibrous material is tough to cut, but not with the new Columbia River Knife & Tool Company's curved *Bear Claw* fixed-blade knife. Designed by Russ Kommer, an Alaskan professional guide and knifemaker, this knife is just right for cutting away clothing from accident victims, slicing through seat belts, or cutting rope. The claw-shaped 2" blade is crafted from AUS-6M stainless steel and is available with a plain or serrated edge. The knife only weighs a mere 2.9 ounces and the versatile thermoplastic sheath allows for a variety of carrying

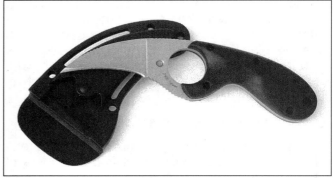

CRKT

For cutting rope, cordage, and fibrous materials, the Columbia River Knife & Tool Company's Bear Claw fixed-blade is the way to go.

positions. In my opinion, this knife should be included in everyone's vehicle emergency kit.

The folks at Ka-bar also make their own version of the Hobo knife. The *Ka-bar Hobo* (Model 1300) is made entirely from stainless steel. It matches up a clip-point knife blade with a spoon and a three-tine fork/bottle opener blade. Each utensil can be separated from one another. Reassembled, the utensil kit is easily carried in its Ballistic® cloth sheath that fastens with a loop and hook closure. Whether you're an outdoors person or not, this knife, fork and spoon set will come in handy in any venue.

Several knifemakers—Camillus, Ka-bar, Remington and others—all make a camp or utility folder. These pocket tool chests have a selection of useful blades, which generally include a spear-point primary blade, can opener blade, bottle cap lifter/screwdriver blade and possibly other tool blades. During my Boy Scout days, I carried such a pocket folder everywhere. You'd be surprised at just how often these American versions of the traditional Swiss Army Knife can help you out of a tight spot.

Ka-bar

When it comes to outdoor dinning, the Ka-bar version of the famous Hobo folder has a complete assortment of eating utensils.

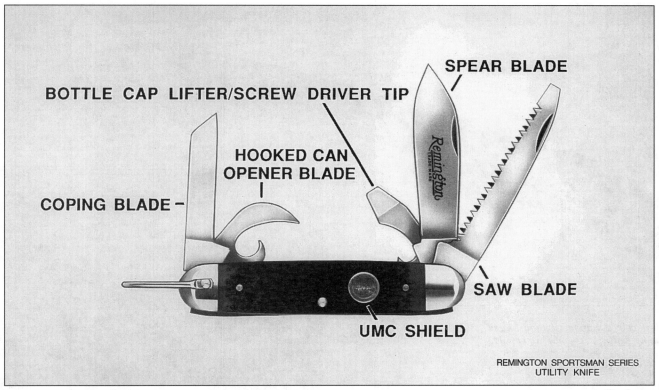

BOTTLE CAP LIFTER/SCREW DRIVER TIP

SPEAR BLADE

HOOKED CAN OPENER BLADE

COPING BLADE –

SAW BLADE

UMC SHIELD

REMINGTON SPORTSMAN SERIES
UTILITY KNIFE

Remington

Several cutlery manufacturers offer camp/utility knives that feature a similar assortment of useful blades.

The handy Spyderco *Snap-It* is a unique folder in that the front of the fiberglass-reinforced handle has a molded snap shackle (with a steel core) that allows the knife to be clipped to a belt loop or D-ring for ready access. The 3" drop-point blade is made from AUS-8A stainless steel and locks open in a fixed position. The Zytel® handle scales feature rubberized Kraton® inserts for a positive, non-slip grip. Weighing in at a mere 2.4 ounces, this useful edged tool is right at home in camp, on the road, or in the field.

Schrade's *Cliphanger* knife series has become quite popular as a general-purpose utility knife.

Images Group/Schrade

For general utility, it doesn't get any better than Schrade's Cliphanger lockblade folders.

Available in a variety of blade lengths, this lock-blade folder is one rugged steel sidekick. The blades are crafted from Schrade+Plus stainless steel in a drop-point pattern. The tough Zytel® molded handles have a patented clip release mechanism. And each knife is packaged with a nylon carrying strap, anodized split ring and an Acetal® thermoplastic hook. Practical, safe and convenient, this is an outstanding outdoor cutlery design.

Camp Knives

Several handmade knifemakers produce a camp knife. Most of these edged wonders are overly-large fixed-blade models. Some may question the usefulness of such a design, but they can be helpful slicing camp bacon, or cutting up venison into appropriate-sized steaks, chops and roasts. Ed Fowler is famous for his hand-forged, carbon steel knives. Ed starts his camp knives with a 7-inch blade, but some guys like them even longer than that. Should your tastes run to Damascus, then you can't do any better than Loyd Thomsen's camp knife. The magnificence of Damascus, set off by an impressive stag handle, will definitely start conversations over a hot cup of coffee. Russ Krommer also makes a fine camp knife that features an ATS-34 blade with a 5-inch cutting edge. Smaller than the competition, nevertheless, a knife of this length can also be useful in the field.

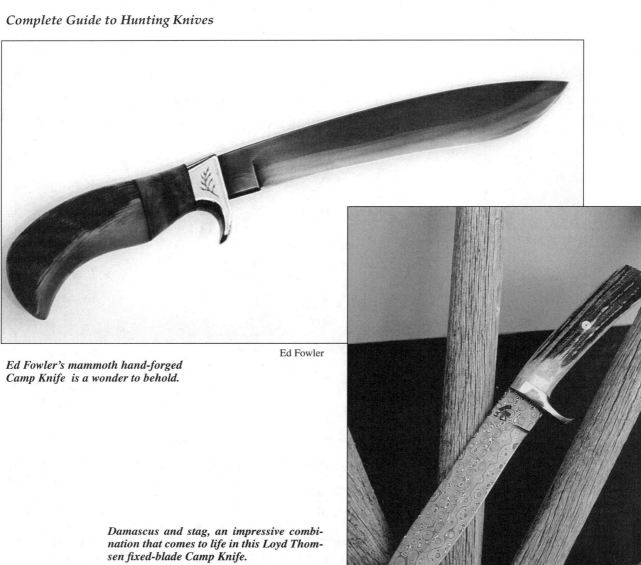

Ed Fowler

Ed Fowler's mammoth hand-forged Camp Knife is a wonder to behold.

Damascus and stag, an impressive combination that comes to life in this Loyd Thomsen fixed-blade Camp Knife.

Jennifer Thomsen-Connell

Handmade by Russ Krommer, this Camp Knife features an ATS-34 stainless steel blade and a desert ironwood handle, with 416 stainless guard and fittings.

Russ Krommer

Emergency Repair

I am forever in need of an assortment of small tools in hunting camp. The Coleman lantern and stove need an occasional repair or adjustment, the truck can often need one thing or another "tweaked," and there's always something to be fixed. In this realm, nothing beats a multi-tool for versatility.

The *BuckTool*™ (Model 360) is one of those "must-have" accessories for anyone who spends time in camp. The original design features folding needlenose pliers with nine other implements (wirecuttters, can/bottle opener, three slotted screwdrivers, a Phillips screwdriver, a plain edge drop-point knife blade, a serrated sheepsfoot blade, and folding lanyard eye. All of the implements lock

Weyer of Toledo

The SOG® Tool Clip contains both knife and tool blades, along with a pair of pliers.

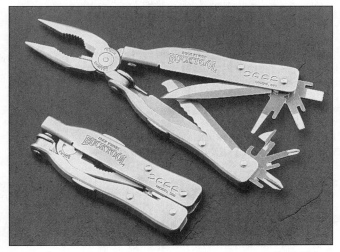

Buck Knives

The Bucktool™ *is a compact, multi-functional tool that features locking blades, one-tool-at-a-time opening and closing, and symbols on the handles to identify all ten of the enclosed tools and blades.*

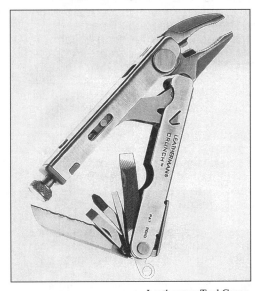

Leatherman Tool Group

Foremost among the features of the Leatherman Crunch™ *is a set of locking plier jaws. Likewise, all of the handle-contained tools and blades also lock positively in place.*

open for safety and when folded are contained within the handles of the pliers. For those who like camo, an *Advantage Classic*® *Camo Version* (Model 360CM) of this same tool is also obtainable. And a lightweight model, the *BuckLite*® *Tool* (Model 355) with non-locking blade is also available. The basic multi-tool design was based on some serious research. This effort resulted in an ergonomically-designed tool that combines user tool comfort (smooth, contoured handles) with all the functional tool application possible in one hand-held personal tool box.

The *Leatherman Crunch*™, with its locking pliers and a whole host of other tools and functions (wire cutters, sheepsfoot blade, wood/metal file, flat and Phillips screwdrivers, hex bit driver, wire stripper, bottle opener, and ruler) is ideally suited for camp duty. The all-stainless-steel construction and the ability to fold down to a compact 4 inches in length makes this tool a fine choice.

The *SOG ToolClip*® is one of the most versatile multi-tools ever conceived. This tool combines a spear-point knife blade, a set of pliers/grippers/wire cutters, two screwdrivers, two wire strippers, a file, bottle opener, and serrated blade that all fold into a single frame. A handy clothing clip provides ready access. If this multi-tool can't put things back into working order, then you'll probably need a fairy godmother.

The Last Cut

Living outdoors often calls for a variety of edged tools and I've only touched on a few in this chapter. Before you leave for hunting camp, sort out all of your camping gear and list those items that are absolutely essential. Pack for unforeseen emergencies, and then pray that none of them come to pass. While our primordial ancestors might have been able to get along with nothing more than a few shards of stone, I think you'll want more of an edge than that!

Afterword

When you come to the end of a project, there are often loose ends to tie up. This is certainly true of this body of work. This book is by no means a technical manual. I have only attempted to condense and simplify cutlery manufacture and knifemaking, so that anyone can gain an understanding of the complex and sophisticated processes. Furthermore, exposure to selected groupings of game-care-appropriate knives and edge maintenance products has also been made. In this effort, there is obviously a strong representation of factory-made edged products. Some may criticize this approach, but I felt compelled to take this avenue for several reasons.

Foremost among the motivating factors was the availability of factory knives. Whether it is a knife shop, gun store, sporting goods outlet, or even the local Wal-Mart, production cutlery has a strong presence. While a small selection of handmade knives can occasionally be encountered at designated outlets, factory-made cutlery far outnumbers that presence.

Consistency of product quality is something that is paramount with factory cutlery. The sophisticated machinery, quality management, and a single-minded devotion to producing the very best possible cutlery at the lowest price are something that cannot easily be matched by an individual knife maker. At the retail end of the production continuum, this results in enhanced cutlery value for the consumer.

All of this should not be interpreted as an assault on handmade or custom knifemakers. I can well appreciate all of the time, effort and skill that go into a particular forged piece. The individuality of design, workmanship, and fine handmade nuances are impossible for a production facility to duplicate at a competitive price.

Consider if you will, that it can take 20-40 hours to produce a hand-forged knife and a quality leather sheath. Just think about all of the effort it takes a knifemaker like Ed Fowler to forge a finished blade from a steel ball bearing approximately three-inches in diameter. At a conservative $25 an hour for labor, this would put blade production costs alone at $500 to $1000 per unit.

Some makers eschew hand forging and cut knife blanks out of sheet steel, then use stock removal to produce the finished product. While this knife making methodology cuts time involvement, the labor costs can still run $100-$300 per unit. And this doesn't even consider expenditures for raw materials, tool maintenance, utilities, bookingkeeping, advertising and a whole host of other costs.

In addition, the cost of subcontracting manufactured components (knife fittings, leatherwork, etc.), or processes not undertaken by the knifemaker (heat treating) must also be added. Should an outside distribution system be used, then the corresponding profit margin markup must be tacked onto the retail price. When you consider all of these factors, it's easy to see why some handmade knives are so pricey. However, those who can't find what they want in production cutlery and are seeking an upscale product, or want a certain level of singularity in their cutlery, a handmade knife can be the solution to those needs.

It should be noted that the most affordable handmade products are found in collaborative efforts with a particular cutlery factory. Examples of this can be found in the Schrade Walker-Lake folder, the Outdoor Edge collaborations with knifemakers Darrel Ralph, Ray Appleton, and Kit Carson, the Browning joint ventures with Michael Collins, as well as several Spyderco collaborations with a host of knifemakers. These aren't the only cooperative efforts with well-known knifemakers, but once again we find ourselves at the doorstep of factory cutlery production.

In this book, both editorial mention and pictorial illustration of factory and handmade cutlery can be seen. Most of the major and many of the minor domestic cutlery manufacturers and importers are represented herein. Also, a representative group of individual knifemakers can be found within these pages. While a number of knifemakers were contacted for inclusion in this book, only a few made an effort to reply. If you provided an answer to that solicitation, your work gained exposure herein. If you failed to reply, no apologies are offered.

This book is not only about knives for hunters. It also covers responsible game care. Hunting provides both recreation and the harvest of consumable culinary resources. The tools you select for that assignment will go a long way to ensure that only top quality wild game, fowl and fish reaches your table.

When your bullet, ball or broadhead has hit the mark, it's not all about knife design and blade steel. You alone are the determining factor. The best knife in the world is nothing more than an inanimate object. It takes human hands to put the knifemaker's work into action. Selected wisely and used knowledgeably, a knife is as essential to the hunt today as it was in millennia past.

Contact Information

Knifemakers:

John Barlow
P.O. Box 568, Nomis
TN 37828
615/494-9421

Keith Coleman
5001 Starfire Pl. NW
Albuquerque, NM 87120
505/899-3783

Edmund Davidson
3345 Virginia Ave.
Goshen, VA 24439
540/997-5651

Jim English
P. O. 167
Jamul, CA 92035
619/669-0833

Ed Fowler
P. O. Box 1519
Riverton, WY 82501
307/856-9815

D. R. Good
65 Bobtail Pike
Peru, IN 46920
765/472-7835

Lynn Griffith
P. O. Box 876
Glenpool, OK 74033
918/322-5414

Russ Krommer
9211 Abbott Loop Rd.
Anchorage, AK 99507
907/346-3339

Jarrell Lambert
Rt. 1, Box 67
Ganado, TX 77962
512/771-3744

William S. Letcher
200 Milky Way
Ft. Collins, CO 80525
303/223-9689

Brett Laplante
110 Dove Creek
McKinney, TX 75069
972/837-4603

Jay Maines/Delta Z Knives
P. O. Box 1112
Studio City, CA 91614
818/786-9488

Joe Malloy
P. O. Box 156
1039 Schwabe St.
Freeland, PA 18224
570/636-2781

Dan McCormick
8915-93rd Ave.
Ft. St. John
BC V1J 4X2 Canada
250/787-1097

Chris Reeve
11625 W. President Dr., #B
Boise, ID 83713
208/375-0367

Joe Szilaski
29 Carroll Dr.
Wappingers Falls, NY 12590
845/297/5397

Loyd Thomsen
HCR 46, Box 19
Oelrich, SD 57763
605/535-6162

Paul J. Turner
P. O. Box 1549
Afton, WY 83110, 307/886-0611

Outfitters/Guides:

Duwane Adams
Arizona Big Game Hunts
204-Ave. "B"
San Manuel, AZ 85631
520/385-4995

John Winter
Two-Ocean Pass Outfitting
P. O. Box 666
Thermopolis, WY 82443
800/RANCH-09

Resources:

A. G. Russell, 1705 N. Thompson St., Springdale, AR 72764, 800/255-9034 *(www.agrussell.com)*
Al Mar Knives, P. O. Box 2295, Tualatin, OR 97062, 503/670-9080 *(www.almarknives.com)*
Bear MGC Cutlery, 1111 Bear Blvd., SW, Jacksonville, AL 36265, 205/435-2227
Benchmade Knives, 300 Beavercreek Rd., Oregon City, OR 97045, 800/800-7427 *(www.benchmade.com)*
Beretta U.S.A. Corp., 17601 Beretta Dr., Accokeek, ML 20607, 301/283-2191*(www.berettausa.com)*
Boker USA, Inc., 1550 Balsam St., Lakewood, CO 80215, 303/462-0662 *(www.bokerusa.com)*
Browning, One Browning Pl. Morgan, UT 84050, 801/876-2711 *(www.browning.com)*
Buck Knives, P. O. Box 1267, El Cajon, CA 92022, 800/326-2925 *(www.buckknives.com)*
Camillus Cutlery, 54 Main St., Camillus, NY 13031, 800/344-0450
C.A.S. Iberia, 650 Industrial Blvd., Sale Creek, TN 37373, 800/635-9366 *(www.casiberia.com)*
Chris Reeve Knives, 11624 W. President Dr., Suite B, Boise, ID 83713, 208/375-0367 *(www.chrisreeve.com)*

Resources (Continued):

Coast Cutlery Corp., 2045 SE Ankeny St., Portland, OR 97214, 503/234-4545

Cold Steel, Inc., 3036-A Seaborg Ave., Ventura, CA 93003, 800/255-4716 *(www.coldsteel.com)*

Columbia River Knife & Tool Co., 9720 SW Hillman Ct. Suite 805, Wilsonville, OR 97070, 800/891-3100 *(www.crkt.com)*

Delta Z Knives, P. O. Box 1112, Studio City, CA 91614, 818/786-9488 *(www.DeltaZ-Knives.com)*

Diamond Machine Tech., 85 Hayes Memorial Dr., Marlborough, MA 01752, 800/666-4368 *(www.dmtsharp.com)*

EdgeCraft Corp., 825 Southwood Rd., Avondale, PA 19311, 800/342-3255

Emerson Knives, P. O. Box 4325, Redondo Bch., CA 90278, 310/542-3050 *(www.emersonknives.com)*

Eze-Lap Diamond Products, 3572 Arrowhead Dr., Carson City, NV 89706, 956/729-7514 *(www.eze-lap.com)*

Fortune Products, 205 Hickkory Creek Rd., Marble Falls, TX 78654, 800/742-7791 *(www.accusharp.com)*

Fowler Custom Knives, Ricky Fowler, P.O. Box 339, Silverhill, AL 36576, 334/945-3289 *(www.fowlerknives.com)*

Fox Cutlery, Via La Mola, 4, Maniago, Pordenone, Italy 33085, 39-0427-71814 *(www.italpro.com/fox)*

Frost Cutlery Co., P. O. Box 22636, Chattanooga, TN 37422, 423/894-6079 *(www.frostcutlery.com)*

GATCO Sharpeners, P. O. Box 600, Getzville, NY 14068, 800/548-7427 *(www.greatamericantool.com)*

Gerber Legendary Blades, 14200 SW 72nd Ave., Portland, OR 97281, 800/950-6161 *(www.gerberblades.com)*

Grohmann, 24000 Highway Seven, Suite 200, Excelsior, MN 55331, 612/470-4457 *(www.grohmannknives.com)*

Gutmann Cutlery, P. O. Box 2219, Bellingham, WA 98227, 800-CUTLERY *(www.schradeknives.com)*

Imperial Schrade Corp., 7 Schrade Ct., Elllenville, NY 12438, 800/351-9658 *(www.schradeknives.com)*

Ka-bar Knives, Inc., 1125 E. State St., Olean, NY 14760, 800/282-0130 *(www.ka-bar.com)*

Katz Knives, Inc., P. O. Box 730, Chandler, AZ 85224, 800/848-7084 *(www.katz-knives.com)*

Kellam Knives, 902 S. Dixie Hwy., Lantana, FL 33462, 800/390-6918 *(www.kellamknives.com)*

Kershaw/kai Cutlery, 25300 SW Parkway Ave., Wilsonville, OR 97070, 503/682-1966 *(www.kershawknives.com)*

Knives of Alaska, 123 W. Main St., Denison, TX 75021, 800/572-0980 *(www.knivesofalaska.com)*

Kopromed, P. O. Box 61485, Vancouver, WA 98666, 800/735-8483

Leatherman Tool Group, Inc., P. O. Box 20595, Portland, OR 97294, 503/253-7826 *(www.leatherman.com)*

L.E.M. Products, Inc. P. O. Box 244, Miamitown, OH 45041, 877-536-7763 *(www.lemproducts.com)*

Manufacturas Muela, Ctra. N-420, Km. 165,500, Argamasilla de Calatrave C. R., Spain *(manufmuela@arrakis.es)*

McGowan Manufacturing Co., 25 Michigan St., Hutchinson, MN 55350, 800/342-4810 *(www.mcgowanmfg.com)*

MeyerCo USA, 4481 Exchange Service Dr., Dallas, TX 75236, 214/467-8949 *(meyerco@bnfusa.com)*

Micro Technology, 932-36th Court SW, Vero Beach, FL 32968, 561-569-3058 *(www.microtechknives.com)*

Mission Knives, 22971 Triton Way, Suite C, Laguna Hills, CA 92653, 949/951-3879 *(www.missionknives.com)*

Normark, 10395 Yellow Circle Dr., Minnetonka, MN 55343, 612/933-7060

Ontario Knife Co. (Queen Cutlery), 26 Empire St., Franklinville, NY 14737, 800/222-5233

Outdoor Edge Cutlery, 6395 Gunpark Dr. , Suite Q, Bolder, CO 80301, 303/530-7667 *(www.outdooredge.com)*

Rickard Knife Co., 10950 Horseback Ridge Rd., Missoula, MT 59804, 406/728-2550 *(www.rkcknives.com)*

Round Eye Knife & Tool, P. O. Box 818, Sagle, ID 83860, 888/801-8858 *(www.roundeye.com)*

Sebertech, 2438 Cades Way, Vista, CA 92083, 888/806-8225, *(www.sebertech.com)*

Smith Abrasives, 1700 Sleepy Valley Rd., Hot Springs, AR 71902, 800/221-4156 *(www.getsharp.com)*

Smith & Wesson (Taylor Cutlery), 1736 N. Eastman Rd., Kingsport, TN 37662, 800/251-0254

SOG Knives, 6521-212th St. SW, Lynnwood, WA 98036, 425/771-6230 *(www.sogknives.com)*

Spyderco, 20011 Golden Gate Canyon Rd., Golden, CO 80403, 800/525-770 *(www.spyderco.com)*

Swiss Arm Brands, 1 Research Dr., Shelton, CT 06484, 800/243-4032 *(www.swissarmy.com)*

Tigersh p Technologies, 4275 D. J. Dr., Missoula, MT 59803, 888/711-8437 *(www.knife.net)*

Tru H e Corp., 1721 NE 19th Ave., Ocala, FL 34470, 800/237-4663 *(www.truhone.com)*

Unit Cutlery, 1425 United Blvd., Sevierville, TN 37876, 800/548-0835 *(www.unitedcutlery.com)*

Utica Cutlery, 820 Noyes St., Utica, NY 13503, 315/733-4663

Viking Knives, 3830 Dividend Dr., Garland, TX 75042, 214/494-3667

W. R. Case & Sons Cutlery, Owens Way, Bradford, PA 16701, 800/523-6350 *(www.wrcase.com)*

Wenger, 15 Corporate Dr., Orangeburg, NY 10962, 914/365-3500 *(www.wengerna.com)*

Wm. Henry Knives, 2125-C Delaware Ave.,Santa Cruz, CA 95060, 831/454-9409 *(www.williamhenryknives.com)*